WHO
TO TRUST
WITH
YOUR
MONEY

BOOKS BY JOHN BARNES

Who to Trust with Your Money
How to Cut Your Taxes
How to Have More Money
Who Will Get Your Money
What Investing Is All About

WHO
TO TRUST
WITH
YOUR
MONEY

JOHN BARNES

WILLIAM MORROW AND COMPANY, INC.
New York

Library of Congress Cataloging in Publication Data

Barnes, John, 1908-
Who to trust with your money.

Includes index.
1. Finance, Personal.   2. Investments.   I. Title.
HG179.B32   1985   332.024   85-11566
ISBN 0-688-04715-7

Printed in the United States of America

First Edition

1 2 3 4 5 6 7 8 9 10

BOOK DESIGN BY BERNARD SCHLEIFER

CONTENTS

stock market for the next 150 years, beginning in 1850 and ending in 1999. For the edification of our readers, the chart is compared to the Dow Jones Industrial Average going back to 1929.

As custodians, banks, savings and loan associations, and credit unions do a good job. They also have federal insurance up to a maximum of $100,000. A banker has very little knowledge of the stock market and real estate. The biggest banks have loaned their entire net worth to third world countries like Mexico, Brazil, and Argentina. Now would you and I do that? The failure of the eighth largest bank, saved by the FDIC and the Federal Reserve Bank, but no rescue for the shareholders. If you want maximum safety for your dollars, don't choose a savings and loan. The financial panic in Ohio. Don't trust a state savings and loan, or a thrift institution, unless it is federally insured. There is always a ratio between risk and reward. Your accountant knows your assets and can compare investment results among his customers, but he will seldom recommend an investment.

Every day a great deal of property and future family security are sacrificed when property owners die. Why? Because they were not aware of the problems created by death, and of the advance decisions necessary to reduce to a minimum the delay, the frustration, the taxes, and the costs involved. Two estates are built during a lifetime—a living estate and a death estate. Meager information about proper estate planning. What is meant by probate anyway? Who do you trust to be your executor? Example of a probate that lasted four years! The importance of trusting your executor. Don't name a family member to be your legal representative. The importance of discussing your plans with the next generation. Your executor is in charge, not the probate attorney. Examples. The importance of a confidential inventory of your assets. An example of one. The inheritance tax appraiser. The State Inheritance Tax return and the Federal Estate Tax return. The long delay of probate.

Two devices to get money for the heirs during probate. A final accounting by the executor. An example. The final decree of distribution by the court and the discharge of the executor. Probate and executor fees. Probate a matter of public record. Anyone can find out what you died possessed of and who received it. How do you avoid probate? Simple. Use correct ownership. If you don't want to do that, you better trust your executor.

To pay more in taxes than the law demands is a deterrent to financial independence. Maintain poor records, keep excess dollars in a

CONTENTS

bank, don't open a Keogh plan or an IRA account, and your accountant can't help you. Four basic ways to reduce your income taxes. There are no "tax loopholes," just legal deductions. Reducing taxes is an all-year problem. Explanation of Form 1040 and Schedules A & B. Difference between a deduction and a credit. Depreciation on property can convert a net income into a sizable loss. Thirteen other ways to reduce your taxes. Explanation of capital gains and losses. Five ways to avoid or defer a capital gains tax. Twelve ways to have tax-exempt income. Explanation of tax shelters. Accountants, swamped before tax time, can't do justice to your return. It's basically your problem. Tax reform and tax simplification are making headlines. If you use the information in this chapter to understand your 1984 and 1985 returns, you will comprehend any changes passed by Congress. It should be understood by everyone that investments made prior to January 1, 1986 will not be affected by any new law.

Trusts are created by people who for good reasons don't want heirs to inherit immediately. Difference between a trustee and an executor. Three basic duties of a trustee. Five reasons why trusts are used. The Clifford trust and an example. The ten basic features of a trust. Often outright distribution to a widow is not wise for five good reasons. How to keep a small business or a valuable piece of real estate intact for heirs by using a trust. Examples. A living trust for a large estate avoids publicity of probate. Example. Use a bank agency account rather than a trust for disability or old age. The use of charitable trusts. Normally, don't name a bank as your trustee.

The Unified Rate Schedule for gift and estate taxes. What is meant by the terms "unified credit," "exemption equivalent," "maximum rate," and "rate on excess"? How to take full advantage of the individual exemption for each spouse. In large estates, don't ignore the interim benefits. Example. Trusts drawn prior to 1981 should be reviewed and probably rewritten. The disclaimer provision. The generation skipping transfer tax. Example. Where it does not apply.

The $250,000 grandchild exclusion clause. The advantage in using powers of appointment. If you name a bank as trustee, give the beneficiary the right to withdraw annually a percentage of the assets. Example of where this was not done. Orphan exclusion clause revoked in 1984. The alternative valuation date. Flower bonds. State inheritance taxes. Gift taxes. The unlimited gift tax marital deduction. Millions may be left to a spouse tax free. Using the $10,000 annual gift tax exclusion. Examples. Lawyers are not much help. More misinformation on estate planning than in any other area of money management. You had better trust yourself because you have learned the rules.

There are eleven estate planning principles that, when used, will provide your estate with simplicity, add cash flow, improve investments, further protect the heirs, and ensure long-term growth to counteract the inroads of inflation. Numerous examples. Also fundamental rules brought out in previous chapters reemphasized here. Estate planning is a must if you are to transfer your estate to your heirs with the least trouble and expense.

Buying real estate today as an investment is difficult because of high prices and high interest rates. Nevertheless very profitable. Many of the great family fortunes have been established this way. Limited partnerships are today's alternative to investing on your own. Four basic benefits, and five additional advantages of partnerships, and the law governing them. Various types—equity, triple net lease, land development, income, leasing. Public and private partnerships. Real estate investment trusts (REITs), either equity or mortgage. Advantages and disadvantages. Oil and gas exploration and development. This is a numbers game. Before placing your trust in the general partners insist upon seven minimum requirements. With the professional expertise available, and viewing the results of the better partnerships, it is hard to make a case for investing in real estate on your own.

CONTENTS

Forty-two million people own stocks and bonds bought through 300,000 registered representatives, but it is an open question how much of this trust is justified. Two examples of fraud involving over $100 million in each case, both recommended by the leading brokerage houses. They conduct business in a way that encourages snap judgments. Example. Protect yourself first by learning as much as you can. History and basic information. Decide on your objectives. Sixteen rules for investing in common stocks. Preferred stocks and bonds. Municipals. Mutual funds and their ten advantages, their charges, and their past performance. Eight guidelines for investing in mutual funds. Money market funds. If daily fluctuations bother you, stay out of the market. Learn by study to trust your own judgment.

A financial planner analyzes your present financial situation and then provides you with a written comprehensive plan on how to improve it. Financial planning is an infant industry, with growing pains and no regulation. A lot of demand. People no longer want to deal with a half dozen different people to achieve their goals. Continuing or future inflation, taxes, economic uncertainty, and proliferation of places to invest has created a financial wilderness. It is increasingly apparent that the ability to make money and the expertise to manage it are seldom found in the same person. Ten questions to test your expertise, with the answers in the Appendix. The International Association of Financial Planners. How to find a competent one. In the future, financial planning will be the major way the financial services industry will function. We recommend the truly professional financial planner, who is fully automated, competent, and dedicated, as someone you could trust.

WHO
TO TRUST
WITH
YOUR
MONEY

1

The Basic Problem

WHEN YOU HAVE accumulated excess dollars, you are confronted with a basic problem: who to trust with your money.

When you ask the average person this question, you will get a reply such as: "Well—I don't know," or, "That's a hard question." Or he or she might say: "I suppose I'd go to a stockbroker," frequently naming some firm they have seen advertised on television, such as Merrill Lynch with its slogan "A breed apart," or E. F. Hutton, with its advertisement "When E. F. Hutton talks, people listen."

Yet when pinned down, most people will admit they have never been to a stockbroker.

Why?

Primarily because of a basic fear that some fast-talking, slick artist will do them out of their money. So they keep their excess dollars in a bank, never talk to anybody, and as a consequence don't invest.

Quite often people turn to a relative or a friend for advice about where to put money to work, or they ask their doctor or lawyer. They tend to consult people who are not going to benefit by giving advice. They feel these people will not be thinking about earning a commission. Even though this assumption is correct, free advice, freely given, is too often the most expensive counsel you can get.

Suppose you ask a relative or a friend, or a well-liked

neighborhood guru, about a specific investment. Usually he will advise you to keep your money where it is, in the bank. Why?

For three reasons.

First, he is apt to see investments in terms of his own needs and interests. Second, he doesn't want to take the time to analyze any investment you might be considering. Third, he can't be proven wrong by advising you to do nothing.

If he does recommend someone for you to see, that individual may give poor advice. Or if an investment is recommended, it may turn out to be a bad one. In that case, the person who made the recommendation has lost a friend or incurred the wrath of a relative; or if he is a professional man, the loss of a patient or a client.

If not from relatives, friends, or professional persons, people then often seek advice from a bank. But your local banker is the wrong person to see. Ask your banker about a loan. He is an expert in this area. Don't ask him about investments.

As mentioned before, stockbrokers are frequently consulted. It's amazing how a person will walk unannounced into a brokerage house, diffident because he or she is in strange and impressive surroundings, and timidly ask what to do with, say, $20,000. It's the wrong way to go about it, yet people do it.

If not from relatives, friends, professional people, and bankers, then counsel is often sought from those who are in the business of advising people about their money, such as stockbrokers, real estate brokers, financial planners, and promoters of investment seminars. Investments are also influenced by columnists and newsletter writers.

One of the best ways to obtain proper advice is to know enough about banks, probate, wills, taxes, and trusts to enable you to ask intelligent questions about whatever concerns you, and to determine the validity of the information you receive.

Besides fear of being sold something they really shouldn't buy, people don't trust outside advice because of the horror stories they have read about investors losing most or all of their money in investments that turned out to be outright frauds.

The following headline appeared in the *San Francisco Examiner* a short time ago.

$100 MILLION MAY BE LOST IN SAN DIEGO INVESTMENT SCAM.

And another one announced a little later:

TAX FRAUD TRIAL OPENS FOR FIVE SENTINEL FINANCIAL TRADERS.

It is headlines like these that frighten people away from trusting anybody, including their best friend, especially since these investments were recommended to their clients by some of the biggest and most respected stockbrokerage firms in the country.

But there are other people in whom you might find occasion to place your trust.

When you have a will drawn, you name an executor to take charge of your assets during the long period of probate, which will certainly take months and in many cases years. It's essential that you trust your executor's judgment because the decisions your legal representative makes are often vital to the financial well-being of your heirs. Since your executor— not the probate attorney—is in charge of your estate, he should be acquainted with the duties of an executor. His ignorance of them can cause needless long delays in the probate process and could cost the estate a lot of money.

I ask you now, did the Internal Revenue Service ever tell you that you didn't take all of the deductions you were entitled to on your income tax return, and therefore you owed less money? Of course not. Since you can't trust the IRS to do this, you would be wise to learn how to keep more of your money for yourself and your family by understanding the deductions and exemptions allowed under the law.

Over 20 million taxpayers use the long form 1040 and itemize their deductions, but through lack of knowledge too few of these people don't reduce their taxes as much as they should. Many taxpayers who use the short form, should not, because they could benefit by itemizing their deductions on Schedule A. Others could benefit by income averaging, or taking tax credits. Everyone should realize that a credit is better than a tax; a credit is deducted 100 percent from taxes, while a deduction simply reduces income.

Estate taxes are not the big problem they were formerly, thanks to the Economic Recovery Tax Act of 1981. If you created a testamentary trust several years ago to reduce your estate taxes when you die, perhaps you should revoke it. Do not expect your trust officer to advise you. He's not going to tell you to take your trust agreement and tear it up. Not if he likes working for the bank.

When people make wills and trusts they should be fully aware of the current regulations regarding estate and gift taxes. They should know that an unlimited amount, even millions, may be given to or inherited by a spouse. They should know about the $10,000 annual gift tax exclusion, which makes the gift completely free of income, gift, and estate taxes, and which may be given to any number of recipients. They should be aware of the grandchild exclusion clause which avoids the generation skipping transfer tax. But how many people know, when considering this tax, that a wife is considered to be of the same generation as her husband no matter how much younger she may be?

But despite fear of salesmen, the hazards of trusting the wrong people, and the big losses incurred by many because of fraud, you should still seek and accept outside advice. Certainly, you can keep your money in a bank or in a savings and loan institution and have the comfortable feeling that government insurance gives you, but you will not become well off, and for sure you will never become wealthy.

Instead you should listen to people about investments. You will learn a lot, and in the process, and in time, you will be able to evaluate their expertise and their suggestions.

Eventually, you should learn to trust a dedicated, competent, fully automated financial planner who can set up a blueprint for your future financial security according to your ability, desires, and assets.

So let's take a closer look at the different people who might be able to give you the financial advice you need and want.

2

Relatives
and
Friends

A WELL-LIKED RELATIVE, especially one who has been considerate and helpful in the past, is frequently turned to for financial advice. These qualities, while certainly admirable, do not necessarily qualify that person for wise counseling on what to do with money.

For example, a broker advised Mrs. Jones on where to invest her money, but she couldn't make up her mind, so she said: "I think I'll ask my cousin Joe."

"That's fine, Mrs. Jones," the broker replied. "Your cousin Joe is undoubtedly a fine man or you wouldn't seek his advice. By the way, has he made a lot of sound investments?"

"Well, I wouldn't say that. I don't believe he has much money."

"What does he do for a living?"

"He's an automobile mechanic."

"I don't know your relative, Mrs. Jones, so I can't insult him, but an automobile mechanic may not be the best person to turn to for investment advice. Under the circumstances, I don't think that you should ask your cousin Joe what to do with your money."

But she did, and he told her to put her money into options "where she would make a lot of money," he said. She didn't though, for she was broke in less than a year.

EXAMPLE TWO

Seeking the advice of adult children, who are often the closest relatives one has, can often be disastrous for the financial well-being of a prospective investor. Mrs. Alden had two married daughters, one generous and outgoing, the other one grasping and self-centered. Mrs. Alden loved them both deeply and was incapable of differentiating between them when it came to their basic qualities.

When her brother died and left her $60,000, she was overwhelmed with emotion and grateful to her brother for being so generous, because she had no money and was barely able to meet her monthly obligations.

The executor of her brother's estate, who also had been his investment representative, was particularly helpful to Mrs. Alden during the many months of probate by keeping her informed about what was going on, and when probate probably would be over. Because of this, and her brother's faith in his financial advice, she told the legal representative she was going to follow his suggestions on what to do with the money when she received it.

Mrs. Alden's brother, prior to his death, told his executor he was concerned that his sister would squander the $60,000 that he was leaving her. As a consequence, he asked the executor in the event of his demise to do what he could to prevent it.

When probate was over, the executor personally delivered the $60,000 check and, mindful of his former client's request, advised Mrs. Alden to keep $30,000 in the bank and place the remaining $30,000 in a sound investment for current income. In addition to receiving more income than the bank would pay her, the money would not be as liquid as a bank account and therefore less likely to be dissipated.

Mrs. Alden agreed, signed the necessary application, and wrote a check for $30,000.

The former executor was relieved, for he was able to

partly accomplish what his former client wanted—which was to protect Mrs. Alden from her spendthrift habits—without too many objections on her part.

But it was all to no avail because Mrs. Alden called him the following morning at 8:00 A.M., saying that she hadn't slept all night from worry and could she have her $30,000 check back?

So the broker sent it back and washed his hands of the whole affair.

Subsequently he heard what happened. After he left that day, Mrs. Alden told her grasping daughter what she had done.

"You can't do that," she exclaimed. "You'll lose the entire thirty-thousand dollars!"

This was why Mrs. Alden couldn't sleep and canceled the investment.

Later on, the grasping daughter persuaded her mother to loan her the $30,000, which she never paid back. The other, softhearted daughter said Mrs. Alden should spend the remaining money rather than leave it to her children someday. After all, they didn't want it, and she reminded her mother that she was already in her sixties and that now was the time to enjoy herself.

Mrs. Alden took the advice, bought a new car (which she didn't need), took a trip to Europe, and spent the rest of the money. So because of the advice and actions of her children, Mrs. Alden dissipated all of the money, which was what her brother thought would happen in the first place.

EXAMPLE THREE

Mrs. Anthony was a widow, living on modest means, who had made a sound investment for income through a financial planner.

When she matured a certificate for $20,000, he suggested that she add $10,000 to her account. She agreed this would be a sound thing for her to do but she wanted to talk to her only son before making a final decision.

The son, who had never been a success financially, suggested that she take the $20,000 and build a duplex with the money, and he would act as the general contractor. Together they would make a lot of money and, who knows, someday they might be wealthy.

The broker tried to dissuade her with sound arguments, but without success.

They built the duplex, but it was so badly designed and constructed that they had a hard time keeping tenants, and when it was put up for sale no one would buy it since, in the small town where Mrs. Anthony lived, the building soon became known as a white elephant. Now, not only did Mrs. Anthony lose the income which she badly needed from the $20,000, but she couldn't recover her money either.

No, well-meaning relatives, and particularly inexperienced adult children, should not be asked for investment advice. Too often the counsel can be disastrous.

Widows in particular are prone to do this. I know that I will be criticized by my female readers for using too many widows in my examples. But it's true that widows, rather than widowers, are more inclined to trust relatives for advice.

If people don't turn to a relative for financial advice, they often seek counsel from a friend.

A competent friend quite often refuses to give advice for two good reasons. One, the person whose advice is sought doesn't have to spend valuable time evaluating the suggested investment; and two, that individual can't be proven wrong if the money is kept in the bank.

Art Linkletter was interviewed one time on the television program *Inside Business.*

The talk show host asked him if he ever advised people on investments, since it was well known that he was many times a millionaire.

"Not anymore," he replied. "Although I used to tell people what I was doing with my money."

The interviewer smiled. "I take it something caused you to change your mind."

"Yes, and it was a small thing really, but it happened too

many times. An acquaintance of mine asked me what I was doing with my money, so I told him about a stock I had bought."

"Then what happened?"

"I ran into him a year later, and he said, 'That was some stock you recommended. I lost my shirt.' I was frankly surprised and told him I didn't know what he was talking about. I never recommended that he buy a stock.

"'Oh yes, you did,' he said.

"And then I remembered that I had casually mentioned this company to him. So I told him that I had sold my stock because I hadn't liked the change in management. He proceeded to berate me for not telling him to sell, too. After that I stopped telling people what I do with my money. People still ask, but I don't tell them."

A friend who is financially incompetent is quite often flattered by being asked for advice and therefore will give it freely. Such a friend, as someone said one time, speaks with the authority of ignorance.

EXAMPLE ONE

A financial planner spent hours of his valuable time with Mr. and Mrs. Andrews, a retired couple, in order to obtain a complete picture of their finances. Some time before, when the husband retired, they had rolled over $40,000 from his company's pension plan into an IRA account. Now that he was seventy and a half years old, Mr. Andrews had to start withdrawing the money, which could present them with an income tax problem.

The financial planner and the couple's accountant agreed that Mr. Andrews could withdraw $20,000 for more income without seriously increasing their income taxes that year. Also, he could withdraw the remaining $20,000 by investing in a real estate tax shelter, which would have the combined effect of tax sheltering the second $20,000 and giving the Andrewses inflationary protection as well.

Unfortunately, before the suggestions were finalized, they visited old friends one evening, and, because their financial decisions were much on their minds, the Andrewses discussed what they were planning to do with the $40,000.

Their friends were horrified. They brought up story after story of retired people who had lost their money. They even brought out articles that they had saved about abusive tax shelters. They said they couldn't believe that their friends would risk so much money at their ages when they had no opportunity to make that kind of money again.

The result? They canceled their next appointment with the financial planner and never saw him again. They argued with their accountant and fired him. Except for the small amount Mr. Andrews had to withdraw each year, as required by law, the money remained in the IRA account, compounding the interest. And for whose benefit if they never withdrew it all? For the benefit of Mr. and Mrs. Andrews' heirs, whoever they might be.

It wasn't their friends who suffered from such advice, for it wasn't their money. But Mr. and Mrs. Andrews lived on a reduced income because of spending an evening with well-meaning friends.

EXAMPLE TWO

Mr. Ansell, a widower, who had worked for forty years for the ABC Company, was retired on a pension. But this was by no means all the money he had. He had been frugal during his working years and with his savings had bought his company's stock, which had increased in value dramatically.

At this point in his life he was introduced to a financial planner who worked for a well-known and respected independent broker with hundreds of representatives from coast to coast. The registered representative had only one suggestion to make. Mr. Ansell should diversify part of his shares into other investments. His investment in the ABC Company, worth $200,000, was simply too much money in one place.

"Mr. Ansell," he advised, "you are violating one of the basic principles of investing, which is diversification. 'Don't put all of your eggs in one basket' is a very old saying. And maybe that is why the expression is so old. It is one of the soundest investment principles around."

"Well, young fellow," replied Mr. Ansell, "I've lived a long time, and the stock has always been good to me. It's gone up and gone down over the years, and I've paid no attention. But in the long run it's gone up."

The investment representative had to smile. "I can't argue with your results," he replied. "Turning ten thousand dollars into two hundred thousand dollars is a remarkable achievement. I have talked to very few people, I might say no one, who has equaled that performance."

"Well, then," replied Mr. Ansell, "I guess I should stay right where I am."

"No," replied the broker, "I have to disagree. It's simply too much money in one place."

"You think the company's going broke?"

"I have no idea. I know nothing about the company. It could be sound, or not sound, but that is not the point. Your two hundred thousand dollars is in jeopardy solely because it is not diversified."

"OK, young fellow. I'll tell you what I'll do. I have a good friend. I'll ask him what he thinks."

So Mr. Ansell sought the advice of his friend, and because he was busy and it was the easiest way out, his friend advised him to sit tight and do nothing.

It was not the best counsel in the world, for shortly afterward the stock of ABC Company started going down. And instead of the price of the stock recovering as it always had in the past, it kept going down until it became worthless when the company went bankrupt. As a consequence Mr. Ansell lost his entire $200,000 because a friend, who was too busy, gave him a careless answer.

But in spite of these examples, and the fact that for the most part relatives and friends are not the best people to ask, if you have a friend or relative who is knowledgeable on investments, or who can send you to someone who has given him sound advice over the years, then by all means consult with that individual. It could be the best investment advice you will receive. But be sure your friend can be trusted to give you the necessary time to evaluate your problem, and that he has the qualifications to act wisely on your behalf.

3

Professional People

DOCTORS ARE OFTEN consulted about money problems because of their affluence. Also, people are inclined to idolize their doctors, setting them on a pedestal as infallible in all things.

As a general rule, however, doctors are terrible investors. By the nature of their profession, they are not in contact with the business world. The only people they see every day are their patients, who have physical problems, real or imaginary.

A doctor's nurse or secretary, as the case may be, is not of any help in this regard. She takes the attitude that the doctor should see no one except his patients. After all, her job is to keep his schedule full every day so he won't have a wasted minute.

But the nurse is wrong. A doctor has to invest his money if he hopes to be wealthy someday. He should occasionally see salesmen as well as his patients.

So let's see what usually happens when a financial planner telephones for an appointment because the doctor's name has been suggested by one of his customers. The conversation takes place like this.

"Doctor's office," the nurse says, as she answers the registered representative's call.

"Is the doctor in?"

"Who is calling, please?"

"John Jones."

"Are you a patient?" The nurse means by this question, are you a patient now, or are you someone who hasn't seen the doctor before in regard to an ailment. Obviously, nobody dares call her busy doctor during business hours except someone who wants to see him because of a physical problem.

"No," the financial planner replies, "I'm not calling as a patient."

"I'm sorry. The doctor is busy and can't be disturbed."

And she hangs up. Unless the caller is unusually persistent, that ends any attempt to see the doctor, and the nurse goes about her business.

Or, let us say, an investment representative succeeds in getting an appointment with a doctor, who is very busy as usual and wants to get back to work, for this is how he earns his money. Which is true, of course, but it is not how he learns to invest his excess dollars.

So the doctor listens impatiently, willing to give the salesman at the most ten minutes of his time.

If the broker is a good one, he insists upon giving an adequate explanation of the proposed investment. The doctor glances at his watch before the financial planner has hardly started on what he wanted to say; thanks the broker for his time; stands up and says he has to get back to work, stating that he is not interested. Not interested in what? He hasn't even found out yet. How can anyone make an intelligent decision on whether or not to invest thousands of dollars in that short a time?

If the broker is an unscrupulous one and only wants to make a sale, not caring how he gets it, he knows he has to give the doctor a fast pitch on a speculative investment, with the promise of a large and quick profit.

After about five minutes of explanation, he asks: "How about it, doctor? Such a good deal is not going to be around very long. Do you want me to write it up?"

"All right," the doctor says, making a snap judgment. "I'll take it. Where do I sign?"

The contrast between the two interviews explains why so many doctors speculate with their money instead of making a sound investment.

So you have an appointment as a patient with a doctor, and you take advantage of this opportunity by asking him about an investment you have in mind.

"After all, doctor," you say, "with the kind of money you make you must have made a lot of sound investments."

If the doctor is flattered, he will give you a snap judgment, so you will get very poor advice indeed, which is not surprising considering the manner in which he makes his own investments.

This does not mean to imply that all doctors are bad investors. A few of them are wealthy, and not necessarily from their practice.

These doctors are smart. They know they are not good businessmen. They listen to proven experts in the investment business, and they read financial publications. They instruct their nurses not to say "no" when a nonpatient calls. They explain that occasionally they will want to see a broker or a financial planner. They will take such calls and decide whether or not to grant an interview.

If you ask such a doctor for investment advice, and if he is willing to take the time to analyze your proposed investment problem, you could obtain good counseling.

Lawyers are even worse than doctors about investing. Many of them have no investable funds, believe it or not, despite their high living standards.

People don't like to consult lawyers because of the poor image the legal profession has with the general public. Many persons feel that once they have placed their problems in the hands of a lawyer, they will be involved with high legal fees, delay, and frustration.

This image, many lawyers will agree, has been created by the legal profession itself. Let's face it, too many lawyers don't work hard. When you go to them with a legal problem, they will ask for all the documents involved with the case, open a file, place the folder on a corner of their desk, and sit back and do nothing. Every time they telephone you, or you telephone them, they charge you for it. If they write you a letter in regard to your problem, you are charged again. In the meantime very little is being done.

I was an executor of an estate one time. I telephoned the probate attorney for an appointment because I was ready to write checks for the heirs now that we had a final decree of distribution from the court. Later in the lawyer's office, after determining the correct amount to be paid to each heir, I sat down and took out my executor's checkbook.

He looked at me in surprise. "What are you doing?" he asked.

"I'm going to write checks to send to the various heirs," I replied.

"What for? There's no hurry. It's noon. How about lunch?"

After lunch he maintained that he was too busy, that he would have to write the checks some other time.

It took me almost three weeks of persistent telephoning to get another appointment with that attorney. At that meeting I insisted upon writing the checks then and there. After his secretary had typed the necessary releases for each heir to sign, I took the releases to the post office myself.

I found out later that the attorney had exclaimed in amazement to his secretary: "You know, it took us just one hour to distribute five hundred thousand dollars to those ten heirs!"

If I had been an inexperienced executor, I don't know how long that attorney would have procrastinated before the heirs were paid what was due them.

Attorneys confuse and intimidate people because they know the law and their clients do not, and partly, too, because they use legal phraseology that most people don't understand.

But in spite of all this, they do a great job of selling themselves.

EXAMPLE

Mrs. Bagley, a widow who was inexperienced in money matters, was nonetheless named executrix in her husband's will. According to the usual practice, she named the lawyer who drew the will as the probate attorney. She felt that since her late husband trusted the lawyer to draw his will, certainly she could have confidence in him when it came to investment advice.

A financial planner, who came well recommended, suggested two investments to her, one for current income and one, because of her relatively young age, for long-term growth.

Mrs. Bagley liked the representative's recommendations, but before deciding what to do she consulted the probate attorney.

"Well," he replied, "those aren't bad suggestions, but I think we can do better with the money."

"What do you suggest?" the widow asked.

"Do you know anything about real estate?"

"No, I don't."

"Well, that doesn't make any difference. I know a good broker who can find a nice duplex for you that will give you what you want. Good current income and a chance for profit. I'll put him in touch with you."

Mrs. Bagley took his advice and bought a duplex that the attorney's broker friend found for her, rejecting the two sound investments that the financial planner had suggested. Although real estate can be an excellent investment in the hands of the right person, this real estate broker sold Mrs. Bagley a building with a negative cash flow (i.e., with no net income, so she had to pay part of the operating expenses from her savings), and because of a poor location, the duplex did not increase in value. So instead of two sound investments, Mrs. Bagley had a poor real estate investment instead.

Why did the attorney make this suggestion? Possibly because he could profit in some way from the sale of the property, or he could split the commission with the real estate broker.

In most states it is against the law to split a real estate commission with an unlicensed person. But many of the legislators who vote for such laws are attorneys. So which people are usually exempt from the above rule about splitting a real estate commission? Lawyers, of course.

It should be fairly obvious it's unwise to ask lawyers for investment advice. Many of them don't have any excess dollars, so they never have invested. If they volunteer investment advice, or advise names of others to see, tell them you want to sleep on it for a while and you will get back to them later.

Go to a lawyer because you have a legal problem. Don't take his advice about what to do with your money.

An investor or prospective investor should read the columns of the nationally syndicated financial writers. Over the course of a year they provide a wealth of information.

One should realize, however, they *have to* write a column, if not every day at least once a week. No matter how good their research or expertise, they are not right every day or all of the time. Like the advice from everyone else, the suggestions and comments they make have to be evaluated.

There is one article by a columnist that I have retained over the years, probably for no reason except my own amusement. Every year or two I take it out and read it again. The article was written by an old college friend of mine, now dead, who became a well-known columnist for a Minneapolis, Minnesota, newspaper.

This article appeared a long time ago, in 1946. It is quoted because the chart in the body of the article is surprisingly accurate, although it starts with the year 1850. It dares to demonstrate the fluctuations of the stock market over a period of 150 years! The column is entitled "In This Corner," and was written by Cedric Adams. Bear in mind, now, that his article originally appeared in 1946, and I quote:

Everybody's been expecting a business boom during the next few years and the economists probably can point to a hundred factors that will justify these expectations. Bill Rehbock sent a chart to This Corner the other day that has quite a background. We ran a paragraph on it, and since then requests for additional information have been so numerous that we decided to reprint the chart. At first glance, it looks a little like a backgammon board, but careful scrutiny reveals some rather startling statistics in connection with it. The original chart started with the year 1810. We chopped a few years off the beginning to fit it into our two-column width. You don't care too much about those early years, anyway. Starting with the year 1850, you get the early panics about which our grade school histories told us. Panic years of 1857, 1873, 1894 are all a matter of record. The top line or "A" indicated years of good times and high prices. That's the time when stocks should be sold, according to the chart. The "B" years are low prices, hard times—the period in which to buy. The "C" years are panic or depression years. Now take a good look at the chart.

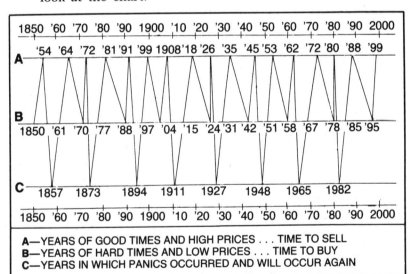

A—YEARS OF GOOD TIMES AND HIGH PRICES . . . TIME TO SELL
B—YEARS OF HARD TIMES AND LOW PRICES . . . TIME TO BUY
C—YEARS IN WHICH PANICS OCCURRED AND WILL OCCUR AGAIN

It's easy [the 1946 article by Cedric Adams goes on to say] to check on the year 1918, for instance, as a prosperous year. You plungers will remember 1929. Note where the chart has 1929. Remember, too, that this chart was made up sometime during or before the Civil War and was found in an old desk in Philadelphia back in 1902. Note that 1931 was a year of hard times and low prices. True? Then we scoot up to 1935, a darn good year. The drop started then and continued till 1942. Up it went again until 1945. But look what happens from 1946 on. There's a nose-dive from 1945 to 1948 which, according to the chart predictions, is a panic or depression year. And that isn't too far off. [Two years from the date of Cedric Adams' article.]

We climb from that low to 1951, a year of low prices. Then comes 1953 which looks like a dandy. There's some ray of sunshine in the fact that after we hit the expected bottom in 1948, it'll take 17 years to go up and back down again. [Author: As a matter of fact, the years 1948 to 1962 marked the longest bull market rise in history.] If some stockbroker would only take the trouble to check back on prices, it would be interesting to see $1,000 invested on the day, for instance, that Lincoln was shot, with the money invested according to the chart. Hetty Green, whose policy was to buy when others were selling and to sell when others were buying, died the richest woman in the world. Maybe she had the chart, huh? Two years more and we'll know how right the document is, anyway.

For the entertainment of our readers, if for no other reason, we have reprinted on page 31 what has happened to the Dow Jones Industrial Average since 1946 in order to compare it with the chart as republished in that year by Cedric Adams. For what it is worth, the chart since 1946 closely follows the Dow Jones Industrial Average. It depicts that 1982 was the last time to buy, and it was right on the money. It's too bad the chart quits with the year 1999. *A word of warning.* We are *not* recommending that you trust the accuracy of the chart.

Newsletter Writers

There are literally dozens of them, mailing out their newsletters weekly, bimonthly, or monthly to thousands of fans all over the country. These newsletter writers are recommending countless different ways to make money, each one claiming to specialize in his or her particular area of investment expertise, from mutual funds to technical analysis (as a way of forecasting the market) to outright recommendations of when to get in and out of the market. One writer was remarkably successful over a period of years, until he told his thousands of readers to sell in the summer of 1982. That advice turned out to be a disaster for his huge following. They sat there in a cash position while the market soared in one of the sharpest and most spectacular rises in recent memory.

Like the columnists, newsletter writers present a sensible argument for whatever course of action they are recommending. Those who religiously believed the doomsday writers of a few years ago who were predicting the coming bad years failed to see it happen. Their readers, with their money stashed in cash and gold, lived to regret the advice.

In practice, economics is not an exact science, but newsletter writers tend to treat investing that way. They predicted over the last several years that we would have high inflation, a bull market in gold, and a U.S. dollar that would be almost worthless. On the contrary we have had low inflation, gold selling around $300 an ounce (down from a high price of over $800), and a U.S. dollar that is the strongest currency in the world.

This doesn't mean that you shouldn't subscribe to two or three newsletters of your choice. These writers are knowl-

Cost of Living Trend, Dividend Income, and Dow Jones Stock Prices from 12/31/46 to 12/31/81

For Purposes of Comparison, All of the Figures Were Adjusted to 100 as of 12/31/45

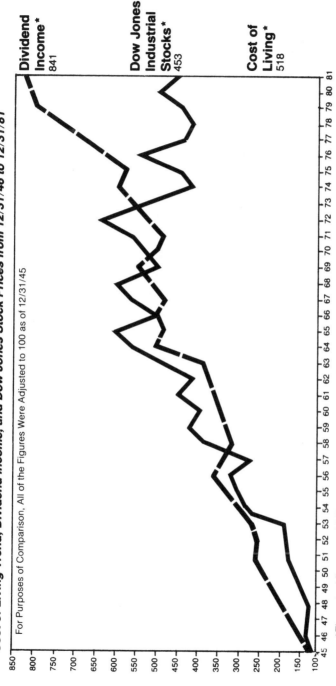

*The actual figures at 12/31/81 were: Dow Jones Industrial Average Stock Prices—875.00; DJ Dividend Income—$56.22; Consumer Price Index—282.6. The chart cannot be considered as an example of future results, and does not reflect any adjustment for income taxes.

edgeable, and you should listen to their observations because you will learn a lot from them. They can be a filter for your own lack of expertise and possibly prevent you from making a serious investment mistake. They are not like Woody Allen who once remarked facetiously when asked what he did for a living, "I'm an investment adviser. I help people with their money until it's gone."

We live in an uncertain economic world, but that doesn't mean that you shouldn't follow a newsletter writer's suggestion about what to do with your money. Despite uncertainty there are ways to invest successfully, just as there are ways of succeeding in your job or your marriage. Economics and investments are not in another world. We live in one world. And despite the fact that no one has a crystal ball, we learn to cope.

4

Thrift
Institutions
and
Accountants

AMERICANS LEARNED LONG AGO to trust banks, savings and loan associations, and credit unions to provide complete security for their money. As custodians, all three types of institutions do a good job, and they should be trusted. In addition, the deposits are insured by an agency of the federal government up to $100,000.

A banker instills confidence by projecting an image of a staid individual, properous, conservative, with vast experience in handling money. After all, money is what he or she deals in every day. But we are not determining here the merits of responsible custodianship or making a good impression. We are trying to decide whom to trust for advice on investments.

What does a banker know about the stock market? Practically nothing, and a smart banker will readily admit it. He doesn't want to recommend a stock because if the price goes down, the customer will have lost money (at least on paper). Naturally, the banker does not want to risk losing an account, or having a customer lose confidence.

What does he know about real estate? He may not know much more than what he knows about the stock market. If you want a real estate loan, he will have your property appraised and lend you a percentage of that value with the protection of a lien on the property. But using real estate as security for a loan does not necessarily qualify a banker to give good advice about investing in real estate.

The average branch officer is limited to a maximum of $100,000 when considering a loan application. If more than this is needed by the borrower, the applicant is referred to the head office. However, this does not mean that the home office is necessarily more competent.

The biggest banks in the United States have loaned billions to the so-called Third World countries in Central and South America and Africa (such as Mexico, Brazil, and Argentina). These loans are in trouble, for the debtor countries are having great difficulty paying the interest, much less meeting the principal payments. They have appealed for relief to the World Bank, but that institution has insisted upon such stringent rules about how to manage their economies in order to obtain more money, the borrowing countries are saying they can't comply, that it would work too great a hardship upon their people.

How much money have the big banks loaned the Third World? The amount is equal to the entire net worth of the banks! Now I ask you, would you and I do that?

And that is not all. A chill went through the banking world when an event occurred in Chicago that has haunted millions of Americans old enough to remember the bank failures of the Great Depression. A major American bank nearly failed.

The Continental Illinois National Bank and Trust Company, the eighth largest in the nation, would have failed if it had not been for an unprecedented bail-out by the Federal Deposit Insurance Corporation, aided by substantial help from the Federal Reserve Bank.

The bank's problems arose not only from loans to the Third World but from bad energy loans, which became what bankers euphemistically call nonperforming loans because nothing was being paid on them by way of principal or interest.

The final result was the ownership of Continental Illinois

Bank and Trust company by the United States government, with the Federal Deposit Insurance Corporation owning 80 percent of the bank's stock, with an option to buy the remaining 20 percent depending upon certain contingencies. The FDIC stoutly maintained that the bank was still a private institution because the new management of the bank (whom the government appointed) came from the private sector and therefore were not federal employees.

This, of course, was a lot of nonsense. When the negotiations were finalized, the Federal Deposit Insurance Corporation owned 80 percent of the bank's stock and under certain conditions could acquire the remaining 20 percent. The only way ownership of the bank could be returned to the private sector would be recovery by the FDIC of most of the billions loaned to Continental Illinois by repayment of the nonperforming loans it acquired from the bank.

No depositor lost any money, no matter how large the account. In this case, the ceiling of $100,000 for bank insurance was ignored. The stockholders of the bank, of course, stood to lose everything. At a meeting convened to obtain approval of the government takeover, the stockholders reluctantly gave it, but only after the chairman of the board told them there was no alternative. It was either approve the arrangement or bankruptcy would be the result.

It is true that with the advent of deregulation some of the bigger banks are attempting to get into the securities business. But until your bank acquires a big, experienced brokerage firm, as Sears, Roebuck did when it took over Dean Witter for the financial services department, the above suggestion of not trusting your bankers for investment advice still holds.

Counsel about investments is also sought from savings and loan institutions. Many people don't differentiate between banks and savings and loans, but they should.

As a depositor of a bank you have a demand account. You have the right to ask for your money when it is due at any time, because you are a creditor of the bank and you receive interest. Your account is insured by the Federal Deposit Insurance Corporation. Failure of a bank results in immediate rescue by the FDIC, either by closing the bank or merging it with a financially healthy one. In either event, the insured depositor loses nothing.

You don't have a demand account with a savings and loan institution. You are not a creditor; and you don't receive interest, you get dividends. Most people know that a savings and loan can demand a thirty-day written notice of withdrawal before it has to honor the request. This is reasonable, for most of the depositors' money is invested in long-term mortgages. A savings and loan, therefore, is not as liquid as a bank that makes short-term loans and, in addition, is required by the Federal Reserve Bank to keep a percentage of its assets in cash.

Deposits in a savings and loan association are protected by the Federal Savings and Loan Insurance Corporation, which is also an agency of the federal government. But the deposit insurance is not the same because the insurance commissioner of the state involved must declare that institution insolvent. And it is not insolvent simply because it cannot pay withdrawal requests.

But the situation is changing with the government's deregulation of thrift institutions. More and more the distinction between banks and savings and loan associations is becoming blurred, and the general public is making less and less distinction between the two. Also, the the Federal Reserve Bank stands ready to assist in the orderly transfer of ownership to a sound financial institution when a savings and loan association fails, resulting in no loss to depositors who have insurance on their deposits up to $100,000.

An example is the failure on March 15, 1985, of the Home State Savings and Loan of Cincinnati, Ohio. This was caused by the collapse of ESM Government Securities Inc. of Fort Lauderdale, Florida, in which Home State had invested over $145,000,000. A loss of this magnitude triggered a panic among the depositors of the other sixty-nine savings and loan associations in Ohio, causing Governor Richard F. Celeste to close them and declare a financial holiday, the first in the nation since the Great Depression.

The financial panic in Ohio caused the value of the U.S. dollar to plunge and the price of gold to soar, resulting in concern among depositors in both banks and savings and loans across the country.

We hasten to add that the Ohio panic was caused because the savings and loans involved were not federally insured. They were state-chartered institutions backed by insurance provided by the Ohio Deposit Guarantee Fund, whose reserves were threatened to be wiped out by the magnitude of the Home State Savings and Loan problem.

After several days the closed institutions were allowed to reopen their doors on a limited basis, permitting withdrawal of $750 per month per depositor, and then only if they could qualify for federal insurance. Paul A. Volcker, chairman of the Federal Reserve Bank, in an effort to calm financial markets across the country stated on March 20 that the federal bank was prepared to lend funds to those Ohio savings and loans that were deemed to be strong enough to reopen. "We are working with the Ohio authorities on the situation," he said.

Under current law, the Federal Reserve Bank is required to provide all depository institutions with access to its discount window, which is a method whereby they can borrow funds for short periods of time at a current rate of 8 percent.

Four days after Chairman Volcker's statement, two thousand customers of Home State Savings and Loan jammed Xavier University's fieldhouse in Cincinnati demanding access to their frozen assets. Despite the reopening of most of the sixty-nine other state savings and loan associations, Home State remained closed. In the meantime Arlo Smith, Ohio conservator for the savings and loan associations, stated that he was trying to find a buyer for Home State and a method of unfreezing its accounts.

There is a lesson to be derived from all of this. Depositors should not trust state-licensed savings and loan institutions whose deposits are backed only by a state insurance agency, or (as in Ohio) by a state deposit guarantee fund. This is true even though the federal government is committed to assist troubled banks and savings and loan associations even when they are not backed by federal insurance.

Trust in our financial institutions is based upon confidence in the banking system. Without that trust federal insurance would be unable to provide the safety demanded by the public, for the FDIC and the FSLIC combined have reserves of only $23 billion, with a line of credit of $4 billion more. This does not insure the approximate $1,000 billion in total deposits.

But depositors have nothing to worry about. Congress has pledged the full faith and credit of the U.S. Treasury for all deposits. This was demonstrated by the billions of dollars that was provided by the Federal Reserve Bank when the Continental Illinois National Bank and Trust Company collapsed in Chicago.

Credit unions were mentioned at the start of this chapter because they are savings institutions whose deposits are insured by the Federal Credit Union Insurance Corporation, but they are seldom used as a source of advice on investments.

Thrifts are also used as though they were savings institutions, but unless they are backed by the FDIC (which is rare because most of them can't qualify), depositors should not trust them as safe custodians for their money.

When you buy a thrift certificate, you make an investment, you don't have a deposit. There is always a ratio between risk and reward. The higher the reward, the greater the risk. Thrifts pay a higher rate of interest than banks and savings and loan institutions because they make mainly industrial loans.

When a thrift fails, the institution goes into bankruptcy, and the investors have to wait while regulators slowly liquidate the firm's assets. In this event, investors would probably recover only a percentage of their investment. In the meantime no interest is paid, which could be a real hardship, particularly for those retired on a low income.

When Western Community Money Center, a thrift based in Walnut Creek, California, failed, it had $99 million in deposits and 12,000 investors. The investors' spokesman claimed that the Department of Corporations failed to properly supervise the company. "We were told that the insurance was the equivalent of the FDIC," he said. "The Department's worst mistake was to permit the Money Center to open an office at the entrance to Rossmore, a retirement community. A lot of these people can't afford to lose. The Department of Corporation of the State of California should admit its responsibility for what happened, or get out of the business of regulating thrifts."

The Western Community Money Center's insurance was provided by the Thrift Guaranty Corporation of California, a private concern, guaranteeing deposits up to $50,000 in industrial loan companies. But the size of the Money Center's loss made it impossible for Thrift Guaranty to meet its obligations. At this writing, investors have received 25 cents on the dollar.

The California state legislature, submitting to public pressure, passed a bill in the Senate which guaranteed a private loan to Thrift Guarantee, which in turn would be required to make payments to the depositors of Western Community Money Center. In addition, the bill would make several reforms to the state's system for regulating and insuring industrial loan companies.

There are a couple of things wrong with this solution. First, it might make people less careful (rather than more so) of where they deposit their money. If the state, in the last analysis, is going to guarantee that the depositors get their money, why bother to be cautious? Second, the thrift institutions' officers may be even more careless than they were before about how they handle their customer's deposits. If they make bad loans, it won't make any difference. The state will bail them out.

One official of a solvent California thrift said: "We've been opposed to the Thrift Guaranty Corporation since its inception because we knew it would be turned into a marketing tool to attract investors, rather than serving as protection."

The answer of whom to trust when depositing your money is fairly obvious. Place your money with those saving institutions where it is insured up to $100,000 by an agency of the Federal Government, meaning the FDIC, the FSLIC, or the FCUIC. Make sure when you open your account that the emblem is prominently displayed.

When an accountant prepares your income tax return he obtains not only a complete inventory of your assets, but facts about you and your spouse, your dependents, and their relationship to you. This information is vital to anyone who advises you on investments. In addition, the accountant probably knows your financial objectives, and how much risk you are willing to assume in achieving them.

On the other hand, friends, relatives, lawyers, doctors, and bankers seldom have information about your assets, mainly because you don't want to give it to them. The average person simply does not divulge such personal information to anyone. It is true that savings institutions would have some information about you, but only on the accounts you have with them.

An accountant has another advantage. He has many customers, and from their records he can compare investment results.

Some of his customers have all of their money in fixed dollars. Others invest, assuming a businessman's risk in order to achieve a profit. Others have various combinations of both.

One of the accountant's customers will have a bigger tax problem than another customer, even though both have the same income and number of dependents. That customer who has a tax problem doesn't keep good records of his disbursements, and often is not aware of the deductions allowed under the law.

Other customers are in such a high tax bracket that they need a tax shelter, yet some of them don't have one.

With all this information at his disposal, you would think that an accountant would give investment advice. But most of them don't. If you want an accountant to advise you, you will have to tell him so. After all, his basic job is to prepare your income tax return. He doesn't want to put himself in the position of losing a customer by making a bad suggestion about investments.

Occasionally, however, without your prompting him, an accountant will suggest that you make a change in your finances. It is usually because he has customers who are making good investments through a registered representative who is well known to him. This individual has proven to be honest, competent, and makes suggestions solely in the best interest of the people he represents.

If you are fortunate enough to have such a tax man, you should see the representative he recommends. The average accountant is not qualified to advise you on investments, but he can certainly suggest that you see someone who *is* qualified.

Before the interview takes place, you should tell your accountant to give the recommended representative a copy of your income tax return. Then it is up to you to evaluate what he tells you. You should not blindly accept the recommendation of your accountant or the suggestions of the financial planner. But because he comes well recommended, you should have some confidence in what the representative tells you about where to put your excess dollars.

5

Probate

EVERY DAY ALL OVER AMERICA a great deal of property and future family security are sacrificed when property owners die. Certainly, after a lifetime of saving and self-denial, this was not their intention.

What then causes this to happen? Usually it is because those who have built a living estate know nothing, or very little, of the complex problems that are created when they transfer their property to their heirs. The property owner mistakenly feels that his heirs will simply take over where he has left off, and that somehow his assets will be transferred to them intact.

Nothing could be further from the truth!

When heirs do not have access to what they rightfully feel is theirs for a period of many months or several years, whose fault is it? Certainly it wasn't the fault of the property owner. He had been careful and had made the right decisions during his lifetime. But he had never been through probate (unless he had at some time been named an executor in a will); therefore he was not aware of the problems created by death and of the advance decisions that should have been made if he were to reduce to a minimum the delay, the frustration, the taxes, and the costs involved.

Too often years elapse before the estate can be enjoyed by the rightful owners, its legal heirs. Too often a lifetime of bitterness is the legacy because of wrangling among the heirs over the division of valuable personal property. Or it is rags to riches in a few short years because incompetent heirs were left property outright when a trust should have been created instead for their protection.

The way to avoid all of this is for the property owner to anticipate the problems and make the right decisions in advance, so that the estate will be transferred to the heirs with the least trouble and expense.

It must be understood by everyone who saves money that two estates are built during a lifetime—a living estate and a death estate.

During the long process of building a living estate, the property owner becomes intimately acquainted with the problems, the decisions, and the difficulties of becoming financially independent. Most people do not inherit money; they must build an estate themselves.

So the first thing to learn is the absolute essential of thrift. A part of all you earn must be yours to keep, and the best way to assure this is to save regularly each month by paying yourself first. If you pay everybody else first out of your monthly earnings, there is seldom anything left. Instead, put a set amount into a bank or an investment account each month, and after that pay your obligations. You'll be surprised how quickly you will adjust to this method of managing your money.

After thrift has been established, it then becomes a matter of learning where and how to invest. Income taxes, too, become a problem. All through life it is a question of how well you learn to arrive at a balance, between saving something to achieve financial independence and spending a little on luxuries so you can smell the roses as you go.

So in building a living estate, difficult decisions are made and the problems are gradually solved. Financial independence is achieved, and the goal of retiring respectably is won.

But what about the death estate? Usually nothing is done. There are those who maintain that nothing should be done, except to make a will and state in it who are your heirs and how your assets should be divided among them. And there are others who, because of superstition and fear of death, refuse to make a will. There are many others who agree that more than a will is needed, but they don't know what to do because it is very difficult to obtain accurate information in the field of estate planning.

Bits of information can be gleaned from here and bits more from there, but the whole picture is not clear; and even from the meager information available there seems to be confusion and contradiction among those who are supposed to know, such as lawyers, trust officers, and accountants. It is true that there is more misinformation and lack of information on the subject of estate planning than in any other area of money management. So, to be able to plan intelligently and to conserve as much as possible of your hard-earned assets for your heirs, let's take a look at the problem, and the step-by-step solution of it.

What is meant by probate anyway?

When you die leaving a will, it has to be submitted to the judge of the probate court (in some states it is called an orphans' court or a surrogate court) to determine that your last testament is genuine and legal.

If it is, the judge issues letters testamentary approving the person named in your will as executor. Armed with this document, your executor can legally take possession of your assets and manage them during the long period of probate administration.

And this is where you as a testator, when having a will drawn, might make your first serious mistake.

Whom do you trust to be your executor?

If he is going to be in charge of all your assets for months and maybe years, he should be honest, capable, and knowledgeable about money and investments. If possible, he should also be acquainted with the complex duties of being an executor.

Mr. Adams, a widower, died in New York leaving a will,

naming his four adult children, three sons and a daughter, as his heirs. He himself was successful in business and should have known what he was doing. He named his sister as his executrix. At his funeral a lawyer friend who drew the will rode in the limousine with the children's Aunt Mamie. Back in the father's apartment after the services, the lawyer produced some legal documents and, without an explanation of them or a reading of the will, suggested that the four children sign the papers he presented.

Fortunately, the daughter's husband was knowledgeable in estate matters, and it had been agreed upon among the four children that he should be the spokesman for all of them. He refused to let them sign, stating that they would see the lawyer later that day in his office.

After lunch, in the lawyer's plush suite on Wall Street, the papers were again placed in front of each child for signature, where everyone, including the lawyer and his partner, the aunt, and the daughter's husband, was seated about a long table overlooking a beautiful view of lower Manhattan.

As the youngest son admitted later, if it had not been for his brother-in-law, he would simply have signed the papers and hoped that someday he would inherit his share. He was at a complete loss, impressed by the plush offices and the air of assurance on the part of the two attorneys.

The brother-in-law was not. He asked to see a copy of the will, which was only a page and a half long, stating that the four children would divide the estate, share and share alike, and that Mr. Adams' sister was the executrix. Two and a half hours later, after the lawyers' fee was established in advance and everyone was satisfied that the first conference had gone well, the papers which were first presented in the deceased's apartment were signed. But even then, with a knowledgeable relative to represent the heirs, it was four years later that the estate was finally distributed to its new owners!

What happened? Nothing, except the exasperating delay of probate. Certainly it was not what Mr. Adams thought would happen. He thought his children would simply sell his investments, take over his bank account, divide the proceeds among themselves, and be grateful to their father for having had the foresight to save an estate and the good judgment to leave it to them instead of to this sister, of whom he was very fond and of whom he had seen a great deal more in recent years than he had of his own children.

Four years! Mr. Adams would have been shocked.

The delay during probate occurs because your assets come under the jurisdiction of the probate court, and the rules and procedures of that court as established by law. As we have said, your heirs do not inherit immediately. How does anyone know who are your legal heirs? "But I named them in my will!" you protest. But the law states that no one but a judge can say who are your heirs, that all of your just debts have been paid, and that your creditors have been satisfied. And, above all, that your taxes have been paid.

These first mortgage demands against your estate must be paid first before the heirs can inherit anything. And you can be sure that everyone is going to get his legal share before the heirs get what is left. The eventual new owners receive no income or capital, and have nothing to do with the estate until probate is over.

Who then manages the assets? Up to the time of death the estate builder was managing his own affairs. He was in legal possession of his property, received the gross income, paid the bills and the taxes, and tended to the myriad details necessary for the proper administration of his living estate. Then who does this now? The executor named in the will takes over; if no executor has been named in the will, the court will appoint someone, who in that event is called an administrator.

The executor's job is to choose the probate attorney; take an inventory of all the assets; pay all just claims; establish a separate trustee account to receive all the income and pay all the expenses; hire an accountant to keep track of all this; arrange for the estate to be appraised; file and pay federal estate taxes and state inheritance taxes, if any; make a final accounting of his stewardship to the heirs; and, after all this is done, obtain a final decree of distribution from the court.

So what do most people do?

They name a relative to be their legal representative. That was what Mr. Adams did when he named Aunt Mamie, who had been a housewife all of her life, as his executrix. And why was Aunt Mamie named? Simply because Mr. Adams thought it would be nice if she collected the executor's fee. An estate that had taken a lifetime to build was placed in the hands of a financial incompetent!

A much better way to arrange a monetary benefit in the will for Aunt Mamie would have been by a special bequest to her for the amount of the executor's fee, and then appoint a qualified person to act as the testator's legal representative.

Another mistake made by a property owner when making his will is reluctance on his part to discuss his estate plans with his heirs. He is naturally secretive about the assets that he has accumulated. He feels that this is nobody's concern but his own; he certainly doesn't want his neighbors to know about them, and many people are especially careful about keeping knowledge of their financial affairs from other members of the immediate family.

Far too often this reluctance to divulge information exists between parents and children. Some parents feel that what they have saved is theirs to enjoy until they die, and for that matter exhaust to the point of zero if that is their desire. Other parents may not feel that way, but the children will generously take the attitude that their father and mother should spend everything before death, and may even balk at a discussion about that eventuality.

Yet strangely the extremely wealthy do not take this attitude and freely discuss among all family members, young and old, about the eventual disposition of a sizable estate to the next generation. If this is the practice among the very wealthy, how much more important it is that the matter be freely discussed in a small estate, where any kind of a loss can be damaging to the family's future security. How much you want to discuss with your heirs about your assets is your business, but to keep them totally in the dark is not wise.

Why does your executor have to appoint a probate attorney? Because only an attorney can go into court and ask for and file the necessary documents. Usually the attorney who drew the will is chosen because the average executor, a family member, feels that there is no alternative. On the contrary, the executor is in complete charge of the estate and may choose any attorney whom he sees fit.

Miss Jones was the sole heir and executrix of her mother's estate. She met with the lawyer who drew the will and took an immediate dislike to him. Because of this she very wisely did not commit herself to anything at the first meeting and went in search of information. Fortunately her investment representative understood estate planning and assured her that she was perfectly within her legal rights to demand that the original copy of her mother's will be turned over to her. This was done, and she then chose another attorney to handle the legal aspects of the probate process for her.

It is important for an executor to be aware of this because the attorney and executor have to work very closely together over the course of many months, and sometimes years, and any friction because of a conflict of personalities, while not disastrous, can be very unpleasant for all concerned.

So the executor's first step is to choose the proper attorney. But once the lawyer is selected, it is important for the executor to realize that he is in charge.

Uncle George died leaving a handwritten will that bequeathed $150,000 to his two nieces and a nephew, all of them in their fifties with children of their own. The older niece was named executrix. Halfway through probate the heirs suddenly realized that the judge was being asked to declare that the handwritten will was not a will but a trust, that only the income from the estate should be paid to the two nieces and the nephew, and that not a cent of capital should be inherited by them. Instead, the estate should be distributed eventually to their children.

The executrix was advised to dismiss the attorney, right in the middle of probate, and petition the court for the appointment of a new lawyer. This was allowed, and the new attorney withdrew the petition asking the court to declare the will to be a trust. As a consequence the two nieces and the nephew inherited the capital, which they knew to be their uncle's wish in the first place.

The angry executrix demanded to know who had petitioned the judge to rule that the will was a trust. She was flabbergasted when the second attorney presented her with a copy of the petition showing that she, as executrix, was the person who had signed it. The first attorney had asked her to sign it, and she had done so automatically, as she had all the other documents, because she knew nothing about her duties and responsibilities as executrix.

Why the original probate attorney felt that the uncle's handwritten will should be declared a trust is a matter of conjecture, but the main thing for an executor to know is that during probate he is in charge, not the attorney, and that he may petition the court for dismissal of the attorney anytime he does not like what is taking place.

Alice, the eldest of three sisters, died in 1980, naming Mildred in her will to be executrix, as she was the older of the two remaining sisters. Mildred was the typical family executrix, knowing nothing about the duties that were suddenly thrust upon her. She hired as the probate attorney the partner of a prestigious law firm that had offices in the town where the three sisters lived.

Months went by during which Mildred heard nothing from the attorney. When she finally tried calling him, she could never get past his secretary. This in itself was strange for it wasn't as if Alice, the deceased, wasn't worth very much. As a matter of fact, she left her two sisters $5 million.

Finally one day Mildred did hear something about the estate. It was a notice from the Internal Revenue Service assessing the estate a penalty of $637,700 for not filing the federal estate tax return within nine months as determined by law!

To put it mildly, Mildred was upset. When she finally

reached the attorney, he didn't have much of an excuse. He simply had forgotten to file the federal estate tax return, he said, thereby incurring the maximum penalty allowed by law, which was 5 percent a month for the five months that the return was overdue.

Mildred fired the attorney and threatened to sue the firm. But she found out that she couldn't sue because the attorney was not legally responsible for the delay. She was the executrix and in charge of the estate, so it was her fault, not the fault of the legal firm that she had hired.

Once the executor is appointed by the court, the first thing that has to be done is to make an inventory of the assets that comprise the estate. The assets, such as securities and deeds to property, are usually found in a safe deposit box (if the testator had one), or in a strongbox or a desk at home. This is usually the first indication of the size and character of the estate. We say usually, but not always.

When Mr. Adams died in New York, the daughter's husband found one document in his apartment the day of the services. It was a whole life insurance policy for $5,000, with the youngest son named as the sole beneficiary. This son, trying to support five children on a low salary, was desperately in need of funds. Without waiting to see the attorney after lunch, the brother-in-law and the son went down to the insurance company's offices and presented the policy for payment of the death benefit, asking how soon the $5,000 would be received. The brother-in-law knew that, regardless of what Mr. Adams' will might say, this sum belonged to the named beneficiary.

The insurance company readily agreed to the request for payment, the claim-for-settlement form was signed by the son, and the badly needed money was paid to him in just five days, although the balance of the estate was not distributed for four years.

At that first conference in the Wall Street offices of the attorney, Aunt Mamie as executrix was concerned. Was it right for the brother-in-law to propose such a thing? The lawyer told her that the insurance policy had nothing to do with the will, and since the brother-in-law had duly reported the facts about the policy everything was in order.

Even armed with letters testamentary, it is not easy for an executor to inventory an estate. A safe deposit box helps. Certainly one can expect that most of the assets will be found there. An estate will consist of a part or all of the following: cash in the form of bank, savings and loan, and credit union deposits; money market accounts; government bonds; life insurance policies; securities; accounts with brokerage firms; and titles to real estate. Notes of money lent to individuals and family members, mortgages on property, and interest in a business may also be found.

Still, in some cases, the executor and the heirs can be left in doubt that everything has been located. It is particularly true if the testator acquired a reputation during his lifetime of being worth a great deal more than the total assets that can be found by the executor. It can be a very nagging thought to the heirs for years to come.

What is the best way for the property owner, in advance, to take care of any possible problem of determining what assets actually did comprise the estate? It is simply a matter of the estate builder himself taking a confidential inventory of the assets and placing it with a copy of his will. If it is frequently updated, this lists of assets is a wonderful relief to the executor when he finds it.

A copy of a Confidential Inventory of Assets is reproduced on the following pages.

The first page is exceptionally important, for not only are the essential statistics given for the property owner and his spouse, such as address, birth dates, telephone numbers, and Social Security numbers, but this information is also supplied for the children. The date and location of the will are also put down. When the testator has trusted advisers—such as an attorney, a life underwriter, an accountant, and an investment representative—information about them is provided too. If the estate builder is still working at the time of the inventory, the business address and telephone number should also be listed.

The second page is the list of the assets and the liabilities, with the net total value of the estate, as of the date of the inventory, stated at the bottom of the page. Total value only of securities is listed; as the note indicates, a detailed list of them is given on the following page. Life insurance is also included. The value should be the face amount that would be paid at death. Double indemnity for accidental death, if provided by the policy or policies, should be ignored for the possibility is minimal. Liabilities listed should first include mortgages on property, particularly on a home on which payments are still being made. The unpaid monthly bills that all of us leave behind are normally small and therefore ignored.

The third page lists in detail the securities that were earlier listed simply as a gross amount.

The fourth page is only for those who own a business, and should be completed by the accountant.

The fifth page is for any comments that the testator might want to leave behind for the benefit of the executor and his heirs.

After a petition is made to the court for a hearing on the will, it is necessary for all possible heirs and creditors to be notified that the testator has died. This is accomplished by publishing a notice of the date, time, and place of the first probate hearing in the local legal newspaper. This has to run for a period of several weeks, the length of time depending upon state law.

The next step is a petition for the appointment of an inheritance tax appraiser, who in most states is a county official. Even though a federal estate tax is due, and therefore the Internal Revenue Service is involved, the federal government usually goes along with the local appraiser's valuation of the estate. This appraisal can be time consuming, for several reasons. Bureaucrats are busy and, as everyone knows, often delayed in their actions by red tape. If the only assets are a

A Confidential Inventory of Assets
Date _____

Name _____ Age _____ Birth date _____

Wife's name _____ Age _____ Birth date _____

Address _____ Telephone _____

City _____ State _____ Zip code _____

Social Security numbers _____

Total value of the estate _____

1. Names of children (name of spouse if child is married), birth date, residence, Social Security number

   _____

   _____

   _____

   _____

2. Last will and testament, date, where kept

   _____

3. Your advisers: name, address, telephone

   Lawyer _____

   Life underwriter _____

   Accountant _____

   Investment representative _____

4. Business address and telephone

   _____

Signature _____ Date _____

Assets

	Value
Bank savings accounts	$ _____
Bank checking accounts	_____
Savings and loan accounts	_____
Credit unions	_____
Money market funds	_____
Securities (see page 55)	_____
Mortgages and trust deeds	_____
Notes receivable	_____
Home	_____
Other real estate	_____
Life insurance death benefit	_____
Business equity (see page 56)	_____
TOTAL ASSETS	$ _____

Liabilities

	Amount
1. Mortgages or trust deeds	
(a) home	$ _____
(b) other	_____
2. Notes payable	_____
3. Other liabilities	_____
TOTAL LIABILITIES	$ _____

Total assets	$ _____
Total liabilities	$ _____
Net value of the estate	$ _____

Securities

Common stocks

No. shares	Company	Costs Basis	Current value	Ownership
____	____	____	____	____
____	____	____	____	____
____	____	____	____	____
____	____	____	____	____
____	____	____	____	____

TOTAL VALUE $ _____

Preferred stocks

No. shares	Company	Costs Basis	Current value	Ownership
____	____	____	____	____
____	____	____	____	____
____	____	____	____	____
____	____	____	____	____
____	____	____	____	____

TOTAL VALUE $ _____

Industrial and municipal bonds

Face amount	Description	Interest	Current value	Ownership
____	____	____	____	____
____	____	____	____	____
____	____	____	____	____

TOTAL VALUE $ _____

Business Data

Firm name _____

Address _____ Type of Business

Nature of business _____ Sole proprietorship

Business position _____ Partnership

Percentage of ownership _____ Close corporation

Are there any family relationships in the business? yes _____ no _____

Business associates

Name	Position	Birth date	Percentage of ownership

Do you intend that the business interest be sold
  when you die?   yes ___ no ___

Is the sale prearranged by a written agreement?   yes ___ no ___

Is the agreement funded by life insurance?   yes ___ no ___

Employee benefits provided by the business

Pension plan: yes ___ no ___   Profit sharing plan: yes ___ no ___

Group life insurance: yes ___ no ___   Group disability: yes ___ no ___

Number of employees _____

Unusually valuable employees in the business

Name	Position

Date business started _____   Original investment _____

Net earnings before taxes

19___	19___	19___	19___	19___
$ _____	$ _____	$ _____	$ _____	$ _____

Comments by the Property Owner

_____

_____

_____

_____

_____

_____

_____

_____

_____

_____

_____

_____

_____

_____

_____

_____

_____

_____

_____

_____

_____

_____   _____

Date   Signature

home and cash the problem is quickly solved, for the appraiser simply has to evaluate the house and is usually quite lenient as to its value; other real estate, however, can be a problem. In one estate the major asset was a ranch, which had been in the family for many years and which had tremendously increased in value since its purchase because the testator had lived into his nineties, had outlived his son and daughter-in-law, and his only heir was a granddaughter. The inheritance tax appraiser valued the property at just under one million dollars! The heiress was fit to be tied because of the state inheritance tax and the federal estate tax involved. She even sued in court, but it did her no good, and eventually the ranch had to be sold.

If a business is a part of the estate, the appraisal can be a sticky one, for quite often the value placed upon it is far and beyond what the heirs feel is fair. The best way to solve this problem in advance is to have the owners enter into a buy-and-sell agreement drawn by a competent attorney, by which they bind themselves individually to sell their interest in the business, in the event of their demise, to the surviving partners. Certainly no one is going to agree to sell for less than the true value of the property. This would simply be another way of disinheriting the heirs. Hence, such an agreement usually results in a fair price, and a bona fide buy-and-sell agreement—or a stock retirement plan if the business is a close corporation—is usually accepted by the appraiser. If the business is large enough, a better way to solve the problem is to go public and sell part of the shares in the open market, thus establishing a price for each share.

Once the estate has been appraised, the executor has to complete and file a State Inheritance Tax return if one is required by state law. If the appraisal by the county official is disputed, a long fight can take place, and sometimes cannot be resolved except by taking the argument before the judge of the probate court.

If the estate appraisal is in excess of the exemption equivalent for the year involved, a Federal Estate Tax Return has to be filed, which means a further delay. (A copy of this return is in the Appendix.) On this return, the executor has two valuation dates from which to choose; he may elect the date of death, or six months later, but he cannot choose any date in between. Many executors insist upon waiting out the six months before they decide which date should be used, for if real estate and/or securities are involved, and there is a declining market during the year, the estate will be appraised for less six months later, therefore the death taxes will be less. But this is a two-edged sword, for if the estate is appraised for less, and the heirs should later sell, the capital gain tax will be greater because of the lower cost basis.

Now six months have slipped by with little or nothing having been accomplished, while the heirs still sit on the sidelines in frustration.

Mrs. Chester died, as a widow with no near relatives, and in her will left her entire $120,000 estate to "my very dear friend, Mary Rogers." Mrs. Chester was not young, and neither was Mary Rogers, who was poorly as well, and as a consequence planned on a trip abroad with the proceeds of her inheritance to improve her health. A year and a half after Mrs. Chester's death, she still had received nothing and could not understand what took the lawyer so long—and for that matter, why she had not heard from him in months. Finally she asked a business friend to intercede for her, to see if he could expedite matters. The executor and the lawyer in this case were not keeping her, as the sole heir, informed and were taking their own time in settling the estate.

In the event of hardship, two devices can be used by the executor to get money over to the heirs while the estate is still tied up in probate. The first method is usually employed when a widow does not have enough income to support herself. A petition is made to the court by the executor, asking for a monthly family allowance to be paid to her. Depending upon the size of the estate and the normal living standards of the surviving spouse, the judge will set an amount and allow the executor to pay her an income by the month. The second method is called a partial distribution. Once again enough time has elapsed to determine that the will is not going to be contested and that all just claims against the estate have been paid. Now a petition is made to the court to allow the executor to pay a lump sum to the heirs out of the assets available. This can be either in cash or in liquid assets such as securities.

You would think that the executor and the attorney would be interested in expediting the estate through probate so they could be paid, since they each earn a good fee. But their motivation is somewhat blunted by the fact that they can collect part of their fees *during* probate, by the partial distribution method. The executor has the attorney petition the court for partial payment of the fees, so that if probate drags on too long, they can be paid in one installment, or more, even though the heirs still receive nothing.

Finally, however, all death taxes and claims against the estate have been paid and a receipt for the inheritance taxes has been presented to the court. Now the executor has to prepare a final accounting of his stewardship to the heirs. The heirs are asked to sign a waiver approving the financial report, which is automatic in most estates, for the heirs assume that the executor is an honest man, which, fortunately, is true most of the time.

A copy of a final accounting for a small estate is reproduced below.

Summary of Account

Assets of the estate, per inventory and appraisement by the inheritance tax appraiser		$41,014.53
Receipts, per Exhibit A		1,122.12
Total estate		$42,136.65
Disbursements, per Exhibit B	$5,206.84	
Distributions, per Exhibit D	500.00	$ 5,706.84
Net estate on hand, per Exhibit C		$36,429,81

Exhibit A—Receipts

Date	Received from	Purpose	Amount
12/2/84	Crocker Bank	Interest payment	$ 151.23
12/2/84	Guaranty S & L	Interest payment	92.35
12/1/84	Guaranty S & L	Interest payment	17.53
	Plaza Galleries	Sale personal effects	
8/08/84	By check		193.79
8/19/84	By check		30.60
8/29/84	By check		167.20
9/04/84	By check		46.49
9/11/84	By check		129.20
12/17/84	Beverly Manor	Refund	99.00
12/28/84	Beverly Manor	Refund	18.75
12/29/84	Final pension	Check to date of death	79.12
12/29/84	Gilbralter S & L	Accrued Interest	96.86
		Total receipts	$1,122.12

Exhibit B—Disbursements

Date	Paid to	Amount
10/11/84	John Baldwin, reimbursement for funeral expenses Catholic Cemeteries	$ 260.00
10/11/84	Dickerson, Higbee, & Lightfoot, funeral expenses, balance on account	184.00
10/15/84	Abbey Rents, for rent of wheelchair	18.55
10/21/84	Alfred Morino, M.D., medical expenses	32.00
10/27/84	Pacific Telephone, closing bill	7.25
11/09/84	Bradford Hull, inheritance tax referee	5.68
11/09/84	County Treasurer, state inheritance tax	2,267.76
12/12/84	Martha Kennedy, executrix	1,200.00
12/21/84	Medical Science Laboratory, last illness expense	40.50
12/21/84	Martin Douglas, attorney, repayment of costs during administration	117.10
12/21/84	Plaza Movers, Baltimore, moving personal effects to auction house	74.00
12/21/84	Redemptorist Mission House, will bequest	1,000.00
	Total disbursements	$5,206.84

Exhibit C—Property on Hand

(1)	400 shares Tandy Corporation common stock, value at death	$ 5,175.00
(2)	100 shares Tandy Corporation common stock purchased March 10, 1985	2,930.75
(3)	200 shares Intel Corporation common stock purchased March 12, 1985	9,648.41

Exhibit C—Property on Hand (cont.)

(4)	200 shares Digital Equipment common stock purchased March 12, 1985	7,980.73
(5)	Bank of America, Com'l acc't 9-01422	157.95
(6)	Bank of America, passbook 5-80502	10,000.00
(7)	Merrill Lynch, brokerage account 286-32105, cash balance on hand	536.97
	Net estate	$36,429.81

Exhibit D—Distributed Personal Property

10/10/84	Distribution to Robert Revoir, personal effects per will	$400.00
	Distribution to Martha Kennedy, personal effects per will	100.00
	Total distribution	$500.00

If the probate judge is satisfied with the accounting he can now issue a final decree of distribution. However, probate is still not over. Two things remain to be done.

For the protection of the executor, the attorney should petition the court for his final discharge. Reprinted below is a copy of such an order.

Order of Final Discharge of Executor

It appearing that all acts of JOHN BARNES, as Executor, were

performed as required by law:

IT IS ORDERED, ADJUDGED AND DECREED,

That JOHN BARNES, as Executor, be discharged as such and

sureties are hereby released from liability for all acts

subsequent hereto.

DATED; _____

_____

JUDGE OF THE SUPERIOR COURT

The second problem that has to be taken care of after the final decree of distribution has been issued involves securities. If they were part of the estate, the ownership has yet to be changed. This is because transfer agents, usually banks, can't issue stock certificates in the names of the heirs until they have received a certified copy of the final decree of distribution.

Now the securities have to be sent to various bank transfer agents all over the country. Each transfer agent has his own documentary requirements that have to be met, depending upon the state where the corporation is domiciled. If fifteen securities or more are involved, the delay will be several months.

One widow had been in probate for two years when the final decree of distribution was issued. In her case only one stock was involved, but the ownership was substantial, consisting of a thousand shares. After waiting two months with nothing happening, she finally had her stockbroker call the trust department of the bank, which was acting as executor, to find out what, if anything, had been done.

It took several telephone calls by her broker, and finally a personal visit by him to the trust department, before it was determined that the individual responsible for handling the probate of the estate had sent the certificate to the stock transfer department on the other side of the banking floor where nothing had been done for two months. The stock was still in the bank's vaults and had not been sent to the transfer agent at all!

There are, of course, probate costs involved in this complicated and long drawn-out process. For a small estate of only $15,000 the fee is 4 percent, or $600. For an estate of $100,000 the fee is $3,150, or 3.15 percent.

A table of probate costs on the first $1,000,000 appears below.

	Percent	Amount	Cumulative cost
First $15,000	4%	$ 600	$ 600
$15,000 to $100,000	3%	$ 2,550	$ 3,150
$100,000 to $1,000,000	2%	$18,000	$21,150

In addition, this sum has to be doubled, for both the probate attorney and the executor receive the same amount. For large estates the fee is 1 percent of anything over $1,000,000. When engaging the probate attorney, the executor should always determine the legal fee in advance. When queried by an Aunt Mamie, a lawyer will usually shrug off the question by saying that his fees are set by law and not to worry about it. He is correct in his reply for most lawyers will not charge more than the table of probate fees shown above. But this doesn't mean that he can't charge more by asking the court to approve an additional fee. Therefore the executor should not be satisfied with a vague reply but should set the legal fee in advance.

The brother-in-law in Mr. Adams' case in New York telephoned the trust department of his firm's correspondent bank on Wall Street and asked the vice president in charge about the procedure in New York State, and if his bank would set the legal fee in advance if named executor. The answer was a positive yes, that the bank would consent to the proposed fee only if it were in agreement with the schedule as set by law.

Most people do not realize that probate is a matter of public record. Anyone can walk off the street into the county clerk's office and demand to see the probate file of a deceased person. No reason for the request has to be given because probate records fall into the area of public domain. Therefore, when you die, any stranger, friend, or relative can find out exactly what assets you owned when you died, down to the last penny, and where you kept them. In the probate file is a copy of your will and a record of the proceedings step by step, including the names and addresses of your heirs and the amount that each received. Most people are appalled when they learn of this and will take every possible step to avoid having this happen to them. In many cases, privacy is of the utmost importance.

Dr. Wilson lived in a small town of 50,000 people, had founded a famous clinic and died wealthy, leaving his estate in a charitable trust to his two daughters, from which they were to receive all of the income during their lifetime.

Since both daughters worked, never married, and inherited their famous father's sense of frugality, they did not spend even the income from the trust but proceeded to build up an estate of their own. The size of the trust also grew over the course of forty years.

The daughters became so secretive in later life that when their banker visited their home and talked a little bit too loudly about the size of their estate while a TV repairman was in the next room, they became very upset. By this time their income was $9,000 per month from the trust fund, and their personal fortune had grown to three-quarters of a million. When one of the sisters died, the subsequent publicity of probate was agony to the surviving sister.

Even a small estate, as little as $15,000, can benefit from knowing the principles of estate planning, as we shall see later. A great many people are not upset so much by the costs of probate as they are by the long delay. There is a feeling of utter frustration by the heirs, and there is nothing they can do about it.

Proper advance planning by the property owner, however, can reduce materially the delay of probate, the frustration of the heirs, and in many instances eliminate entirely bitterness and lifetime enmity among children and other heirs. Trusts, too, can be created to reduce taxes and protect incompetent beneficiaries. In many cases the judicious use of gifts is valuable. And if it is advisable and desired, it is possible to eliminate the probate process entirely.

First, however, before an explanation of any of this can be undertaken, a thorough understanding of taxes is essential, because so much of estate planning revolves around this all-important problem.

But remember, if you should decide probate is the best way to transfer your assets to your heirs, you better be sure you trust your executor.

6

Ownership

How do you avoid probate?

Simple. By holding all of your assets in joint tenancy with right of survivorship. This way the surviving joint tenant automatically inherits everything.

This method is highly recommended for a husband and wife when they want the survivor to own all of the assets with the least amount of trouble.

Oh, I can hear objections pouring in from attorneys, trust officers, and accountants. "You can't advise people to do that. What about estate taxes, failure to use the marital deduction, and the fact that only one-half of the property is entitled to a new cost basis upon death of one of the joint tenants? And don't forget that the survivor can will the entire estate to anyone he or she pleases."

I know, I know. But let's go back to the original premise, that a married couple wants the survivor to inherit with the minimum amount of trouble. This is their major consideration. If estate taxes are owed, they don't care. The heirs will have to inherit less. It's all right, too, with both joint tenants for the survivor to control the ultimate disposition of the property.

But since, apparently, there are arguments against holding property in joint tenancy, let's take a closer look at this type of ownership, and particularly at the four objections raised above.

OBJECTION ONE

You can't have joint tenancy if you have an estate tax problem. We agree. But how many married couples do? Each individual who dies has a personal exemption of $400,000 in 1984, $500,000 in 1985, and $600,000 in 1986, where it levels off.

Example. Mr. and Mrs. Benson had a total estate in 1984 of $400,000. They held all of their assets in joint tenancy. In November of that year Mr. Benson died, and Mrs. Benson inherited the entire estate. But she doesn't have a federal estate tax problem, because when she dies the entire $400,000 will be tax exempt because of her personal exemption.

This is true, of course, for any estate of a husband and wife whose total assets are *less* than $400,000. As a consequence, in the majority of estates of married couples with assets from nothing up to $400,000, the ownership of their property should be held in joint tenancy.

OBJECTION TWO

You can't have joint tenancy and take advantage of the marital deduction.

This also involves estate taxes. Let's assume that the Bensons had a total estate of $500,000. Then Mrs. Benson would have inherited $100,000 over her individual exemption, which would have meant that her estate would have had to pay 34 percent on the excess when she died, or an estate tax of $34,000 instead of a tax-free estate.

Perhaps, if the Bensons' estate had been worth $500,000 and they had two children, joint tenancy should not have been used. Instead, Mr. Benson could have willed $100,000 directly to the children, or left it in trust for them, using that much of his personal exemption (or call it his marital deduction if you will) that would once again have resulted in Mrs. Benson's estate paying nothing in federal estate taxes when she subsequently died possessed of the remaining $400,000.

OBJECTION THREE

With joint tenancy only one-half of appreciated assets acquires a stepped-up cost basis at death. The other one-half retains the cost basis of the deceased.

Assume that Mr. and Mrs. Benson bought a stock years ago for $30,000 that had a market value upon Mr. Benson's death of $100,000. Only one-half of the $100,000 would have taken on a new cost basis of $50,000. The other half would have had a cost basis of $15,000. If Mrs. Benson should sell the stock, she would incur a capital gain tax on $35,000 ($50,000 − $15,000). It is unlikely, however, that Mrs. Benson would sell, considering how well the stock had performed. But even if she did, the maximum capital gain tax would have been only $7,000 ($35,000 × 20 percent).

OBJECTION FOUR

The surviving joint tenant controls the ultimate disposition of the assets.

It is true that Mrs. Benson could remarry and leave the entire estate to a second husband, thereby disinheriting the children. This is unlikely today, where premarital property agreements are common in second marriages.

Nonetheless, it is a valid argument against joint tenancy, because it is possible for this type of ownership to result in heirs being treated unfairly.

Mr. McAfee, a widower with three children, had married a second time to a widow who had one child. He was the 100 percent stockholder of a close corporation, which at the time of his second marriage didn't have much value. He placed this stock in joint tenancy with his new wife.

With the passage of many years, however, the corporation prospered, and the stock greatly increased in value. Mr. McAfee then died, and shortly thereafter his second wife also died. Now something happened, due to joint tenancy with right of survivorship, that neither one of them had intended.

Mrs. McAfee inherited all of the stock and in her will left everything of which she died possessed to her only child. Mr. McAfee's own three children were disinherited of a sizable sum of money!

Even so, after discussing the four objections above, we return to our original recommendation. Most married couples should avoid probate by holding all of their assets in joint tenancy, because they don't have any of the problems that this type of ownership might create.

Nevertheless, there are other reasons, besides the four basic objections, for not holding assets in joint tenancy.

Quite often joint tenancy ownership should not be used where the surviving spouse is completely inexperienced in money matters. In such an instance, a trust might be advisable to provide experienced management.

Normally, joint tenancy should not be used with children. The surviving spouse should retain the assets in his or her name only, even though the children are adults, because they should not be given control over one-half of the property solely to avoid probate. The heirs will simply have to endure the probate process.

Often when joint tenancy is used some of the assets are held in single ownership without the property owners realizing it. Now the survivor is in probate even though the joint tenants didn't intend this to happen. Therefore if probate is to be avoided, a married couple should review the ownership of their assets, including their cars, their home, and their securities, to be sure that joint tenancy is held on all of them.

Even though probate is avoided, it is true that joint tenancy still has to be dissolved. Then why hold your assets this way at all? Why not just go through probate?

This objection to joint tenancy is not valid because dissolving a joint tenancy is not that much of a problem.

What then, exactly, has to be done?

Ownership of real estate can be changed by supplying the county recorder with a certified copy of the death certificate and an "Affadavit—Death of a Joint Tenant," a simple form that can be obtained from a stationery store. Ownership of securities can be changed by writing the bank transfer agents who are named on the face of the certificates and asking them for the forms required. Normally a stock power, with the signature of the survivor guaranteed by a bank officer, a certified copy of the death certificate, and the stock certificate are all that are necessary.

Deposits in banks, savings and loan associations, credit unions, and thrifts can be transferred to the survivor's name by a certified copy of the death certificate and an inheritance tax waiver (required in those states where this tax is a part of state law). Savings bonds can be cashed by this same method, and car ownership can easily be changed at the state motor vehicle department.

Life insurance proceeds can be obtained by going to the local office of the company, as was done in Mr. Adams' estate (chapter 4). If there isn't any local office, the claim form can be requested from the home office, enclosing a certified copy of the death certificate.

Of course if death taxes are owed, returns will have to be filed and the taxes paid. In this event help should be elicited from an accountant.

Admittedly all this takes time, but in small estates sixty to ninety days should see an end to the problem, which is certainly a lot better than going through probate. If a widow is the survivor and she doesn't want to go to the trouble, she can always hire an attorney to dissolve the joint tenancy for her. The fees will be about one-third of the probate costs, and the delay will be far less.

There are two other ways to avoid probate, both of them the result of proper ownership.

NAMING A BENEFICIARY

The average person is acquainted with this method because it is widely used with life insurance policies. Life insurance companies will pay the death benefit to the named beneficiary regardless of the provisions of a will. We have seen an example of this in Mr. Adams' estate in the probate chapter.

For insurance policies only, contingent beneficiaries can also be named. This takes care of the possibility that the first beneficiary could die before the insured. Take as an example a father, who is the insured, with a wife and three children.

The beneficiary designation can now read as follows: "To Mary Doe, wife, if living; if not, to the lawful children of the insured and his wife, Mary Doe, equally, the survivors equally, or the survivor." Now all possible contingencies have been taken care of without further changes in the beneficiary designation, right down to the death of the last child.

While it is convenient and it avoids probate, there are a couple of hidden pitfalls in this type of ownership.

If most of the estate consists of a large amount of decreasing term life insurance, which is often the case with young families where the breadwinner hasn't had the time to build an estate, then outright payment to a named beneficiary could be a mistake. This occurs when the beneficiary is inexperienced in money matters.

A beneficiary designation naming individual heirs would also be inadvisable where the proceeds of the policies might be needed by an executor to pay death taxes and other administration costs. A frequent example of this is where most of the estate consists of real estate and there is a liquidity problem. If the heirs receive the proceeds of the policies outright, this money will not be available to the executor. In such estates the beneficiary designation should read: "Payable to my estate."

There is a basic difficulty with this type of ownership, however. You can't name a beneficiary for real estate and securities. Therefore its use is limited.

A LIVING TRUST

This is complicated and is used only by the wealthy to avoid publicity. This method is discussed later in the chapter on trusts.

It is obvious from the above discussion on how to avoid probate that you can't trust your attorney, a trust officer, or even your accountant to give you correct advice on this type of ownership. Why? Because it is not in their best interest to have you hold your assets this way. It will be to their financial advantage to have you in probate.

There are three other ways to hold your assets in joint names, besides normal joint tenancy, and still avoid probate.

JOINT TENANCY AS A MATTER OF CONVENIENCE

This is joint tenancy with right of survivorship, but with a tax difference. When this is used, the joint tenants are not spouses. It is often used by a widow or widower with a child or children as the other joint owner. The purpose of this ownership is to avoid probate, but since one joint tenant originally owned all of the property and continues to receive all of the income, the asset is 100 percent taxable in that person's estate.

Mrs. Crane was a grass widow for twenty years and decided to place the property she had acquired as a schoolteacher in joint tenancy with her spinster daughter, who had followed in her mother's footsteps by becoming a teacher, acquiring along the way a Ph.D. and a full professorship in an endowed college. When Mrs. Crane put her assets in joint tenancy she wasn't trying to reduce death taxes, but she did want to avoid probate, and joint tenancy achieved this. Since she received all of the income from her assets, and her daughter admittedly received none, it was a joint tenancy of convenience. Probate was avoided, but the entire property was included in her estate for death tax purposes.

TENANTS BY THE ENTIRETY

This is another form of joint tenancy. It may be used only by a husband and wife and, when used, can apply only to real estate. The advantage to be derived from this type of ownership is that the property cannot be attached by a creditor of either the husband or the wife. Upon the death of either spouse, title rests with the survivor.

This ownership is used most frequently by retired people with meager resources, where one spouse may not handle money wisely. The creditor of the financially irresponsible spouse cannot have recourse to legal action to collect that debt by placing a lien against the property when real estate is held this way.

DECLARATION OF HOMESTEAD

This is a joint tenancy allowed in many states. It can be used only between husband and wife, and then only on their home.

It is accomplished by filing a declaration of homestead with the county recorder and paying the appropriate fee. Once the property is so recorded, the declaration is micro-filmed (or otherwise filed), and the original is returned to the married couple to be placed with their other valuable documents.

The declaration is a simple one and can be obtained from a stationery store, or it can be prepared by an attorney. Home-steading is used for virtually the same reason as tenancy in the entirety. Now, however, instead of protecting the property from the rash financial actions of one of the co-owners, the home is protected from seizure as the result of a judgment being obtained against either or both of the joint tenants be-cause of an unpaid obligation.

A lien can be obtained against the home even when it is homesteaded, but the property cannot be taken away from the owners to satisfy that lien. If the property is sold, of course, the lien or liens must be satisfied.

When available, it is used by couples as a prudent precau-tion against possible future financial reverses, and by many more couples as an immediate protection because of present financial difficulties. It is not protection against two possible creditors—the holder of the mortgage on the property and the Internal Revenue Service. As a practical matter, however, the IRS is loath to move against a married couple, taking their home away from them by legal action and putting them out on the street, though they have the legal right to do so.

So far we have discussed ways to avoid probate that pertain to most of the fifty states. But there is another ownership that avoids probate in just a few states.

This is community property.

It's available only in the eight community property states of Arizona, California, Idaho, Louisiana, Nevada, New Mexico, Texas, and Washington. These states have a sizable population; therefore this type of ownership can't be ignored.

Community property law is complex, so let's try to keep it as simple as possible.

Community property, for one thing, is a matter of domicile. You are considered to be living in a community property state if you have your domicile there. You can have only one domicile, although you may have more than one residence.

Your domicile is a place of abode fixed and permanent, or at least of indefinite duration. The question of domicile is one of intent; you intend a given state to be your permanent home in order to claim it as your domicile. A temporary residence may be a matter of months or even years, while a domicile may be established the first moment you occupy the property. Also, the domicile of a wife, generally speaking, is the domicile of her husband.

California, Nevada, New Mexico, Arizona, and Texas were once a part of Mexico, which before that belonged to Spain. Therefore the common law in these states goes back to Spain, where community property has always been recognized. Louisiana was originally French territory, so its state law reflects the community property law of France. Washington and Idaho simply adopted community law. All the other states in the Union go back to the common law of England, where the husband has always died possessed of the entire estate and is taxed accordingly.

Community property is all property, not falling within the definition of separate property, acquired by a husband and wife during their marriage while they are domiciled in a community property state. The husband and wife each have a half-interest in all such property, according to state law. Death of either spouse dissolves the community, and an absolute decree of divorce also dissolves it.

In Louisiana, however, the community is dissolved by a separation from bed and board, while in Arizona, community property may be divided upon grant of a divorce *a mensa et thoro*, which for all practical purposes is synonymous with the Louisiana definition.

Separate property is all property owned separately by the spouses prior to their marriage, and all property that is acquired after marriage by one spouse as a gift, devise, or inheritance.

It wasn't until the serious escalation of the federal estate tax during World War II that the rest of the country became aware of the community property law and the advantage, say, of dying in California, with the husband being taxed on only one-half of the estate, as against dying in New York, for instance, where he was taxed on it all.

The outcry when this became widely known was justifiably great, and Congress eventually had to take recognition of this injustice in the tax laws by passing the marital deduction rule in 1948. This rule holds that people dying in non-community property states have the same estate tax advantage as those who die owning community property, namely only one-half of the estate is taxed upon the death of the first spouse. It must be stressed, however, that the tax advantage derives from a different reason—because of a law passed by Congress, and not by the common law of the state in which you happen to be domiciled.

Qualifying for the marital deduction rule is simple. All you have to do is leave your one-half of the estate to your spouse, whereby she receives all of the income, payable at least annually.

Residents of community property states still retain one tax advantage. This involves the capital gain tax. As we have seen in joint tenancy, only one-half of the property inherited by the survivor receives a stepped-up cost basis upon death. But if you hold property as community in the eight states mentioned above, both halves of the property are entitled to the stepped-up cost basis. This means that the survivor can sell and not pay a capital gain tax at all.

A word of warning. When you own real estate as community property, it is not as easy to remove the deceased's name from the title when compared to owning it as a surviving joint tenant. You have to hire a lawyer to petition a court for permission to change the ownership, and when it is granted, take this document to the county recorder.

Probate Assets

When title to property is held so that it is a probate asset, the property will pass through the executor's hands and be distributed according to a will or a trust agreement. There are seven different ownerships that are subject to probate.

1. Tenants in common. With this ownership both owners want their names on the asset, yet each desires to distribute his or her one-half by will. In this case the surviving joint tenant does *not* automatically inherit. This ownership is employed by spouses with large estates in excess of $600,000 because they have an estate tax problem.

   Mr. and Mrs. Darby have an estate of $1,250,000. If Mr. Darby should die leaving his one-half of the estate to his wife, she would die possessed of the entire $1,250,000. Assuming that Mr. Darby should die in 1987 or later, this would subject her estate to an estate tax of $255,000. To avoid this, they held their assets as tenants in common, with Mr. Darby willing $600,000 to their three children, thereby making full use of his 1987 individual exemption. This way Mrs. Darby would subsequently die possessed of only $650,000, which would cause her estate to pay $17,000, an estate tax saving to the Darbys of $238,000!

For the sake of simplicity, willing to the children is used in the example. Actually Mr. Darby left his $600,000 marital deduction in trust for the children, with the income paid to his wife during her life, resulting in the same tax savings. The reader is asked to refer to the chapter on trusts.

Most assets, including securities, may be held as tenants in common.

2. Individual ownership. This is widely used by single persons who want their assets to pass by will. There are millions of single people who have never married, or who have yet to marry, and millions more who are divorced. These people usually leave their assets to several relatives and in varying amounts. Individual ownership with distribution by will, using percentages to each one, is the simplest solution.

There is also little desire upon the part of such a testator to avoid probate, or to reduce the impact of death taxes if the estate is that large. "Let the ax fall where it may" is the general attitude.

3. A testamentary trust. Property left in this manner goes through probate, the same as assets left by will. And like a will, nothing takes place until the testator dies, at which time an executor takes over, passing on the assets to the trustee upon the conclusion of probate.

4. Ownership by a minor. Assets owned by a minor come under the jurisdiction of the probate court. This is for the protection of minor children, for without it many of them would be victimized by more knowledgeable adults.

When parents (who are the natural guardians of their own children), or guardians of minors appointed by the court, desire to change the minor's funds from one asset to another, they have to petition the court through an attorney for permission to do so.

It used to be that minor children's funds could only be invested in legalized investments such as bank accounts, government bonds, and mortgages. In recent years the courts have become more lenient, particularly in those states that have passed the Prudent Man Rule, which allows guardians to invest in common stocks, including, of course, mutual funds.

This rule has been adopted by at least forty states. It lays down broad principles by which fiduciaries can invest money that is entrusted to their care for the benefit of others. The Prudent Man Rule states in part:

> All that can be required of a trustee . . . is that he shall conduct himself faithfully and exercise sound discretion. He is to observe how men of prudence, discretion, and intelligence manage their affairs, not in regard to speculation but in regard to the permanent disposition of their funds, considering the probable income as well as the probable safety of the capital to be invested.

In those states that have the Prudent Man Rule, a petition for the child to own securities or mutual funds receives almost automatic approval by the judge. The attorney simply sees the clerk of the court who obtains the judge's signature on a standard form. The whole procedure usually takes only a few minutes. If the minor should die, the property is inherited by operation of law. It is therefore a probate asset.

5. A guardian. Guardians are appointed by the court (or in a will) as we have seen above when minor children are involved. Guardians are appointed also to handle the affairs of people who are financially incompetent for mental or physical reasons, or both. The elderly, the physically handicapped, and the mentally impaired all

fall into this category. An individual may be named guardian of the person, or guardian of the property, or both. When a guardian is named in a will, it is because a personal relationship is desired, and therefore the guardian is usually placed in charge of both the person and the assets. Where protection and payment of property only is required, the testator normally creates a trust instead.

Mrs. Greenfield was appointed by the court to act as guardian for her widowed sister. Years before, her sister had fallen on her head, and the injury had so damaged her brain that eventually she could no longer take care of herself or her affairs and had to be placed in a mental institution. Mrs. Greenfield, as guardian, not only managed her assets and paid all her bills for several years until she died, but also took care of her personal wants and needs, such as overseeing a practical nurse when she was still at home, and buying her clothes and personal necessities.

During this time she opened a separate fiduciary account in a bank and hired a public accountant to keep books and prepare an annual report to the court. When her sister died, Mrs. Greenfield took over as executrix and eventually distributed the assets according to her sister's will.

6. Conservator. This is also a fiduciary ownership like a guardianship. A conservator is appointed where an adult is the owner of a sizable estate and has been declared legally incompetent by the court. The purpose is to conserve the estate against the rash or unwise acts of the present owner for his or her protection, as well as conserving the estate for its eventual heirs. The estate will be inherited according to the will of the owner drawn before he or she was declared incompetent.

Frequently a spouse is named conservator for the other spouse when he or she becomes mentally incapacitated through senility or a stroke.

Mrs. Alderman was named conservator for her husband because he became senile. As far as she was concerned, this was just like inheriting both halves of the estate, for now she had to make all of the investment decisions. This is quite a responsibility, and many wives because of their lack of experience are not able to assume it.

Mrs. Alderman felt this way, so she sold all of their securities and put them into a balanced mutual fund in order to obtain diversification and professional management. As a fiduciary agent for her husband's one-half of their estate, she acted in a responsible and sensible manner. She did not have to obtain a court order to change the assets. She already had approval when she was named conservator. All she had to do was supply each transfer agent with a certified copy of her court appointment.

In the case of Mrs. Peck, an attorney was appointed as conservator of her estate when she was declared incompetent by the court. Her net worth was $1 million, which would eventually be inherited by distant relatives according to the terms of her will. In this case, because of the amount of money involved, a professional man was appointed by the court, rather than a relative. This would lessen the possibility of a suit by the heirs claiming malfeasance by the conservator.

7. Custodian under the Uniform Gifts to Minors Act. This act allows outright gifts to minors of any kind of property, without the custodian having to obtain a court order to withdraw the funds.

For years, about the only asset that a minor could own and later withdraw to pay for, let us say, a college education was life insurance. This was seriously objected to and contested by banks and stockbrokerage firms, resulting in the passage of the Uniform Gifts to Minors Act.

Now virtually any kind of asset may be held in this

type of ownership. When money is needed for the benefit of the minor, the company involved is empowered to honor the redemption request over the custodian's signature.

As a result of the passage of the Uniform Gifts to Minors Act there has been widespread use of this method of making gifts to minors. Many parents and grandparents prefer to build a college education fund by an equity investment, with its opportunity for profit, rather than by the medium of a fixed dollar asset, as long as it can be withdrawn without a problem.

It must be understood by anyone using this form of ownership that it is an outright gift to the minor and as such is part of the minor's estate, and if not used will become the property of the minor when he or she becomes legally of age. If the custodian dies, a successor custodian may be appointed.

There are a couple of adverse features about this ownership. If the donor names himself as custodian, and he should die, the gift will be taxed in his estate. If the donor has a death tax problem, he should name some other member of the family to be custodian. This presents no problem when a grandparent is the donor; he or she simply names one of the child's parents to act in that capacity.

Secondly, the asset can't be transferred into another type of security. When mutual fund shares are involved, as part of a group of funds under the same management which permits a free transfer privilege, this rule results in a sale and a new commission.

As we have seen, ownership is divided between probate and nonprobate assets. As a consequence, in too many estates title is left to chance. Assets that are acquired over a period of a lifetime are bought without regard to correct title. In other estates where ownership was chosen with care, conditions changed, usually because of a death, birth, marriage, or divorce. Titles that were correct, or that seemed to be correct at the time that the assets were acquired, no longer apply. And yet mainly through inertia, they were never changed.

If assets in an estate are held in the name of an individual alone, and the property owner leaves no will, the estate will pass to his heirs by operation of law. The distribution will depend upon the law of the state where the deceased was domiciled. This varies widely from state to state. It would be wise for everyone to determine the law of succession where they reside.

The result of dying interstate, with all of the assets held in individual ownership, may be so shocking as to prompt some people who have no will to go to a competent attorney and have one drawn at once. In some states, where there are no children, and a widow and the deceased's parents are the surviving relatives, the widow receives one-third and the parents two-thirds of the husband's estate. If the widow desperately needs all of the assets, the result could be disastrous.

In the state of Ohio if a person dies without a will, and all of the deceased's assets are held as an individual, the estate will be divided by state law among first, second, and third cousins, if these people are the only relatives.

Mildred Cameron, a retired maiden schoolteacher, age eighty, died in Columbus, Ohio, without a will, with her assets in her name alone. She was an only child, with one aunt and an uncle, both deceased. She had two widowed cousins, who lived nearby, of whom she was very fond. She always felt that she would leave what little she had to them. But it didn't happen that way.

When Mildred Cameron died, the probate division of the Court of Common Pleas appointed an attorney as the administrator. Her entire estate consisted of $24,000 in two equal savings accounts. The attorney was faced with locating all of the heirs, who by Ohio state law (as said above) are first, second, and third cousins if they are the only relatives, which was the case with Mildred Cameron.

Almost four years after she died, one of her first cousins

who lived in Florida received an unexpected long-distance telephone call one day from Columbus, Ohio.

"Is this Mr. Robert Cameron?" the voice asked at the other end of the line.

"Yes, it is."

"I'm John Hull, attorney-at-law in Columbus, Ohio. Do you happen to know a Mildred Cameron of Columbus?"

"Yes, I do. I'm her first cousin."

"I hoped you'd say that. I've been looking for you. She died several years ago, and you are one of the heirs."

"Mildred Cameron," mused the cousin. "That's a name out of the past. I haven't seen her for forty years. Why would she leave me anything?"

"Well, she didn't, really. She died without a will, and I'm the administrator of her estate. Her heirs by state law are her cousins. Unfortunately, there seem to be quite a few of you. I have spent the last several years tracing the family tree."

"What is the estate worth? Do you know?"

"Oh, yes. Twenty-four thousand dollars, all in cash."

"How many cousins are there?"

"Sixteen, including you."

"That doesn't leave much to divvy up, does it?"

"No, it doesn't."

"What do you want me to do?" asked the cousin.

"Nothing, actually, now that I've located you," replied the attorney. "You're the last one I had to find. I'll mail you a court summons for a Hearing on Complaint to Determine Heirship. But you don't have to appear. The court should declare the sixteen of you as heirs. Not in identical shares, however. As a first cousin, you inherit one-tenth. Since there are five first cousins, the five of you will inherit one-half of the estate, the other eleven will divide the other half."

"Well, thanks anyway for calling."

"Don't mention it."

What was the result? Mildred Cameron's estate was distributed four years after she died among sixteen people, fourteen of whom she had never seen, or hadn't laid eyes on for thirty or forty years! Her two first cousins, living right in Columbus and whom she wanted to inherit her estate, actually received one-tenth each, after attorney's fees and probate costs of $4,875.60.

· If Mildred Cameron had understood proper ownership, she could have made it easy for her two cousins in Columbus to inherit the entire estate. She could have named them as beneficiaries on her two savings and loan accounts. This way there would have been no delay, no probate, and no expense, except for the Ohio estate tax.

From the previous discussion, the importance of proper ownership is obvious. It can be of *overriding* importance in many estates.

Since you can't trust anyone to give you proper advice in this vital area, your understanding of the various types of ownership is essential.

7

Wills

EVERYONE SHOULD HAVE A WILL.
If you don't have a will, the state in which you are
domiciled will determine by law who will inherit your assets.
That is what happens when you die intestate, or without a
legal will. Most people don't want this to occur. They prefer
to leave their assets to relatives and friends of their own
choosing.

Then why do people die intestate?

There are several reasons, but the main one seems to be
procrastination. They don't intend to die without having a will
drawn; they just never get around to it. It's too easy to delay
making a decision, particularly one that can be put off because
there is no apparent reason for doing it now. No one plans on
dying. Young people under thirty think they are immortal;
older people know they are going to die someday and have
philosophically learned to accept this fact, but the unhappy
event is always at least ten years away, so there is plenty of
time.

As Bernard M. Baruch, the famous financier and adviser
to presidents, once said: "Old people are those who are fifteen
years older than I am," and this was true with him even when
he was in his eighties. This makes for a healthy mental attitude about the golden years, but it is not conducive to the
drawing of a will.

People also die intestate because they are superstitious. They feel they will die soon after having a will drawn. Mr. Marks felt this way so he left no will. He died in a state where, with no will, the widow receives one-third and the children two-thirds of the estate. As a result, his two sons could have claimed two-thirds of the estate and left their mother in difficult financial circumstances. Instead, they signed over everything to their mother, because that was the way their father wanted it. However, there are many children who wouldn't do this, retaining instead what is legally theirs.

Some married couples feel they don't need a will because they have all of their assets in joint tenancy, thereby avoiding probate, with the survivor automatically inheriting everything. It is true that when the first spouse dies no will is necessary; but what is going to happen when the second spouse dies?

"Oh," you say, as the survivor, "I can make a will."

You can, but will you? The two of you didn't bother to make a will when you were married, so probably you won't get around to it as the survivor. And even if you do, it would have been much better to have made the decision together rather than deciding alone.

Everyone should have a will. And it should be drawn by a competent attorney, for only then will it hold up in court and be declared legal. But choosing an attorney is often a problem. Many people are not in touch with a lawyer. They don't know one because it may have been years since they sought legal advice, and surprisingly enough, many people have never seen an attorney for any reason.

If once upon a time they had an attorney, he may have retired or died, or they themselves may have changed their residence and moved to another state. A great number of retired people move thousands of miles away from where they have spent most of their lives in order to be near their adult children and grandchildren, or to live in a milder climate.

The choice of an attorney to draw your will is an important one. Lawyers specialize just as doctors do. You should not go to an attorney who has spent a lifetime in corporate tax law and ask him to draw your will. You should go to an attorney who is competent in estate work and probate.

How then can you find an experienced lawyer to draw your will?

One of the best ways is to ask an officer in the trust department of your bank. This department handles probate on a regular day-to-day basis and employs attorneys to handle the legal aspects. When you query an officer of the trust department about an attorney, he will usually suggest three different legal firms—one large one, one small one, and one to suit your own race or creed. You should see all three lawyers, and then choose the one you like the best.

Another way to choose an attorney is to call the Attorney Reference Panel listed in the pages of your telephone book and ask them to recommend someone who is competent to draw a will. This service is available in over 250 cities in the United States. However, don't expect too much; some are good and some bad.

We personally checked out one in a large city and found it to be nothing but a telephone service. The office was primarily in the business of providing secretarial and computer services. The name Attorney Reference Panel wasn't even printed on the door. The girl we talked to admitted that her service, which was only a sideline with her, consisted of giving the caller the name and telephone number of an attorney from a list she had. If you went to see the lawyer recommended, the cost was $7.00, whether or not you engaged his services.

Another way to find an attorney is to ask a friend, particularly one who recently has had a will drawn and is satisfied with it.

But despite the care you take in choosing an attorney, you can still choose the wrong one.

Dr. Elliot had become a millionaire as an orthodontist to famous movie stars in Hollywood. He gave up his practice of dentistry when in his fifties and moved to a rural part of the state, where he lived handsomely in retirement for twenty years. When he and his wife were in their seventies, they sought advice from the head of the trust department of their bank in regard to estate planning, and in particular for the name of a competent legal firm to draw their will.

Unfortunately, they chose a large firm in the financial center of the west, San Francisco. There wasn't any question that the firm was competent. The mistake they made was choosing a firm that was too technical. Everything was agreed upon among Dr. and Mrs. Elliot, the head of the trust department, and the attorney in regard to the will, except for one point.

The Elliots had three children—two married daughters and a son. They insisted upon disinheriting their son, refusing to tell the attorney the real reason, except to say that he had disappeared for twenty years, causing great mental anguish for his mother, who did not know whether he were alive or dead, and had only reappeared when he discovered that his parents had become millionaires. The Elliots insisted that the attorney include a clause in their will specifying that the son inherit one dollar and no more.

The attorney was equally adamant that the son should inherit $50,000. Why? Because if the son were left only one dollar he would probably contest the will; but if he were left $50,000 he would probably accept it, rather than sue and maybe inherit nothing. The attorney was right, but he was insistent for another reason. He was not going to be put on the witness stand at some later date, he said, and admit that his prestigious firm had drawn a will that probably shouldn't have been written in the first place.

So the will was drawn and mailed to the Elliots for their signature, with the stipulation that the son inherit $50,000. The good doctor and his wife were so incensed when they read the will that they tore it up and asked the law firm to send them a bill. Three months later the doctor died, leaving over $2 million to his wife.

Dr. and Mrs. Elliot chose the wrong firm. When the impasse took place they should have gone to another lawyer, who probably would have drawn the will the way they wanted it. And by the use of a trust agreement, a fortune would have been saved in estate taxes. Instead, through joint tenancy, Mrs. Elliot became the sole owner of the entire estate.

The effect of dying without a will can be disastrous, especially when you consider the following nine possible ways, depending upon state law, that an estate can be distributed when a property owner dies intestate.

1. Upon the death of husband or wife, when there are no descendants, parents, brothers, sisters, or their descendants—

   all property goes to the surviving spouse.

2. Upon the death of husband or wife, where there is one child—

   one-half goes to the surviving spouse;
   one-half goes to the child.
   (Except in community property states, all to spouse)

3. Upon the death of husband or wife, where there are two or more children—

   one-third goes to the surviving spouse;
   two-thirds is divided among the children.
   (Except in community property states, all to spouse)

4. Upon the death of husband or wife, where there are no descendants, but a father and a mother—

   one-half goes to the surviving spouse;
   one-quarter goes to the father and one-quarter goes to the mother, unless only one parent survives, then one-half goes to the surviving parent.

5. Upon the death of a widow, widower, or single person, where there are no descendants, but a father and a mother—

one-half goes to the father;
one-half goes to the mother;
and if one parent survives, all the property goes to the
surviving parent.

6. Upon the death of a widow, widower, or single person,
where there are no parents or descendants but brothers
and sisters—

all property goes to the brothers and sisters;
descendants of deceased brother or sister take his or
her share.

7. Upon the death of husband or wife, where there are no
descendants and no parents, but brothers and sisters—

one-half goes to the surviving spouse;
one-half is divided among brothers and sisters;
descendants of deceased brother or sister take his or
her share.

8. Upon the death of widow or widower, where there is a
child or children—

the estate is divided equally among the children.

9. Upon the death of a widow or widower or single person
where there are no descendants, parents, brothers, or
sisters, or their descendants—

all property goes to the next of kin.

To avoid one of these arbitrary divisions of your estate you
should have a will drawn by a competent attorney.

After deciding on your attorney and your executor, the
next step is to arrange a conference with the lawyer. Here is
where a Confidential Inventory of Assets plays an important
role (see chapter 5). A copy of this inventory should be sent to

the attorney several days in advance of your meeting, because if he has this vital information beforehand, it will considerably reduce the time you have to spend with him. If he can have the family information on page one, and a complete inventory of your assets, he will have much of the information that he would have to obtain from you by tedious questioning. After all, he does charge by the hour for his time, therefore his charges will be less.

If you have an existing will, drawn several years ago by another attorney, it would be of considerable help to him if you sent this, too, along with the inventory of assets. This tells the attorney quite a bit about your family and what would have happened if you died yesterday. It also gives him an insight into your thinking the last time you made a testamentary disposition. If there have been changes in your family status since the last will, a covering letter to this effect should be sent.

You should also be prepared to give him the exact ownership of your various assets. For instance, you can't will anything you have in joint tenancy, as we have seen in the chapter on ownership, so your attorney must know how you hold the assets in your estate, or he can't draw a proper will. Again, it will save time if you examine the title to your assets in advance and not trust your memory in this regard.

Once the attorney has drawn your will and sent you a copy, you should read it carefully before you sign it to be sure that there has been a complete meeting of the minds between you and your lawyer. Does he understand exactly what you are attempting to accomplish by this testamentary disposition of your living estate to your heirs?

With a small estate and a simple will, this shouldn't be a problem. A two-page document, saying that you leave everything of which you die possessed to your beloved spouse, both real and personal, and whereever situated; and if your spouse should predecease you, then you leave your estate to your children share and share alike, certainly shouldn't be misinterpreted by you or your attorney.

In larger estates, however, particularly those involving trusts, the legal terminology can become quite technical, and therefore a clear understanding of what is being accomplished by this document is essential. Here is where a financial-planning team is important, so that you can discuss the will before you sign it with your tax accountant, your investment representative, and your life insurance underwriter. The function of the financial-planning team is discussed in a later chapter.

All wills, however simple or complex, have certain essential phrases that lawyers use. It will be easier for you to comprehend your will if you understand these terms. They are listed below in the usual order they appear in the average disposition.

1. "I revoke all wills and codicils previously made by me."

   When drawing a new will, it is automatic that you should revoke all previous wills and codicils. Your attorney will insert this phrase even though you assured him that you never had a will drawn before; after all, no harm is done, and it does revoke completely all previous testamentary documents. Sometimes people feel, when contemplating having a new will drawn by a different attorney, that they would rather not go ahead with it because they will have to inform the first attorney that the will he drew is no longer valid. This is not necessary. Your new will automatically revokes the previous one, and that is that.

2. "I direct first that my executor shall pay all inheritance, estate, or other death taxes, all expenses of administration of my estate, and all legal claims against my estate."

   These first demands against your assets have to be paid, and then the balance of your estate will be distributed to your heirs. If, on the other hand, you should state that your heirs get their inheritance first, and then everyone else should be paid—the IRS, your executor, the probate attorney, and your creditors—

there would be nothing with which to meet these obligations. The effect would be to have your will declared invalid. In this event you would die intestate, which is exactly what you were trying to avoid when you had your will drawn in the first place.

3. "I have the following children," and then you proceed to name them.

Supposing you said in your will that you have several children, and they shall share and share alike if your wife predeceases you, but you did not name them. This is wrong, as demonstrated by the following case.

Mr. Reese, who had seven children, left a will stating that they should share and share alike, but he didn't name them. He had married twice, having three children by his first wife, whom he divorced, and four children by his second wife, who died. When he divorced his first wife, he had been young and without money, but the court had awarded him the custody of their three children anyway. He found it financially impossible to take care of the youngest child, who was a daughter only a year old, so he put her out for adoption, stipulating to the foster parents that he, the real father, would never contact her until she was twenty-one, or they had died.

He kept his promise, but when her foster parents died, he contacted her, which came as no surprise to his daughter for she had been told that she was adopted and that her real father was still alive.

However, when Mr. Reese died many years later, his will was contested by a woman living in Chicago, his former residence. She claimed through her attorney that she was one of the seven children mentioned in his will; that the daughter who had been legally adopted was not one of the seven; that she, though illegitimate, was one of the seven children.

The claim was undoubtedly false, but it effectively

tied up the estate in probate court for five years. Finally, the executor settled out of court, paying the woman $5,000 just to get rid of her in order to distribute the balance of the estate to the rightful heirs.

4. "If my executor shall fail, be unable, or cease for any reason whatever to act as executor hereunder I hereby appoint the following corporate executor."

When you have named an individual executor in your will, this clause ensures continuity in your choice of your legal representative. You direct that an institution, usually a bank, would take over if that should be necessary.

5. "My executor shall have the right to dispose of any or all of my assets."

This phrase is used so your executor will have enough money to pay taxes, expenses of administration, and just claims against your estate. However, if you don't want the possibility of all of your assets being sold, this phrase should be carefully reviewed with your attorney, and perhaps changed to read that your executor shall have the right to sell only those assets that are necessary to pay these costs. You may prefer to pass on most of your carefully chosen investments to your heirs, and not have your executor sell them and distribute cash. Giving your executor the right to sell all of your assets may be too broad a power and unnecessary in your case.

6. "If my wife and I should die as the result of a common accident, and should she survive me by a period of six months or less, it is presumed that she predeceased me."

This is known as a common-disaster clause and is inserted by your attorney to avoid having your estate taxed twice within a short period of time. First in your estate because you died first, and then again in your wife's estate because your will provides that she inherits from you. Some states have a Simultaneous Death

Act which acts as a common-disaster clause in the event that your will does not contain this provision, but it is good usually for only the first twenty-four hours following the accident.

7. "I give, devise, and bequeath all of my property, both real and personal, and whether separate, joint, or community, and whereever situated."

This is an all-inclusive term and certainly covers everything in your estate. You have the right to give your property away. Devise means to transfer real estate by will, and bequeath means to transfer personal property by will. And "wherever situated" couldn't be a broader term as to location. By this phrase, therefore, there is no question that you are willing your entire estate.

The above explanation of frequently used phrases in wills should enable you to read your will more intelligently when it is presented by the attorney for your signature.

Another reason for having a will drawn now instead of procrastinating indefinitely is the possibility of living so long that you arrive at the point where, because of age, you are no longer capable of making the right decisions. We are not discussing senility here, for many people live until they are ninety, and beyond, in full retention of their faculties. It is simply that they have outlived most of their generation. They belong to another time. They refuse to make decisions that are imperative, or they decide on the wrong solution.

Mr. and Mrs. Stevens had everything in joint tenancy, so when he died his wife inherited everything. Mrs. Stevens lived until she was ninety-two years old, remaining in remarkably good health, but drastic changes had taken place in her family in the twenty years that she survived her husband. They had three married children, two sons and a daughter. The two sons and their wives had died during that twenty-year period, and by the time Mrs. Stevens was eighty-five her remaining child, her married daughter, was already sixty years of age.

In all that twenty years she had held on tightly to a comfortable estate and given nothing to her children. Of course, Mrs. Stevens had the right to retain the estate; it was hers, and if she wanted to keep possession of it until she was gone, it was nobody's business but her own. But when she reached her eighties, it certainly was time to take cognizance in her will of the fact that her two sons had died. Finally, at ninety, she decided to make a change.

But the change she made was to virtually disinherit her only remaining child! She didn't like her son-in-law, and since she had already lost two children, she falsely reasoned that the third one would die relatively soon after she did. In this event, what property she left to her daughter would go to her husband, and she didn't want that to happen.

So she changed her will, leaving her daughter only $20,000 of a sizable estate and placing the balance in a bank trust for the benefit of her six grandchildren. When she died at ninety-two, she left behind a very bitter daughter. The daughter's husband, who was retired, had never made much money, and she saw her rightful inheritance left for the most part to grandchildren. Mrs. Stevens had lived too long to make the right decision.

In another case Mr. Rodney, a widower, also lived to be over ninety. He had been an engineer in China most of his adult life, and he and his wife had found it relatively easy to amass a fortune living in a land where the cost of living was cheap. At ninety he was alert, his hearing was excellent, and he felt well enough to live alone in a big house. His interest in national and international affairs was very keen, especially since he had lived in Asia for so many years. He was receptive to new ideas and displayed an avid interest when a financial planner told him about the death-tax savings that could be achieved through proper estate planning. But he had become too old, at ninety, to make a decision. His reply was always: "I'll think about it." He refused to face up to the reality of his great age. He was convinced that he would live to see one hundred, and more, but he was dead at ninety-three.

Living so long that he could no longer make a major decision cost Mr. Rodney's children dearly in unnecessary estate taxes. He should have made estate-planning decisions years before.

Two apparently minor but actually important items in regard to a will seem to puzzle a lot of people.

First, and the more important of the two, is how they should divide their assets. Should they leave each heir a specific dollar amount? Or if there are bequests, should these be made first and then the residue divided? Or what? The simplest and most effective method is to think of your estate in terms of percentages (the whole estate being 100 percent), and divide your total assets by percentages instead of willing dollar amounts.

Mr. Bowman had a $40,000 estate that he was leaving to his three sons. His youngest son was a high school teacher with four children. His earned income was low, while at the same time demands on his money were great. Financially, raising four children is a problem, much less sending them to college. Since Mr. Bowman's other two sons were good money-makers with small families, he decided to leave unequal shares to his children. He left 50 percent to the high school teacher and 25 percent each to his other two sons. This was the *correct* way to arrange the division of his assets in his will.

Supposing, instead, that Mr. Bowman had divided the $40,000 in dollar amounts, stating that the neediest son was to inherit $20,000 and the other two sons the residue of his estate share and share alike. Now let's take a look at what might have happened.

First, Mr. Bowman might have spent half of his estate by the time he died. This way the schoolteacher son would inherit $20,000 and his other two sons would receive nothing. Secondly, assuming that instead of spending half of his estate Mr. Bowman, by sound investing, had increased his estate from $40,000 to $80,000 by the time he died. Now the needy son would still inherit $20,000, but the other two sons would divide the remainder, or $60,000.

Neither of these events actually took place, but even though they had, Mr. Bowman had foreseen the possibility and wisely arranged to have his schoolteacher son receive 50 percent of his estate no matter what happened. By the percentage method of division, the neediest son would inherit one-half of his estate whether its value was $20,000, $40,000, or $80,000 by the time he died.

A word of caution. If you do leave uneven shares to children for some good reason, have your lawyer insert a clause in your will stating why you did it. It will avoid ill feeling among your children as to why you didn't treat them equally.

The second apparently minor but important problem is how to divide your more valuable personal belongings. Leaving your personal property for your children to wrangle over can cause a lifetime of bitterness. In many households there are a few pieces of furniture and items of personal belongings that have an unusual monetary or sentimental value: a tea set that belonged to Grandma, a piano, a brand-new bedroom set. These are called chattels by your attorney.

The best way to handle the problem is to make a decision on these items and then state in your will who gets them. Or if you don't want to mention them in your will, use an old-fashioned method that still works, even though it may not be legal. On the underside of each valuable item put the name of the heir who is to receive it. This clearly states your wishes, and most of the time your heirs will cheerfully abide by your thoughtful decisions. The balance of your personal property that has little value will be divided without argument, or for that matter discarded or sold.

Mr. and Mrs. Page had three married sons and ignored the division of their personal estate. The sons didn't fight over who got what, but their wives did! A grandfather clock was literally stolen by one daughter-in-law, according to the other two, just because she happened to be there first. And a very comfortable, new bedroom set was bitterly wrangled over but seized by the family that needed it the least, or so it was contended. The backbiting that went on eventually disrupted the three families to the point where the three sons seldom saw one another anymore.

Sometimes personal property includes business furniture or equipment. It makes sense to leave farm equipment, for instance, to a son who is managing the farm, not to your widow, or to all of the children share and share alike. A business or professional person would do better to leave his office equipment to his business associates rather than to heirs who have little or no use for it.

One of the possibilities that should be avoided in your will is ancillary administration of part of your estate. This means probate of those assets that are physically in another state, in addition to the state in which you are domiciled. The asset most commonly involved is real estate.

Mrs. Edie was a widow who retained ownership, until she died, of a mountain cabin in an adjoining state which she used every summer for about three months. She enjoyed the cabin immensely, but eventually she became too old to enjoy it, so that her son and his family were the only ones who made use of it, mainly during his two-week annual vacation. Mrs. Edie should have given it to her son during her lifetime, which would have avoided ancillary probate proceedings of the cabin in the adjoining state.

Sometimes, however, giving up ownership of real estate by the property owner is not advisable. Then other arrangements should be made.

Mrs. Woods lived in a large and expensive house in Philadelphia, which had been her home for most of her adult life. For her security and protection she saw no alternative but to retain the ownership. She died, leaving her estate, including the house, to her only daughter, who lived in New York. Since most of her estate was in securities these presented no problem. But the ancillary probate administration because of the house in Philadelphia became a headache, which was not settled for several years. The big old home, though valuable, was a white elephant because of the existing poor real estate market in Philadelphia.

Ancillary probate administration is required for several reasons.

1. The state in which the property is located wants to be sure it collects its share of inheritance taxes.
2. The creditors in that state have to be protected.
3. Heirs want to be sure that title to the real estate is not clouded, which could happen if probate of the property was not carried out in the state in which it was located.

Where assets other than real estate are held in another state they should be physically brought into the state of domicile, particularly since some states require ancillary administration of all tangible personal property, including stocks and bonds and bank accounts. The careless retention of a bank account in Vermont, for example, simply because you formerly lived there and go back to visit once in a while, could cause trouble, when it would be so simple to transfer the account to your new permanent home in Florida.

Real estate, as we have indicated, presents the major problem. There are actually five different ways to solve it:

(a) by an outright gift to your heirs;
(b) by retaining a life interest in the property, including the right to sell;
(c) by placing it in joint tenancy;
(d) by placing it in a revocable living trust (discussed in the trust chapter);
(e) by incorporating the property, if it is sizable. Now it is no longer real estate, but stock, which in most states would not make it subject to ancillary administration.

Liquidity is another problem frequently not considered by the testator when having a will drawn. An estate can be completely debt free, but in the next instant, because of death, be subjected to sizable bills. Death creates cash requirements for the following reasons:

(a) funeral expenses;
(b) doctor and hospital bills;
(c) administration costs;
(d) cash bequests in the will;
(e) federal estate taxes;
(f) state inheritance taxes;
(g) income taxes.

An estate consisting almost entirely of real estate presents the biggest liquidity problem to an executor. Sometimes the above obligations cannot be met except by mortgaging the property, or selling it in a hurry, usually at a sacrifice. An alternative method would be for the testator to sell some of the real estate at a favorable price during his or her lifetime.

Income taxes have to be paid by the executor, as we can see from the above list. There are two returns involved: the personal income tax of the deceased during that part of the year in which he survived; and the income tax of the estate itself, for it is a separate tax-paying entity that has to report the income the estate has received during probate administration (if this amount exceeds $600).

Your executor should understand that on the estate tax return he has the option of reporting on a calendar year or a fiscal year basis. Let us say that death occurs on February 1. Your executor could choose a fiscal year and not owe any income taxes in the year of death by transferring that obligation, very advantageously sometimes, to the following first of February. Also, your executor may charge the expenses of administration of your estate either to the deceased's personal income tax return or the estate's income tax return, whichever is the more advantageous.

*   *   *

It is possible, but not advisable, to draw a will yourself and thereby avoid the expense of hiring an attorney. A handwritten will drawn by the testator is called a holographic will. The main objection to drawing your own will is the possibility that it will be declared illegal. It has to meet certain rigid standards, and even these can vary from state to state. Generally speaking, it must be written entirely in the testator's own hand on a perfectly plain piece of stationery; there can be absolutely no printing of any kind on the paper. It must be dated, of course, and, in most states, witnessed by at least two persons.

Some attorneys will recommend a holographic will as a stopgap device. A client, for instance, might telephone in the middle of the night upset because he is having a heart attack, or thinks he is, and suddenly realizes that he doesn't have a will. Quite often it's not possible for the attorney to see his client immediately—say, the next day—so under these circumstances he may suggest that the testator write his own will, which is better by far than dying intestate.

Reproduced below are two samples of holographic wills that were admitted to probate court and declared legal. Names, places, and dates have been changed. The wording, however, is identical, including misspelled words and bad punctuation.

San Jose, Calif.
March 14, 1984

I, Mae Morse, hereby make my last will—I, give all the property of which I die possessed to my husband George T. Morse—I appoint my said husband executor of this will without bonds. I give him power to sell all or any of my estate without an order of court I case my husband George T. Morse should die before I do—I want the estate to be divided into equal parts and given to each of my living sisters amd brother.

I want Anna Jones to serve as executor of this will without bonds.

If anyone contests this will—they shall receive the sum of one dollar ($1.00)

This is my last will and declare this will is entirely written and dated and signed by my hand.

MAE MORSE

45 N. Street,

San Jose, Calif.

San Francisco, Calif.

February 14, 1984

I, Mary Doe, being of sound mind and not acting under fraud menace, or the undue influence of any person do hereby make and declare this to be my last will and testament in the following manner: I give, devise and bequeath all of my property of every kind nature and description and whereever situate to my brother, Thomas Doe.

I appoint as my executor to serve without bond James Doe of 100 Main Street, San Francisco, California.

I hereby affirm that this my last will and testament is entirely written by my own hand and signed by me.

Mary Doe

Whether your will is drawn by your own hand or by an attorney, it should be under periodic review. Too often a testator takes the attitude that once his will is drawn the job is done. It has been done, for the time being, but unfortunately assets entail responsibilities, and as far as your will is concerned this means keeping it up to date. Any material change in circumstances should alert the property owner that perhaps his will should be reviewed. Events such as a marriage, a divorce, or birth of children or grandchildren should serve as a red flag. Your will would not necessarily have to be altered, but it is just as well to take it out of your safe deposit box and look it over to be sure.

Quite often a will should be reviewed if an estate is reduced in size due to financial reverses. Cash bequests, for instance, could be eliminated because the principal beneficiaries will need the entire estate. A change in family or financial circumstances, therefore, is the key.

To repeat again, your will should be drawn by a competent attorney. But you can't trust him in regard to its provisions. Remember, the average attorney wants your estate in probate court because his fees will be higher. For the same reason he will try to talk you out of joint tenancy, even though that is the correct ownership for you.

You have to stand your ground with him. After all, it is your estate and your heirs, not his.

And before you sign your will, be sure that you understand it.

8

Income
Taxes

MOST PEOPLE OVERPAY their income taxes.

If you are skeptical about this, take a look at your last year's U.S. income tax return. Did you pay more than 15 percent of your adjusted gross income in taxes? You did? Then you probably paid too much.

We say "probably" because no one can make a flat statement about the finances of the more than 100 million people who file an income tax return each year. But if you feel that you are paying too much in taxes, we suggest that you find out what you can do about it.

No one should pay more in taxes than the law demands. To do so is a deterrent to financial independence. Contrary to popular opinion, the Internal Revenue Service does not want you to pay more than you owe, but on the other hand they will not tell you how to pay less. Paying less is entirely up to you. You must know how to take all of the deductions allowed under the law. More than one taxpayer has claimed: "I deduct everything but the kitchen sink."

You shouldn't do that. But let's suppose that you deducted more than you should, and you are one of those unfortunates chosen for an audit by the Internal Revenue Service. What then? Nothing, except you will have to pay more taxes. Taxpayers have nothing to fear from the IRS as long as they report all of their income. It's people who conceal income who get into trouble, and sometimes go to jail.

"But I have my accountant make out my return," you protest, "so I get all of my deductions."

Maybe you do, but I wouldn't count on it. The Internal Revenue Service recently estimated that over 70 percent of all tax returns are incorrectly filled out. This includes millions of returns prepared by accountants. How much of a tax preparer's time do you feel you can hire for fifty dollars, or even a few hundred dollars, especially at his busiest time of the year during the ninety days before tax time? And if you go to a national firm that trains part-time tax preparers who are paid on a commission basis, the chances for a sketchy, poorly prepared return are even greater, for the more returns they grind out, the more they are paid.

But let's suppose that you are making enough money to pay a handsome fee to your accountant, and that he has given you good advice in the past. You should still not assume that you have reduced your taxes to a minimuim.

Why?

Because your accountant can only work with the figures that you give him. His hands are tied if you maintain poor or insufficient records, insist upon keeping all of your excess dollars in a bank or a savings and loan instead of investing them, don't open an IRA or Keogh account, and don't say anything about deductions or credits that only you can know about because you are the only one intimately enough acquainted with your particular financial situation. Your accountant has no alternative but to make out your return according to the figures you have submitted to him.

In the last analysis, then, it is up to you to reduce your taxes, just as the knowledgeable investor knows that it is his responsibility to make the final investment decisions, and not rely entirely on the judgment of a financial adviser.

There are four basic ways you can reduce the income taxes that you owe every year.

1. You must learn about—and take—all of the deductions and credits you are entitled to under the law.

    These deductions and credits make for a significant

difference between an individual taxpayer's *gross* income and the *taxable* income on which he actually pays his income tax. Within reasonable limits, this variation is intended by Congress and is inherent in our income tax system. It is only net income that is subject to tax, after recovery of the expenses and capital consumed in earning it, and after setting aside a basic sum for personal expenditures of the taxpayer and his family.

2. You must, if you can, rearrange the source of your excess-dollar income.

   You should not keep your excess dollars where they earn interest only. You should invest them, and find out how current income can be translated into capital gain which will be taxed at much lower rates. This double benefit will be explained in detail later.

3. You should have your money at work so that part of the income you receive is tax exempt. There are twelve different ways to invest whereby the income is completely tax-free, also explained later.

It should be realized, too, that our tax system is one that is based upon self-assessment and voluntary compliance. It is the taxpayer, not the Internal Revenue Service, who reports his or her income, itemizes deductions (as millions of us do), and determines the amount of tax that is owed.

The IRS usually accepts income tax returns as filed. However, some returns are audited. This is because the service has a random audit system that will choose returns for audit without any justification for their being singled out from the millions of returns sent in each year. Returns are also audited because the computer discovers discrepancies in arithmetic, or unusual deductions which depart from the norm.

In the past most people have been willing to pay what they owe (even though they grumble about it) because they have assumed that everyone was paying his or her fair share of the tax burden. But this attitude is changing so that tax reform and tax simplification are the order of the day.

The income tax is a progressive tax, meaning that the higher the income the higher the tax rate, which theoretically assesses a taxpayer on his ability to pay. The tax schedule apparently supports this for the tax rate rises with an increase in the taxpayer's income.

We said this is apparently so. And we mean exactly that. There are many persons with incomes of one or two million dollars and more who pay the same amount in taxes as people with incomes of only $20,000 to $30,000. Even people with identical income pay taxes in highly varying amounts. And finally there are tax deductions that are subject to wide abuse.

You often hear tax experts, and others, say that these "tax loopholes" enacted by Congress should be abolished. Let's set this expression straight right now. There are no tax loopholes. There are only tax deductions approved by Congress and the Internal Revenue Service. These deductions are legal and, while they are still available, should be used by everyone, not just by those who have enough money to hire the top tax brains in the country in order to take full advantage of them. True, the more money you have, the greater are the chances of benefiting by many of these deductions. But this does not mean that you should not use them, too.

What is sauce for the goose is sauce for the gander. It is time to end the old cliché about taxes: "The rich escape them; the poor don't pay them; therefore the whole burden falls upon the middle class." On the contrary, equity in taxation should be the privilege of paying as little as somebody else. This lower- to middle-income tax burden can be changed if everyone becomes fully aware of what can be done to reduce his or her income taxes.

Let's suppose by reading this chapter that you learn how to reduce your taxes by only $1,000 every year. You should realize this is not just $10,000 saved in the next ten years, or $20,000 saved in twenty years. When $1,000 of saved taxes is put to work every year for ten years at 8 percent compound interest, $10,000 becomes worth $21,590. And if $1,000 is put to work every year for twenty years at 8 percent compound interest, $20,000 becomes worth $46,610, a sizable sum of money. And if your tax savings are more than $1,000 a year, they could be worth a small fortune.

Reducing your income taxes to a minimum is not a last-day affair or a three-month problem starting on January 15 of each year. It's an all-year problem. Sound gruesome? It shouldn't, and besides that it's worth it. The few hundred dollars, or the few thousand dollars, by which you can cut your taxes and thereby keep these dollars for yourself and your family are definitely worth the time and trouble. You should not, year after year, hand over to the Internal Revenue Service more money than the law requires.

First, as a help in solving the problem, take a look at Form 1040, which is the basic two-page form used to file an income tax return, and which is reproduced on the following pages.

Form 1040 is not complicated. It comes in five basic parts. The first three are on page one. The first part consists of basic information concerning your name, address, Social Security number, filing status, and personal exemptions. The second part lists the sources of your income. The third part enumerates the eight adjustments to income to which you might be entitled. The net total of these adjustments, if any, reduces your total income to your adjusted gross income. The one most commonly used is payment to an IRA or a Keogh plan.

The final two of the five basic parts of Form 1040 are on page two, which is the reverse side of the form. Part four is your tax computation. The first step is to take your adjusted gross income from the bottom of page one and deduct from it your personal deductions that you listed on Schedule A, which is the amount by which your personal deductions exceed the standard deduction (the zero bracket amount). Next you deduct the dollar amount of your exemptions that are listed at the top of page one, Form 1040, which is the number of your exemptions times the amount allowed for each exemption. You have now determined your taxable income. With this sum you determine the amount of income tax that you owe. That is, with one exemption.

Form **1040**	Department of the Treasury—Internal Revenue Service **U.S. Individual Income Tax Return**	1984	(O)		

For the year January 1-December 31, 1984, or other tax year beginning _____ , 1984, ending _____ , 19 _____   OMB No. 1545-0074

Use IRS label. Other- wise, please print or type.	Your first name and initial (if joint return, also give spouse's name and initial) Last name	Your social security number
	Present home address (Number and street, including apartment number, or rural route)	Spouse's social security number
	City, town or post office, State, and ZIP code	Your occupation
		Spouse's occupation

Presidential Election Campaign ► Do you want $1 to go to this fund? . . . . Yes ☐ No ☐
If joint return, does your spouse want $1 to go to this fund? . . Yes ☐ No ☐

Note: *Checking "Yes" will not change your tax or reduce your refund.*

For Privacy Act and Paperwork Reduction Act Notice, see Instructions

Filing Status

Check only one box.

1 ☐ Single
2 ☐ Married filing joint return (even if only one had income)
3 ☐ Married filing separate return. Enter spouse's social security no. above and full name here. _____
4 ☐ Head of household (with qualifying person). (See page 5 of Instructions.) If the qualifying person is your unmarried child but not your dependent, write child's name here. _____
5 ☐ Qualifying widow(er) with dependent child (Year spouse died ► 19 _____). (See page 6 of Instructions.)

Exemptions

Always check the box labeled yourself. Check other boxes if they apply.

6a ☐ Yourself   ☐ 65 or over   ☐ Blind
b ☐ Spouse   ☐ 65 or over   ☐ Blind
} Enter number of boxes checked on 6a and b ►

c First names of your dependent children who lived with you _____

Enter number of children listed on 6c ►

d Other dependents: (1) Name	(2) Relationship	(3) Number of months lived in your home	(4) Did dependent have income of $1,000 or more?	(5) Did you provide more than one-half of dependent's support?

Enter number of other dependents ►

Add numbers entered in boxes above ►

e Total number of exemptions claimed (also complete line 36). . . . .

Income

Please attach Copy B of your Forms W-2, W-2G, and W-2P here.

If you do not have a W-2, see page 4 of Instructions.

Please attach check or money order here.

7	Wages, salaries, tips, etc.	7	
8	Interest income (also attach Schedule B if over $400)	8	
9a	Dividends (also attach Schedule B if over $400) _____ , 9b Exclusion _____		
c	Subtract line 9b from line 9a and enter the result	9c	
10	Refunds of State and local income taxes, from the worksheet on page 9 of Instructions (do not enter an amount unless you itemized deductions for those taxes in an earlier year—see page 9)	10	
11	Alimony received	11	
12	Business income or (loss) (attach Schedule C)	12	
13	Capital gain or (loss) (attach Schedule D)	13	
14	40% of capital gain distributions not reported on line 13 (see page 9 of Instructions) . .	14	
15	Supplemental gains or (losses) (attach Form 4797)	15	
16	Fully taxable pensions, IRA distributions, and annuities not reported on line 17 . . .	16	
17a	Other pensions and annuities, including rollovers. Total received 17a _____		
b	Taxable amount, if any, from the worksheet on page 10 of Instructions	17b	
18	Rents, royalties, partnerships, estates, trusts, etc. (attach Schedule E)	18	
19	Farm income or (loss) (attach Schedule F)	19	
20a	Unemployment compensation (insurance). Total received 20a _____		
b	Taxable amount, if any, from the worksheet on page 10 of Instructions	20b	
21a	Social security benefits. (see page 10 of Instructions) 21a _____		
b	Taxable amount, if any, from the worksheet on page 11 of Instructions	21b	
22	Other income (state nature and source—see page 11 of Instructions) _____	22	
23	Add lines 7 through 22. This is your **total income** . . . . . . ►	23	

Adjustments to Income

(See Instructions on page 11.)

24	Moving expense (attach Form 3903 or 3903F)	24		
25	Employee business expenses (attach Form 2106) . . .	25		
26a	IRA deduction, from the worksheet on page 12 . . .	26a		
b	Enter here IRA payments you made in 1985 that are included in line 26a above ► _____			
27	Payments to a Keogh (H.R. 10) retirement plan . . .	27		
28	Penalty on early withdrawal of savings	28		
29	Alimony paid	29		
30	Deduction for a married couple when both work (attach Schedule W)	30		
31	Add lines 24 through 30. These are your **total adjustments** . . . . . . ►		31	

Adjusted Gross Income

32	Subtract line 31 from line 23. This is your **adjusted gross income**. If this line is less than $10,000, see "Earned Income Credit" (line 59) on page 16 of Instructions. If you want IRS to figure your tax, see page 12 of Instructions . . . . ►	32	

Form 1040 (1984)

Tax	33	Amount from line 32 (adjusted gross income)	33
Compu-	34a	If you itemize, attach Schedule A (Form 1040) and enter the amount from Schedule A, line 26	34a
tation		**Caution:** If you have unearned income and can be claimed as a dependent on your parent's return, check here ▶ ☐ and see page 13 of the Instructions. Also see page 13 if:	
		• You are married filing a separate return and your spouse itemizes deductions, OR	
(See		• You file Form 4563, OR • You are a dual-status alien.	
Instruc-	34b	If you do not itemize deductions, and you have charitable contributions, complete the worksheet	
tions on		on page 14. Then enter the allowable part of your contributions here	34b
page 13.)	35	Subtract line 34a or 34b, whichever applies, from line 33	35
	36	Multiply $1,000 by the total number of exemptions claimed on Form 1040, line 6e	36
	37	Taxable Income. Subtract line 36 from line 35	37
	38	Tax. Enter tax here and check if from ☐ Tax Table, ☐ Tax Rate Schedule X, Y, or Z, or ☐ Schedule G	38
	39	Additional Taxes. (See page 14 of Instructions.) Enter here and check if from ☐ Form 4970, ☐ Form 4972, or ☐ Form 5544	39
	40	Add lines 38 and 39. Enter the total . . . . ▶	40
Credits	41	Credit for child and dependent care expenses (attach Form 2441)	41	
	42	Credit for the elderly and the permanently and totally disabled (attach Schedule R)	42	
(See	43	Residential energy credit (attach Form 5695)	43	
Instruc-	44	Partial credit for political contributions for which you have receipts	44	
tions on	45	Add lines 41 through 44. These are your total personal credits	45
page 14.)	46	Subtract line 45 from 40. Enter the result (but not less than zero)	46
	47	Foreign tax credit (attach Form 1116)	47	
	48	General business credit. Check if from ☐ Form 3800, ☐ Form 3468, ☐ Form 5884, ☐ Form 6478	48	
	49	Add lines 47 and 48. These are your total business and other credits	49
	50	Subtract line 49 from 46. Enter the result (but not less than zero). . . . . ▶	50
Other	51	Self-employment tax (attach Schedule SE)	51
Taxes	52	Alternative minimum tax (attach Form 6251)	52
	53	Tax from recapture of investment credit (attach Form 4255)	53
(Including	54	Social security tax on tip income not reported to employer (attach Form 4137)	54
Advance	55	Tax on an IRA (attach Form 5329)	55
EIC Payments)	56	Add lines 50 through 55. This is your **total tax** . . . . ▶	56
Payments	57	Federal income tax withheld	57	
	58	1984 estimated tax payments and amount applied from 1983 return.	58	
	59	Earned income credit. If line 33 is under $10,000, see page 16 .	59	
Attach	60	Amount paid with Form 4868	60	
Forms W-2,	61	Excess social security tax and RRTA tax withheld (two or more employers)	61	
W-2G, and W-2P	62	Credit for Federal tax on gasoline and special fuels (attach Form 4136) . . .	62	
to front.	63	Regulated Investment Company credit (attach Form 2439) . . .	63	
	64	Add lines 57 through 63. These are your **total payments** . . . . ▶	64
Refund or	65	If line 64 is larger than line 56, enter amount OVERPAID . . . . ▶	65
Amount	66	Amount of line 65 to be REFUNDED TO YOU . . . . ▶	66
You Owe	67	Amount of line 65 to be applied to your 1985 estimated tax . . . ▶ 67	
	68	If line 56 is larger than line 64, enter AMOUNT YOU OWE. Attach check or money order for full amount payable to "Internal Revenue Service." Write your social security number and "1984 Form 1040" on it . . . (Check ▶ ☐ if Form 2210 (2210F) is attached. See page 17 of Instructions.) $	68

Please Sign Here Under penalties of perjury, I declare that I have examined this return and accompanying schedules and statements, and to the best of my knowledge and belief, they are true, correct, and complete. Declaration of preparer (other than taxpayer) is based on all information of which preparer has any knowledge.

Your signature   Date   ▶ Spouse's signature (if filing jointly, BOTH must sign)

Paid Preparer's Use Only

Preparer's signature ▶	Date	Check if self-employed ☐	Preparer's social security no.
Firm's name (or yours, if self-employed) and address ▶		E.I. No.	
		ZIP code	

Beginning with 1984, one-half of Social Security payments could be taxed. If your adjusted gross income computed in part one, plus one-half of your Social Security benefits, plus tax-exempt interest, exceeds $25,000 if single, or $32,000 if married and filing jointly, the excess is subject to tax.

In part five you list tax credits, if any. The two most commonly available are the credit for the elderly and the credit for child and dependent care expenses. The other tax is the self-employment tax, which is the Social Security tax paid by the self-employed. Under payments, you put down the amount of income tax witheld by your employer and/or your estimated tax payments.

To recapitulate what you have done in part five, you subtracted credits from the tax you computed in part four, added any additional taxes, and subtracted your tax payments. If the result is larger than your final computation (in part five), the IRS owes you a refund; if not, you owe them a payment.

So, we repeat our original contention that Form 1040 is not that difficult.

Perhaps one other area of confusion should be clarified, which is Schedules A & B, the only other form that the average taxpayer fills out besides Form 1040.

Schedule A itemizes the six personal deductions. Remember our earlier statement that only *net income* is subject to tax after setting aside a basic sum for personal expenditures. This basic sum is the standard deduction (zero bracket amount), which is constantly being changed by Congress. Married couples receive the greatest allowance, single persons about two-thirds of this sum, and married persons filing separately one-half.

Your six basic personal itemized deductions of medical and dental expenses, taxes, interest expense, contributions, casualty and theft losses, and miscellaneous must *exceed* the amount of the standard deduction (which is the amount stated at the bottom of Schedule A). If they do not, you don't have any itemized deductions to report in part four of Form 1040.

In this event the standard deduction is all that you are entitled to, which is automatically included in the Tax Tables.

Schedule B (on the reverse side of Schedule A) is used to report the amount and source of your interest income in Part I, and the amount and source of your dividend income in Part II. You have nothing to report if neither one exceeds the amount stated in the income section on page 1, Form 1040. Schedules A & B are reproduced on the following pages.

Before proceeding, we should also clarify the difference between a deduction and a credit. A deduction reduces your reportable income; a credit reduces your tax. Therefore a credit is far better than a deduction.

To illustrate: if you enter a $1,000 deduction on your income tax return, and you are in a 40 percent tax bracket, you save $400. If you are entitled to a $1,000 credit, you save $1,000 (regardless of your tax bracket) because it is deducted directly from your tax. This is clearly demonstrated by an examination of Form 1040. The adjustments to income at the bottom of page one are deductions (except for the penalty on early withdrawal of savings) that reduce your income. The credits in part five decrease your taxes.

We are now ready to discuss the four basic ways to reduce your taxes, besides the adjustments to income and the credits provided for on Form 1040.

You must learn about, and take, all of the deductions to which you are entitled under the law. Remember, you can't trust your accountant or tax preparer to do this for you.

The first of these deductions is a sum for each person who qualifies as your dependent, which reduces your reportable income by that amount. Don't assume that someone who is living with you, or whom you are partly supporting, doesn't qualify. Have your accountant look up the regulations.

Next, buy a home if you can. I know most young people can't qualify, either because they don't have the down pay-

| SCHEDULES A&B
(Form 1040)
Department of the Treasury
Internal Revenue Service (O) | **Schedule A—Itemized Deductions**
(Schedule B is on back)
▶ Attach to Form 1040. ▶ See Instructions for Schedules A and B (Form 1040). | OMB No. 1545-0074
1984
07 |

Name(s) as shown on Form 1040 · Your social security number

Medical and Dental Expenses (Do not include expenses reimbursed or paid by others.) (See Instructions on page 19)	1 Prescription medicines and drugs; and insulin	**1**	
	2 a Doctors, dentists, nurses, hospitals, insurance premiums you paid for medical and dental care, etc.	**2a**	
	b Transportation and lodging	**2b**	
	c Other (list—include hearing aids, dentures, eyeglasses, etc.) ▶		
	....	**2c**	
	3 Add lines 1 through 2c, and write the total here	**3**	
	4 Multiply the amount on Form 1040, line 33, by 5% (.05)	**4**	
	5 Subtract line 4 from line 3. If zero or less, write -0-. **Total medical and dental** ▶	**5**	
Taxes You Paid (See Instructions on page 20)	6 State and local income taxes	**6**	
	7 Real estate taxes	**7**	
	8 a General sales tax (see sales tax tables in instruction booklet)	**8a**	
	b General sales tax on motor vehicles	**8b**	
	9 Other taxes (list—include personal property taxes) ▶	**9**	
	10 Add the amounts on lines 6 through 9. Write the total here. **Total taxes** ▶	**10**	
Interest You Paid (See Instructions on page 20)	11 a Home mortgage interest you paid to financial institutions	**11a**	
	b Home mortgage interest you paid to individuals (show that person's name and address) ▶		
		11b	
	12 Total credit card and charge account interest you paid	**12**	
	13 Other interest you paid (list) ▶		
		13	
	14 Add the amounts on lines 11a through 13. Write the total here. **Total interest** ▶	**14**	
Contributions You Made (See Instructions on page 20)	15 a Cash contributions. (If you gave $3,000 or more to any one organization, report those contributions on line 15b.)	**15a**	
	b Cash contributions totaling $3,000 or more to any one organization. (Show to whom you gave and how much you gave.) ▶		
		15b	
	16 Other than cash (attach required statement)	**16**	
	17 Carryover from prior year	**17**	
	18 Add the amounts on lines 15a through 17. Write the total here. **Total contributions** ▶	**18**	
Casualty and Theft Losses	19 Total casualty or theft loss(es). (You must attach Form 4684 or similar statement.) (see page 21 of Instructions) ▶	**19**	
Miscellaneous Deductions (See Instructions on page 21)	20 Union and professional dues	**20**	
	21 Tax return preparation fee	**21**	
	22 Other (list type and amount) ▶		
		22	
	23 Add the amounts on lines 20 through 22. Write the total here. **Total miscellaneous** ▶	**23**	
Summary of Itemized Deductions (See Instructions on page 22)	24 Add the amounts on lines 5, 10, 14, 18, 19, and 23. Write your answer here.	**24**	
	25 If you checked Form 1040 { Filing Status box 2 or 5, write $3,400 / Filing Status box 1 or 4, write $2,300 / Filing Status box 3, write $1,700 }	**25**	
	26 Subtract line 25 from line 24. Write your answer here and on Form 1040, line 34a. (If line 25 is more than line 24, see the Instructions for line 26 on page 22.) ▶	**26**	

For Paperwork Reduction Act Notice, see Form 1040 Instructions. · Schedule A (Form 1040) 1984

Schedules A&B (Form 1040) 1984   **Schedule B—Interest and Dividend Income**   08 OMB No. 1545-0074 Page **2**

Name(s) as shown on Form 1040 (Do not enter name and social security number if shown on other side.) | Your social security number

Part I
Interest
Income

If you received more than $400 in interest income, you must complete Part I and list ALL interest received. If you received interest as a nominee for another, or you received or paid accrued interest on securities transferred between interest payment dates, or you received any interest from an All-Savers Certificate, see page 22.

(See
Instruc-
tions on
pages 8 and 22)

Also complete
Part III.

Interest income		Amount
1 Interest income from seller-financed mortgages. (See Instructions and show name of payer.) ▶	1	
2 Other interest income (list name of payer) ▶..............................		
....		
....		
....		
....	2	
....		
....		
3 Add the amounts on lines 1 and 2. Write the total here and on Form 1040, line 8 . ▶	3	

Part II
Dividend
Income

If you received more than $400 in gross dividends (including capital gain distributions) and other distributions on stock, or you are electing to exclude qualified reinvested dividends from a public utility, complete Part II. If you received dividends as a nominee for another, see page 22.

(See
Instruc-
tions on
pages 8 and 22)

Also complete
Part III.

Name of payer		Amount
4		
....		
....		
....	4	
....		
....		
5 Add the amounts on line 4. Write the total here	5	
6 Capital gain distributions. Enter here and on line 15, Schedule D.*	6	
7 Nontaxable distributions. (See Schedule D Instructions for adjustment to basis.)	7	
8 Exclusion of qualified reinvested dividends from a public utility. (See page 23 of Instructions.)	8	
9 Add the amounts on lines 6, 7, and 8. Write the total here	9	
10 Subtract line 9 from line 5. Write the result here and on Form 1040, line 9a . . . ▶	10	

*If you received capital gain distributions for the year and you do not need Schedule D to report any other gains or losses, do not file that schedule. Instead, enter 40% of your capital gain distributions on Form 1040, line 14.

Part III
Foreign
Accounts
and
Foreign
Trusts
(See
Instruc-
tions on
page 23)

If you received more than $400 of interest or dividends, OR if you had a foreign account or were a grantor of, or a transferor to, a foreign trust, you must answer both questions in Part III. | Yes | No

11 At any time during the tax year, did you have an interest in or a signature or other authority over a bank account, securities account, or other financial account in a foreign country? (See page 23 of the Instructions for exceptions and filing requirements for Form TD F 90-22.1.) . . . .

If "Yes," write the name of the foreign country ▶ ....

12 Were you the grantor of, or transferor to, a foreign trust which existed during the current tax year, whether or not you have any beneficial interest in it? If "Yes," you may have to file Forms 3520, 3520-A, or 926. . .

For Paperwork Reduction Act Notice, see Form 1040 Instructions.   **Schedule B (Form 1040) 1984** ment, or because they can't meet the payments on the necessary loan, or both. But if you do own a home, you are entitled to two fine deductions, the interest on the mortgage and the amount of the property taxes.

Remember our statement that only net income is subject to tax, after recovery of the expenses and capital consumed in earning it. If you own a business, expenses are deducted first; only net income is reported.

The same is true of income property. But now because you have investment property (not a home), you can deduct depreciation of the building, a major reason people buy income property, besides the opportunity for a long-term profit.

Most people who have never owned income property don't understand depreciation. In contrast to other operation expenses, such as property taxes, interest on the mortgage, repairs, utility charges, and janitorial services, depreciation is not an out-of-pocket expense. It is a bookkeeping entry, which can convert a property that is actually producing a net income into one that has a sizable loss. This loss can then be used to offset other income.

Douglas and Mary Abbott, who were in a 50 percent tax bracket, bought an apartment house for $210,000. They paid 25 percent down, or $52,500, and financed the balance of the purchase price with a first mortgage of $157,500 for 30 years at 12 percent. The building was valued at $200,000 and the land at $10,000. They assumed a useful life of 15 years, allowed under the Accelerated Cost Recovery System (ACRS) passed in 1981. This allowed them to take a depreciation rate of 6 ⅔ percent on the $200,000 building (you can't depreciate land), for a deduction of $13,333 a year.

Now let's take a look at the Abbotts' tax advantage because of depreciation at the end of the first year. Their apartment house returned them $3,100, which was 5.9 percent on their $52,500 investment. Yet for tax purposes, because of depreciation, their apartment house showed a sizable loss.

Their tax figures looked like this:

Gross rental income	$36,000	
Operating expenses	14,000	
Net income		$22,000
Mortgage interest @ 12%		18,900
Income before depreciation		$ 3,100
Depreciation deduction		13,333
Net loss		($10,233)

The depreciation deduction gave the Abbotts two tax advantages. They had a $3,100 net income they did not have to report, and they had a $10,233 tax loss which they used to offset other taxable income which, in their 50 percent tax bracket, saved them $5,116 in income taxes.

There are other less dramatic deductions that are available to reduce your income taxes.

A personal bad debt (except to a relative), but the deduction can't be taken until the debt is worthless.

A benefit received from an employer because an employee died, up to $5,000.

Car pool receipts.

Child support payments.

Damages from libel, loss of life, personal injuries, slander.

Grants under the Disaster Relief Act.

Life insurance dividends, but not the interest on them.

Employment agency fees.

Labor union assessments for out-of-work benefits.

Nonrecoverable loss if a bank fails.

Interest you pay, except on a loan to buy tax-exempt securities, or to pay for life insurance under a systematic plan to borrow against the increasing cash value.

Medical expenses taken in Schedule A.

Doctors' fees and prescription drug costs are combined. They must exceed 5 percent of adjusted gross income. Only the excess over this percentage can be deducted, which eliminates many people from a medical expense deduction, particularly when any payment by Medicare must also be deducted from the total of your medical expenses.

The best way to keep records of medical expenses is to list them in a ledger as they occur, and subtract your insurance or Medicare payment when it is received. For example:

Provider	Amount	Insurance or Medicare	Net Cost
Dr. John Jones	$45.00	$36.00	$9.00

Casualty and theft losses taken in Schedule A must exceed 5 percent of adjusted gross income, after *each loss* is reduced by $100.

Miscellaneous deductions taken in Schedule A include union dues and initiation fees, tax preparer fees, uniforms required for work, and safe deposit box rent if used for investment or business purposes.

(Every year some deductions are modified or repealed. Check with your accountant in regard to current regulations.)

Secondly, you must, if you can, rearrange the source of your excess-dollar income.

You should invest your excess dollars rather than keep them at interest in order to take advantage of the capital gain deduction. Special income tax treatment is granted the taxpayer when money is made by selling a capital asset at a long-term profit. *The capital gain deduction is 60 percent of the long-term profit.* In other words this much is tax exempt. The other 40 percent is taxed as ordinary income, just as though it were interest or a raise in salary. This is one of the finest tax deductions available. The wealthy and the well-to-do always strive to make money this way, and so should you.

A profit from the sale of a capital asset is considered long-term when it is held for a minimum period of time (currently six months and one day). A capital asset is any property not used in the operation of a business. Examples of capital assets are common stocks and real estate.

The tax computation on a hypothetical sale for $20,000, which realizes a long-term profit of $10,000 with a cost basis of $10,000, looks like this:

$20,000 sale
10,000 cost basis
$10,000 long-term profit
    60%
$ 6,000 the capital gain deduction
$ 4,000 or 40%, ordinary income

The statement is often made that the capital gain tax is a maximum of 20 percent, which is true. To illustrate from the above example, if you are in the maximum tax bracket of 50 percent, you would pay 50 percent of the above $4,000 in taxes, or $2,000. This is 20 percent of the long-term profit of $10,000.

Of course if your tax bracket is less than the maximum, say 32 percent, you would pay a capital gain tax of only 16 percent, which is 4 percent less than the maximum. When you consider that millions of people are in a tax bracket that causes them to pay considerably more than this on their ordinary income, this is a cheap way, tax-wise, to make money.

Obviously, when capital assets are bought and sold, they could be sold for capital gains or capital losses. Likewise gains or losses can be either short-term or long-term.

We have already discussed the tax treatment of long-term gains. Short-term gains (capital assets held six months or less) are 100 percent taxed at ordinary income rates.

A *capital loss* is a *long-term loss* if the property is held for longer than six months. Only one-half of a long-term loss is deductible, up to a maximum of $3,000. Any amount in excess of this amount must be carried forward to future years, but it can be carried forward indefinitely until it is exhausted. Note, however, that it takes a $6,000 long-term loss to obtain a $3,000 deduction.

A *capital loss* is a *short-term loss* if the property is held for six months or less. A short-term loss is fully deductible dollar for dollar against ordinary income. But the loss deduction is limited to the smallest of the following three items: (1) the taxable income for the year, computed without regard to either capital gains and losses or deductions for personal exemptions; (2) $3,000; or (3) the *net* capital loss as described below.

If a taxpayer has both capital gains and capital losses, they must be balanced against each other. Thus a *net* capital loss is determined by using the following three rules:

1. If you had a net short-term capital loss and a net long-term capital gain, your capital loss is the excess of your net short-term capital loss over your net long-term capital gain.
2. If you had a net long-term capital loss and a net short-term capital gain, your capital loss is one-half of the excess of your net long-term capital loss over your net short-term capital gain.
3. If you had both a net short-term capital loss and a net long-term capital loss, your capital loss is your net short-term capital loss plus one-half of your net long-term capital loss.

To illustrate number 3, assume that you had wages of $16,000, and a $600 net long-term capital loss, and a $500 net short-term capital loss. Your capital loss deduction is computed as follows:

Net short-term capital loss	$500
One-half of net long-term capital loss	
(½ of $600)	300
Total capital loss deduction	$800

Remember, your net capital loss cannot exceed your income, which is why wages were mentioned in the above example. Also, the above three rules are easy to understand if you remember that a short-term loss is 100 percent deductible, a long-term loss is only one-half deductible, and if you have both long-term and short-term losses both of them are deductible.

How can a taxpayer avoid or defer the capital gain tax? There are five ways.

When a property is exchanged for another of similar kind, no capital gain tax is imposed provided both properties were held for business or investment purposes.

When a sale is made by a homeowner who is fifty-five years or older, no capital gain tax is owed on the first $125,000 of long-term profit. The homeowner must have used the home as his principal residence for three out of the last five years. If the homeowner is married, only one spouse has to be fifty-five years old, but the exclusion may be used only once in a lifetime. The IRS considers a person to be fifty-five years old the day before his birthday.

When a taxpayer's property is taken over by the federal government (or a state or local government) under its right of eminent domain, the capital gain tax does not have to be paid provided the money is used to buy similar property. If it is nonbusiness property, the replacement—if not similar—must be related in service or use. If it is business property, it must also be of like kind.

If a property owner, regardless of age, sells his home and buys or builds another one within two years before or two years after the sale, the seller does not have to pay a capital gain tax provided the amount invested in the new home is at least equal to the sale price of the old one.

An individual who transfers ownership of property by giving it to someone else, rather than selling it, does not have to pay a capital gain tax.

For example, if you transfer ownership of a ranch to your son, no tax is imposed on this transaction. However, if your son should later sell the ranch, the cost basis upon which to determine any profit he makes is based on what the ranch cost you.

The third way to reduce taxes is to invest where the income is tax exempt.

Believe it or not, there are many ways to obtain income that you don't have to report at all. It is yours completely tax free. There are twelve sources of tax-exempt income.

1. The dividend exclusion. If you receive dividends, you are allowed to deduct a certain amount from them. This sum is stated in the income section of page one, Form 1040. Let us say that for the year in question a married

couple is allowed a dividend exclusion of $200. Assuming a 5 percent return, this is the dividend that would be paid on $4,000 worth of stock. If you don't own any securities, it might be advisable to buy that much in order to obtain the tax-exempt income.

2. Income earned on an IRA (Individual Retirement Account) is tax exempt. Actually it is only tax deferred; when you start drawing on the account, both the income and the principal are taxed at ordinary rates. Nevertheless, it is one of the best ways to accumulate a retirement fund. Everyone should have an IRA.

3. Income earned on a Keogh plan is tax exempt. This is a retirement plan exclusively for the self-employed. While this income is also tax deferred, rather than tax exempt, a Keogh plan owner obtains a special tax break upon withdrawal. He or she is allowed a ten-year averaging method to reduce the tax. A Keogh plan holder is also allowed to have an IRA.

4. Interest on state and municipal bonds issued by state and local governments, commonly called tax-exempt bonds, or municipals. This is the most widely used investment for tax-free income, especially by the wealthy. Municipals are taxed at the state level, however, unless they are issued by the state in which the taxpayer resides. Their value fluctuates inversely as to interest rates. If interest rates go up, bond prices go down, and vice versa.

5. Ordinary income that is sheltered by investing in tax shelters. Obviously, income that is not reported is tax exempt.

6. The income from U.S. government E bonds. This interest is either tax deferred or tax exempt. The income is tax exempt if they are never redeemed, but taxable to the heirs if they are. It is tax deferred if redeemed in a person's lifetime, or if the U.S. government declares it will not extend the maturity date of the bonds (usually after forty years from date of issue).

7. The return earned on money invested in a company

pension or profit-sharing plan. This is tax deferred until you retire. However, you may roll over any part of a lump-sum payment into an IRA and continue to defer the tax. Warning: if you do, you lose the special ten-year averaging privilege.

8. The cash surrender value of life insurance (if redeemed) is not income to you, unless the value exceeds the premiums you paid. Then only the excess is taxed.

9. Disability income is exempt up to $100 a week for 52 weeks for disability payments made by or financed by your employer. However, if your adjusted gross income exceeds $15,000, your disability exclusion is reduced for every dollar that your adjusted gross income exceeds $15,000.

10. The 15 percent depletion allowance for independent oil and gas producers is tax-exempt income. The maximum daily rate of production for oil is fixed at 1,000 barrels a day, and for gas at 6,000,000 cubic feet a day. The percentage depletion allowance for the major oil producers was repealed on January 1, 1975.

11. Sheltered income because of depreciation. See page 117.

12. The capital gain deduction for a long-term profit (already discussed).

Fourthly, if you are in a high tax bracket, you should invest in bona fide tax shelters.

The laws that allow tax shelters to exist deliberately encourage investments in certain sectors of the economy that need additional capital to achieve economic and social goals. Without tax incentives, this money would not be invested. But the law also states that there has to be an economic benefit and a profit motive, not just a tax incentive, or the deduction will be disallowed.

Bona fide tax shelters invest their customers' money in real estate, cattle feeding, oil and gas, agriculture (such as vineyards or almond orchards), and research and development of new products. They should be evaluated by how much of the original investment is tax sheltered, the amount of risk involved, the reputation of the general partners, past performance, and, particularly, for the chance of recovery of the investment. Emotions should not be involved. Tax shelters are unique legitimate investments that provide tax benefits. This is how they should be judged.

Tax shelters are subject to the "at risk" rules of the Internal Revenue Service. Generally, the investor can't shelter any more than what he has at risk. For instance, if the amount invested is $10,000, the maximum that can be sheltered is 100 percent, or the $10,000. Many tax shelters provide less. The one exception is real estate. Real estate is not subject to the at risk rule. Therefore there are bona fide real estate tax shelters that shelter ordinary income from the IRS up to 200 percent of the original investment.

Much has been said about "abusive" tax shelters, which are those that abuse the tax laws on which they are based. The IRS has defined abusive tax shelters as those that involve transactions with little or no economic reality, inflated appraisals of the property, unrealistic allocations among partners, etc. The IRS tends to have little patience with those that don't adhere to the regulations.

The individual investor should avoid *non-real estate* ventures that offer more than a 100 percent deduction, and *real estate* tax shelters that offer more than 200 percent. Also, it should be understood that this much is not available except in the early months of the tax year. The IRS rightfully says that an investor who invests in the fall of the year is not entitled to the same amount of tax shelter as the investor who becomes a limited partner, say, in January. The decline in the deductible percentage is approximately at the rate of 8 percent per month, so that a 200 percent deduction in real estate in January becomes only a 100 percent deduction by November or December.

Tax-shelter limited partnerships may be either public or private. Public partnerships must be registered with the SEC and are offered in several states or nationwide. Private partnerships are offered, for the most part, only to the residents of the state in which they are domiciled and, depending upon state law, are confined to a limited number of investors, say, thirty-five. They are not registered with the SEC, but only with the state regulatory agency involved.

Tax shelters are not for everyone. Primarily the taxpayer has to be in a high tax bracket and be able to meet the high suitability requirements that are stated in the prospectus. Usually these are:

An individual net worth of $250,000, or a joint net worth of the same amount with the investor's spouse, or a net worth of $150,000 with an annual taxable income, some portion of which will be subject to a combined federal and income tax rate of 44 percent.

The objectives of the partnership are also stated in the prospectus, usually as follows:

(a) To preserve and protect the partnership's invested capital
(b) To realize appreciation upon the sale or other disposition of the property
(c) To provide federal income tax deductions during the early years of property operations
(d) To generate future distributable capital gains

Also in the offering memorandum is a financial projection. The one opposite was taken from a memorandum for the fall of the year on a specified 202-unit apartment house. The minimum investment is for $74,000, with payment spread over a period of six years.

Note from the opposite projection that, because of the tax write-off of $118,302, giving the taxpayer in a 50 percent tax bracket a tax saving of $59,149, the net investment is only $13,301. The result is that the taxpayer sheltered almost $60,000 of ordinary income that would otherwise have gone to the tax collector.

Tax-shelter annuities are also available. They do not provide a tax deduction when they are acquired. Instead, they shelter income over the usually long period of time until retirement. *Regular annuities* in the past have paid a very low rate of

SUMMARY OF FINANCIAL PROJECTIONS
Based on a minimum investment of $74,000
Assumes a 50 percent federal tax rate

Year	Investment	Tax Loss	Tax Savings	Cash Income	Total Invested	Percent Tax Loss
1985	$ 5,180	$ (6,293)	$ 3,146	——	$ 2,034	121%
1986	17,760	(30,875)	15,437	——	4,357	174%
1987	15,540	(21,785)	10,892	——	9,005	140%
1988	13,320	(17,359)	8,679	——	13,646	130%
1989	12,580	(14,544)	7,272	——	18,954	116%
1990	9,620	(10,996)	5,498	300	22,776	114%
1991	——	(8,290)	4,145	500	18,131	11%
1992	——	(8,160)	4,080	750	13,301	11%
Total	$74,000	($118,302)	$59,149	$1,550	$13,301	160%

return. *Tax-shelter annuities* enhance their income by investing in certificates of deposit and mutual funds. The annual premium is tax sheltered and compounds tax free. The proceeds, however, are actually tax deferred and not tax exempt.

The above discussion of the income tax is not meant to be comprehensive, for it is only one chapter. Accountants and tax preparers, swamped before tax time, can't do justice to your return. In the last analysis it's your problem. All that you should expect from your accountant is the accurate filing of your return, not advice on how to cut your taxes.

At the present writing (the summer of 1985), tax reform and tax simplification are making headlines and are being endorsed by President Reagan. If the reader will take the time to review and understand his or her 1984 tax return along the lines laid down by this chapter, he or she will be rewarded for the effort. If you can understand the forms and regulations existent in 1984 and 1985, you will be better able to understand the changes that may be enacted by Congress in 1986. It should be understood, too, by everyone that investments made prior to January 1, 1986 will not be affected by any new law. Real estate purchased in 1985 (or before), for example, will have the same tax advantages as before. Or if tax-exempt securities are no longer tax-exempt, such securities purchased before the new law is passed will still be tax-exempt.

9

Trusts

TRUSTS ARE CREATED mainly by people who, for various good reasons, do not want their estates to be inherited immediately by the heirs. As we have seen, a will states who gets the property, and when probate is over, title passes to the new owners who may then use the assets as they see fit. In a trust, title passes to a trustee who then administers the property according to the terms of the trust for the benefit of someone else. Disposition of the capital and/or the income for the beneficiaries of the trust estate usually takes place over a period of many years.

When considering a trust, most people are confused about the difference between a trustee and an executor. An executor and an attorney are still necessary in a testamentary trust because the property has to pass through the probate court. At the conclusion of probate, instead of the assets being given to the heirs, they are turned over by the executor to the trustee, who then, and only then, starts to function as the fiduciary agent. Thus, the trustee takes over from the executor, and at that point starts managing the estate and distributing the income and/or the capital to the beneficiaries of the trust according to the written instructions of the grantor in the trust agreement.

A trustee of a trust has three basic duties:

1. to protect the property
2. to provide an adequate return for the income beneficiaries
3. to carry out the terms of the trust

Since the trustee takes title and is responsible for properly managing and investing the assets, great care must be taken in the choice of who will be trustee. A trust institution is usually chosen, witness the fact that trust departments of banks currently manage over $200 billion. There is no question that banks know how to protect trust property, and, of course, they are completely reliable. Therefore they do a good job with that responsibility.

However, the second basic duty—to provide an adquate return for the income beneficiaries—is often a different story. A banker by his very training is ultra-conservative; therefore the results in the form of income and long-term growth are often disappointing.

In 1975 Mr. Turner, for tax reasons and upon the advice of his attorney, put one-half of the total estate that he and his wife had acquired over a lifetime in a testamentary trust. His bank was named trustee, with instructions to pay the income to his wife during her lifetime and, upon her death, to terminate the trust and divide the assets equally among their children. His wife made the same arrangement on her one-half of the estate. As an added precaution, each made the survivor co-trustee with the bank. As it so happened, Mrs. Turner was the first to die, so Mr. Turner became co-trustee with the bank on his wife's one-half of the estate, which amounted to $100,000.

After a period of many years Mr. Turner became completely dissatisfied with the way the bank was managing the money, and with the poor return on it, compared to the income that he was receiving on his own $100,000 which he had placed in a mutual fund.

Finally he went to the head of the trust department and demanded that the bank place his wife's property in the mutual fund also, agreeing that the bank could remain as trustee and continue to collect the trustee fee. Mr. Turner had two interviews with the bank, both times bringing with him his investment representative.

At the end of the first interview, at which the bank had unsuccessfully tried to convince Mr. Turner that the performance on his wife's money was satisfactory, the trust officer stated that he would submit the matter to a committee for its consideration.

The second interview was a repeat of the first interview, except that at its conclusion the trust officer stated that the committee's decision was a flat rejection of Mr. Turner's request.

At this point the investment representative spoke up. He reminded the head of the trust department that the $100,000 the bank was managing was, after all, Mr. Turner's money that he and his wife had saved. Certainly it was not the bank's money, and therefore his wishes should be considered, particularly since he was co-trustee with the bank. The investment representative then proceeded to ask a direct question.

"As co-trustee with the bank on his own money," he asked, "does Mr. Turner have any rights?"

"Certainly," was the reply.

"What are they?"

"If he doesn't like our decision, he can sue the bank."

The result was that the bank continued to manage the money until Mr. Turner died.

How should the trust agreement have been drawn? Obviously the testator shouldn't have trusted his attorney.

Mr. Turner should have been named sole trustee. He should not have been named co-trustee with the bank; a bank trust department, as a matter of policy, simply ignores anyone who is supposed to function in this capacity. As sole trustee Mr. Turner would not have had to appeal to a co-trustee for a vital investment decision, only to be turned down. He would simply have invested his wife's money in the mutual fund.

Until well into the twentieth century, most property

owners left their estates outright by will to members of their families. Death taxes and income taxes did not pose a threat to future family security; and state laws were strict and inflexible, leaving little opportunity for the trustee to invest in anything but legalized investments which were mostly fixed dollar in nature, such as government bonds and real estate mortgages.

However, with the advent of the estate tax, the effect of inflation on the dollar value of estates, and the liberalization of state laws allowing the trustee more latitude in investing, trustees have been given broader powers. As a result, trusts have come to play a larger and more important role in effective estate planning.

Today trusts are created for the following reasons:

(a) to save estate and income taxes
(b) to protect beneficiaries
(c) to retain a business interest or a valuable piece of real estate intact
(d) to avoid probate
(e) to provide personal security to the grantor

In most trusts today the underlying motive of the grantor is to save taxes. Both estate taxes and income taxes can be reduced by the judicious use of trusts.

By far the most common use of a trust *to reduce estate taxes* is by the creation of a marital deduction trust in order to reduce the impact of taxes on the estate of the second spouse to die.

The trust most often used *to reduce income taxes* is the short-term reversionary trust, most commonly called a Clifford trust. This is a living trust, meaning that it is in effect during the lifetime of the grantor, as opposed to a testamentary trust which, like a will, does not come into being until the grantor dies. As the name implies, in the Clifford reversionary trust the trust property reverts back to the grantor because that person is not wealthy enough to give away more than the income. Someday the creator of the trust wants the property back.

This type of trust must last for a minimum period of ten years and one day, at which time title to the property and its income reverts back to the grantor.

Dr. Strum, a surgeon in his forties with a lucrative practice, had yet to build a sizable estate. However, because he was in a 50 percent tax bracket, he had a serious income tax problem. Upon the advice of his investment representative he put $70,000 of common stocks, earnings $3,500 a year in dividends, into a ten-year reversionary trust for the benefit of his son, who was just entering college with the intention of becoming a doctor. The income from the trust would help defray the cost of an expensive education.

By shifting the trust income from his high income tax bracket to his son's income tax return, Dr. Strum saved handsomely on his family's income taxes. As a matter of fact, the son didn't have to pay an income tax at all. The doctor, however, in his 50 percent tax bracket would have had to pay one-half of the $3,500 dividend income to the IRS, or $1,750 a year. In ten years he thus saved $17,500.

Since the doctor was not wealthy, he would get the $70,000 back at the end of ten years for his own retirement. In addition, he didn't lose the dependency deduction for his son, for he continued to pay more than one-half of his son's support as a full-time student.

Before placing property in a trust, it is important to understand certain basic features of a trust agreement.

1. No trust is allowed to last forever. It must cease to exist sometime, at which time the trust property will be distributed to its eventual heirs. Unless sooner terminated, each trust must cease to exist twenty-one years after the death of the last surviving heir (who must have been alive at the time the trust was created).

   In a trust where grandchildren are beneficiaries,

the maximum time the trust could last would be twenty-one years after the death of the last grandchild. Where they are minors, this could be a very long time indeed, as much as one hundred years.

2. The trustee has to be given the right to manage the property. Years ago the grantor often gave very restricted powers to the trustee. For example, the trustee might be instructed to hold real estate intact, with instructions that it could not be sold for any reason. It was discovered, however, that the heirs of such a trust could be disinherited by such a limited power of investment. Shifts in population could occur, resulting in once-high-income property becoming slum dwellings, in which event the income would not be sufficient to pay even the costs of property taxes and insurance, much less provide an income for the beneficiaries. Yet the trustee could not sell, even though in some instances the eventual remaindermen would inherit property not worth the accumulated liens for back taxes. Today broad powers are given to the trustee to take care of unforeseen developments.

When creating trusts, most lawyers do not draw their own broad trustee powers. Banks are most frequently named trustees, and each bank supplies to the legal fraternity printed copies of the trust powers they prefer to have delegated to them. Some attorneys use a legal handbook instead, which again spells out the powers of a trustee without their having to do the research that would otherwise be necessary.

When having a trust drawn, a grantor should not assume the attorney has worked hard in framing the powers granted to the trustee, which constitute most of the legal document. They simply have their secretaries copy standard forms.

Reproduced below are trust powers granted in an actual trust agreement which was drawn in the state of California.

Powers of Trustee. To carry out the purposes of any trust created under this Paragraph Fifth, and subject to any limitations stated elsewhere in this will, the trustee is vested with the following powers with respect to the trust estate, and any part of it, in addition to those powers now or hereafter conferred by law.

A. To continue to hold any property and to operate at the risk of the trust estate any business received or acquired under the terms of the trust by the trustee as long as the trustee shall deem advisable.

B. To manage, control, grant options on, sell (for cash or on deferred payments), convey, exchange, partition, divide, improve and repair trust property.

C. To lease trust property for terms within or beyond the terms of the trust and for any purpose, including exploration for and removal of gas, oil, and other minerals.

D. To borrow money, and to encumber or hypothecate trust property by mortgage, deed of trust, pledge, or otherwise.

E. To carry, at the expense of the trust, insurance of such kinds and in such amounts as the trustee shall deem advisable to protect the trust estate and the trustee against any hazard.

F. To commence or defend such litigation with respect to the trust or any property of the trust estate as the trustee may deem advisable, at the expense of the trust.

G. To compromise or otherwise adjust any claims or litigation against or in favor of the trust.

H. To invest and reinvest the trust estate in every kind of property, real, personal, or mixed, and every kind of investment, including corporate obligations of every kind, stocks, preferred or common shares of investment companies, and mutual funds, which men of prudence, discretion, and intelligence acquire for their own account.

I. With respect to securities held in the trust, to have all the rights, powers, and privileges of an owner, including the power to vote, give proxies, and pay assessments.

J. Except as otherwise specifically provided in this will, the determination of all matters with respect to what is principal and income of the trust estate and the apportionment and allocation of receipts and expenses between these accounts shall be governed by the provisions of the California Principal and Income Law from time to time existing.

K. In any case in which the trustee is required, pursuant to the provisions of the trust, to divide any trust property into parts or shares for the purpose of distribution, or otherwise, the trustee is authorized in the trustee's absolute discretion, to make the division and distribution in kind, or partly in kind and partly in money, and for this purpose to make such sales of the trust property as the trustee may deem necessary on such terms and conditions as the trustee shall see fit.

When an individual trustee is named, broad powers are granted in order for the trustee to have the widest possible latitude in investment decisions. However, when a bank is named trustee, these powers can have an adverse effect, particularly if the grantor would prefer to have the assets retained in the trust rather than sold. Too many banks will immediately sell the investments they receive and buy a whole new list, because they feel they know more about investments than any individual grantor. If the estate is over $100,000, they will buy individual securities. But if the estate is below this figure, the bank usually will not manage the trust assets on an individual basis. Instead, the property will be sold and the money invested in the bank's common trust fund, which is similar in operation to a no-load mutual fund.

If the grantor is aware of this and does not want his investments sold, he may state his wishes in this regard in the trust agreement. The trustee is not legally bound to hold the investments under this arrangement, but most trust officers feel they should, if possible, carry out the investment desires of the grantor.

Nevertheless, even though trust assets may be disposed of against the wishes of the grantor, the power to sell should be expressly given in the trust agreement. In some states real estate can't be sold unless the right to sell has been given to the trustee, and some states even require that the trustee be specifically given the right to decide on the terms and conditions of the sale. The trustee not only should be given the right to sell, but also the right to retain any real estate in the trust; some states require that the property has to be sold if this power is not given, even though this may be against the expressed wishes of the beneficiaries of the trust.

As a general rule, it is better to grant a power that is not needed than for the trustee to be without a power when it is needed.

3. Not all assets have to be placed in a trust. That little red wagon called a trust is a very convenient vehicle. Any property may be put into it, and any property may be left out of it. The most frequent asset not placed in trust is a home owned jointly by husband and wife. Since the survivor usually wants to occupy it for the rest of his or her life, the house is kept in joint tenancy. A small joint bank account is frequently excluded from the trust also, thereby providing immediate cash to the survivor.

4. When contemplating a marital deduction trust, it is important for the grantor to know that physical segregation of the property is not required. If a hundred

shares of General Motors stock are involved, for example, they may be retained in one stock certificate. Two stock certificates, one in the name of the trustee and one in the name of the surviving spouse, are not necessary. However, the trustee must keep separate accounts for the different undivided interests. Income, either distributed or left to accrue, must be shown as being attributed to the appropriate owners.

5. A trustee must make a fiduciary report once a year to the taxing authorities. Proof must be supplied that the trust property is truly being held in trust for the benefit of the income beneficiaries and the eventual heirs, and that income taxes are being paid. With a marital deduction trust this is a simple matter and should not disturb a widow if she is the trustee. She can simply turn the matter over to her accountant.

6. When an individual trustee is named by the grantor, a successor trustee should always be appointed for the first trustee might not be able to serve for a variety of reasons, including death. For this same reason a trustee of last resort should be named in the agreement to be sure that a trustee will always be available. For obvious reasons this is usually a bank, particularly if the trust will not terminate for many years. As we have stated before, a corporation never dies.

7. Corporate trustees are automatically bonded; individuals are not. Therefore when no bond is required of an individual trustee, the grantor must specifically state this in the agreement.

8. A trust is a separate tax-paying entity. If income accrues to the trust, the trust itself must pay taxes. The trust enters the tax tables as an individual taxpayer with, however, only a $100 deduction.

9. A trust may be revocable or irrevocable. Most trusts are of the former type, which means they may be revoked like wills. If the grantor changes his mind, he has the right to do so. He can either revoke the trust entirely and not draw a new one, deciding to dis-

tribute his assets by will, or he may create a new trust agreement. Occasionally trusts are made irrevocable, usually for estate tax reasons.

10. Trusts may be testamentary trusts or living trusts. Most trusts are testamentary, which means they do not go into effect until the grantor dies. In this respect they are similar to wills and, for that matter, are quite often referred to as trust wills. Living trusts go into effect while the grantor is alive.

The second basic reason grantors establish trusts is to protect their beneficiaries. An heir who is otherwise intelligent simply may not be competent in money matters. The most frequently protected heir is a widow who has been a homemaker all of her life with no interest or experience in managing investments. Even in these days of excellent federal and state laws, unknowledgeable widows who are left estates are too often destitute in four or five years.

Outright distribution to a widow who has no knowledge of money matters is therefore not wise for the following good reasons.

1. The widow is presented with management problems and investment decisions that she cannot resolve intelligently.
2. She may have loan requests from relatives. She frequently does not know how to say no to these people, so the money is soon frittered away and never repaid, despite good intentions.
3. She has to deal with the varying interests of her children. One may be in grave need of funds and the others well off, yet she feels she has to treat them all alike.
4. Advice on how and when to invest is offered by well-meaning friends who have little to offer in the way of experience. Following this advice can be very costly.
5. As we shall see in the estate and gift tax chapter, outright distribution to a widow can result in unnecessary federal estate taxes.

Unknowledgeable widows are not the only heirs who need to be financially protected. Where minor children are involved, the only practical solution is a trust, normally with a bank acting as trustee. Trusts for minors usually extend beyond age twenty-one, most grantors feel that outright distribution at this age is not justified. It is too much to expect someone twenty-one to handle money properly. The usual distribution is to have the heirs inherit one-third at age twenty-five, one-third at age thirty, and one-third at age thirty-five. It is a mistake for a grantor to try to protect minor children forever. If by the time children are thirty-five they have not learned how to manage money, it is probably just as well to let them dissipate their inheritance and start to learn the hard way about how to save for the future.

Many families have a mentally or physically handicapped family member who must be protected by a lifelong trust, with the trustee being given full powers over income and principal in order to meet the changing conditions that such a situation can present. In dealing with this kind of problem, it is fortunate that bank trusts are available.

The third basic use of trusts is to protect a business or a valuable piece of real estate. Let's consider a business first, starting with a business that is incorporated.

Quite often ownership of a close corporation stock is the major asset of an estate. A close corporation has been defined by the courts as "a corporation in which the stock is held in a few hands, or in a few families or one family, and wherein it is not at all, or only rarely, dealt in." Quite often the owners, the directors, and the officers are all the same people who own 100 percent of the common stock. When 100 percent of the stock, or the majority of it, is held by one property owner, it can become a problem of how to will it.

Mr. Spencer, a widower with three children and a profitable business, owned 100 percent of the stock of his close corporation, which was the major asset of his estate. His only son managed the business with him and was very competent. His two married daughters and their husbands, however, had no desire to enter the firm and help run it. In his will Mr. Spencer wanted to divide his estate equally among his three children, but if he left each of them one-third of the corporation, he knew that the business would not long survive him because, by splintering up the stock, no one person—including his son—would have control. He solved his problem by creating a trust.

His son, as trustee, was given control of the corporation with the right to vote all of the stock. His two daughters, although they each inherited one-third of the business, were given no say in the management.

Mr. Spencer recognized, however, that there was still one unfair possibility in this arrangement, for the son as sole trustee could claim that all of the net profits were needed in the business and refuse to pay dividends on the corporation stock. This would result in no income being paid to his daughters, while the son would be handsomely rewarded by his salary as president of the firm.

So Mr. Spencer further stipulated in his trust agreement that his bank would be co-trustee with his son with, however, the bank having only one specific power, the right to determine how much the dividends should be each year. The bank would determine the net income, after taxes, annually by using the services of an outside independent accounting firm. Now the corporation would be run for the benefit of all the family members, with each child inheriting one-third of the business.

Mr. Childs, married with two children and owning 100 percent of his close corporation, had a different problem. He wanted to retire and allow the business to be managed by his two competent sons who were respectively president and executive vice president of the firm, but he could not retire without an income from the company. His solution was recapitalization of the company and the creation of a trust.

In the recapitalization, preferred stock paying 8 percent was issued to Mr. Childs and his wife, which was declared to be a tax-free dividend by the Internal Revenue Service. In other words, the transfer of most of the common stock to a new preferred stock was not a taxable event. Upon the death of either Mr. or Mrs. Childs, the preferred stock would qualify for the unlimited marital deduction and be owned outright by the survivor.

A small amount of voting common stock (but still 100 percent) was issued and placed in trust, with Mr. Childs's two sons as co-trustees. This gave them voting control of the corporation.

By recapitalization and a trust agreement, Mr. Childs accomplished several objectives simultaneously.

1. He gave himself and his wife an adequate retirement income.
2. He gave complete control of the business to his two sons as co-trustees with power to vote the stock as they saw fit.
3. He saved substantially on estate taxes by not piling up a 100 percent ownership of a growing corporation in the hands of the surviving spouse. Instead, the common stock, the growth asset of the corporation, would be held in trust for the sons and would not be taxed again when the second spouse died.
4. The dividend from the preferred stock would be paid to Mr. Childs and his wife until they both died. In the meantime the sons would be rewarded for managing the corporation by their salaries as president and executive vice president of the firm.

A valuable piece of real estate can be left in trust by incorporating and issuing shares of stock to the heirs, with control as trustee being given to the most responsible relative.

The fourth basic reason for creating a trust is to avoid the publicity of probate. This is accomplished by the creation of a revocable living trust, which is a trust created during the property owner's lifetime. It should be emphasized at once that a revocable living trust is never created for the purpose of saving estate taxes. It does not save estate taxes.

Mr. and Mrs. Jack Yates had a $700,000 estate which they had accumulated as the result of owning the only hospital in a small town. Since they had no children, they decided that after they both died their estate should go to their favorite charities. They had been exceptionally frugal in building an estate of this size. As Mr. Yates said to his lawyer: "I'm like a squirrel. I bury those nuts and I forget about them." As a consequence, no one in their small town had any idea of the size of their estate. When Mr. and Mrs. Yates found out about the publicity of probate, and that anyone could walk into the county courthouse when one of them died and find out from the probate file what they were worth, they were appalled and could hardly wait to set up a living trust.

When Mr. Yates died, the complete lack of information about the size of his estate so frustrated people that Mrs. Yates would be stopped on the street with leading questions, such as: "I assume that Jack left you pretty well off?" But she would just smile and walk on. If privacy in estate matters is desired, a living trust will guarantee it.

The fifth basic reason trusts are created is to provide personal security for the grantor. Managing assets in sizable estates, particularly when compounded by the frailty of advancing years, may pose a problem that can be solved by a living trust with a bank as trustee. However, while this is true, many people are changing their thinking and, instead of creating a living trust to solve their problem, they are opening an agency account with the trust department of a bank instead. This provides professional management without the expense and trouble of creating a living trust. A bank trust department will take over the problem of management by a simple written agreement, which is completely revocable at any time by a thirty-day written notice. It is hardly necessary to enter into a living trust when the same objective can be more easily accomplished. Besides, a living trust can have a bad result.

Dr. Frisbee had several heart attacks, the last a severe one. He made up his mind that he wasn't going to recover and therefore placed all of his sizable list of stocks in a revocable living trust with his bank, giving broad powers to the trustee.

Some two years later, to the doctor's amazement, he had recovered to the point where he was again practicing medicine, and he felt well enough to revoke the trust and ask the bank to return his stocks to him. He anticipated no difficulty because his living trust was revocable at any time.

He found out to his dismay that the bank had sold out all the excellent stocks that he had spent a lifetime accumulating. The new list that the bank's trust department had bought had declined in value, with a considerable loss to the doctor, and in addition, to his frustration, he was completely unfamiliar with the portfolio. He was furious, but he could do nothing about it because of the broad discretionary powers he had given the bank. An agency account would have served his purpose just as well, giving the bank no authority to make any change in his investments without his prior consent.

This explanation of the basic use of trusts should give you a better understanding of them. As we have said, most people don't trust attorneys. And if you don't especially trust your attorney but decide to have him draw a trust anyway, at least you will know now what to look for in a properly drawn trust agreement before you sign it.

Charitable Trusts

Before these trusts are used, even by the wealthy, the rules of charitable giving must be understood. A taxpayer may deduct donations made to religious, educational, and public charitable institutions that receive a substantial part of their support from the general public or the government. But there are limitations in the amount that may be given. The donor is limited to 50 percent of adjusted gross income if cash is given, and to 30 percent of adjusted gross income if the donation consists of appreciated personal property (such as securities) or real estate held long term.

The usual donation is a lifetime deferred gift to obtain several attractive advantages for the donor. The vehicle used is a charitable remainder unitrust. With such a trust, the income from the trust is paid for life to the donor, with the charity receiving the remainder interest upon the death of the grantor. The amount of the remainder interest depends upon the age of the donor at the time of the gift, and varies by IRS tables from 40 to 65 percent.

Mr. Granger was a millionaire many times over. He had made his money in electronics and decided to give 2,500 shares of stock in his corporation to his alma mater, Stanford University at Palo Alto, California. The stock had cost him $2.00 a share and had a market value of $40.00 a share. He decided to give this $100,000 worth of stock as a lifetime deferred gift, using a charitable remainder unitrust, in order to avoid the capital gain tax. There wouldn't be a capital gain tax on the appreciation when he transferred the stock to the trustee, and the trust would not pay a tax when it was later sold. After selling, the trust could diversify the investments, and, in addition, the entire $100,000 would be working for Mr. Granger.

Another advantage would be the opportunity for an increased rate of return. If we assume that the stock was returning 2 percent, and the trust invested the money at 8 percent, Mr. Granger would quadruple his income, from $2,000 to $8,000 a year.

In addition, when he created the trust, Mr. Granger was entitled to a federal income tax charitable deduction of the remainder interest given to charity. If we assume because of his life expectancy that this would be 60 percent of the $100,000 donation, he would be entitled to a $60,000 deduction, and if he were in a 50 percent tax bracket, this would give him a tax saving of $30,000.

This tax saving is additional capital and if invested at 10 percent would provide an additional income of $3,000 a year. Thus, because of his charitable gift Mr. Granger's income increased from $2,000 to $11,000 a year on his $100,000 donation.

While charitable trusts are not primarily created for income or tax benefits, because it is the intention of the grantors for charities to benefit, nevertheless, in sizable estates important economic benefits can be the result.

10

Estate
and
Gift
Taxes

THE INTERNAL REVENUE SERVICE estimates that by 1987 only 3 percent of all estates will owe a federal estate tax. The federal estate tax exemption per individual is $400,000 in 1985, $500,000 in 1986, and $600,000 in 1987, where it levels off.

The Unified Rate Schedule for Gift and Estate Taxes is not difficult, but it is necessary to become familiar with a few terms such as the "unified credit," "exemption equivalent," "maximum rate," and "rate on excess" if you are to comprehend the schedule. A simplified Unified Rate Schedule is reproduced below.

If an individual estate does not exceed $400,000 in 1985, no federal estate tax is due, as the table discloses. But if the estate of the deceased is $500,000, the federal estate tax is $34,000. (The rate is 34 percent of the excess over $400,000.) Note from the table that in 1986 and 1987 the estate tax is zero because the exemption has increased to $500,000 and $600,000 respectively in those two years.

Because of the size of these exemptions, taxpayers should not carelessly assume that their estates are not large enough to be subject to the estate tax. When they add up their assets, they may find to their surprise that they are worth more than they think, especially when the increased value of their home is taken into account.

Let's take one more example from the table, making an assumption that an individual dies in 1985 with an estate worth $750,000. With this amount of property, an estate tax would have been due if he had died in any one of the three years. On the excess above $400,000 (the exemption amount in 1985), the federal estate tax is computed as follows. On the first $100,000, 34 percent or $34,000; and on the next $250,000, 37 percent or $92,500, for a total tax of $126,500. The tax is lower in 1986 and 1987 because of the increased individual exemption.

The term "unified credit" will be used frequently in this chapter. For an explanation of this term we need to take a look at the *complete* rate schedule (rather than the previous simplified one), which is also reproduced on the following pages.

At the bottom of the table the unified credit is listed for six years going back to 1982, and opposite this is the exemption equivalent. The estate tax is computed by ignoring, at first, any credit or exemption. To take the example above of a $750,000 estate, the table discloses that the estate tax on this amount is $248,300. However, $121,800 is deducted from this sum, which is the unified credit for 1985, thus reducing the actual tax to $126,500, as stated above.

(The larger table shows six years for the unified credit and the exemption equivalent because readers may be concerned about the estate of someone who died in 1982 and whose estate is not yet settled.)

How do we know that the exemption equivalent of the unified credit is the correct amount? This can be proved easily.

If we enter the table in 1985 with a $400,000 estate, we see that the estate tax on the first $250,000 is $70,800, plus 34 percent of the excess $150,000, or $51,800. By combining these two figures we see that the estate tax is $121,800. But when we deduct the unified credit for 1985 (which is the identical $121,800), the estate tax is zero. Thus a $400,000 estate that is not taxed in 1985, because of the unified credit, has an exemption equivalent of this amount.

There is one other point. The table discloses that the maximum estate tax rate is 55 percent. This rate is assessed on any estate in excess of $3,000,000. It was scheduled to be reduced to 50 percent in 1985, but the Tax Reform Act of 1984 eliminated this reduction. The maximum estate tax rate is now scheduled to be reduced to 50 percent in 1988.

This discussion refers mainly to married couples because they are best able to take advantage of the deductions and exemptions allowed under the law. Single persons can do little about reducing estate taxes except by making gifts during their lifetime.

A spouse has an unlimited marital deduction. This means that any amount, even millions, may be left to the surviving spouse completely free of the estate tax. What is meant by the expression "marital deduction"? This is simply the amount that is left by the deceased spouse to the survivor, either outright or in trust.

A spouse also has an unlimited gift tax deduction, which means that one spouse may give to the other spouse an unlimited amount without being subject to the gift tax.

Note that the rate schedule is a *unified* table, meaning that it applies to both estate and gift taxes. This means that the unified credit may be used to reduce either gift or estate taxes, or a combination of both. It does not mean that you can use the full unified credit to reduce each tax. In other words, the unified credit does not double.

This important change in the law, granting a married person an unlimited marital deduction, makes estate planning simple for those couples who are not concerned about the amount of estate taxes that will have to be paid by the beneficiaries after the death of the second spouse. Each spouse provides by will that upon the death of the first spouse, the assets go to the survivor.

And if it is their desire also to avoid probate upon the

death of the first spouse, all of the assets should be held in joint tenancy.

On the other hand, if you are like most married persons and want to leave as much of your assets as possible to your children, grandchildren, or other heirs, then your goal is to minimize estate taxes. In that event, your estate planning has to take full advantage of the estate tax credits and exemptions available to each spouse.

It should be realized that each spouse is entitled to the unified credit. This means that a married couple may have a maximum combined estate of $1,200,000 which can be completely free of the estate tax (in 1987). But *only* if each spouse provides in his or her will that the allowed exemption does not go to the surviving spouse, but to the heirs.

In other words, each spouse should not leave his or her one-half to the survivor outright. If this is done, the survivor will die possessed of the entire $1,200,000, and, by referring to the combined rate schedule, the estate tax will then be $235,000 ($345,800 plus $82,000, minus the unified credit of $192,800).

There are two ways for each spouse to take full advantage of the individual exemption and thus escape the imposition of a $235,000 estate tax because the survivor dies possessed of property worth $1,200,000.

Obviously the first spouse to die can leave his or her exemption amount directly to the heirs. Thus the survivor will die possessed of only the remaining $600,000, which will also be estate tax exempt because of the survivor's individual exemption.

The second—and better—way is for the first spouse who dies to leave his or her exemption amount in trust for the eventual heirs, with the income to be paid to the surviving spouse for life. This way the survivor can enjoy the economic benefit from the entire estate, with no estate tax being due upon the death of the second spouse. And, if it is desired, the surviving spouse can be named trustee.

This type of trust is sometimes referred to as a "credit

equivalent trust," or a "bypass trust." The income goes to the survivor until death, when the balance goes to the children or other beneficiaries exempt from the estate tax.

Mr. Bannon died in 1984, leaving $325,000 in a credit equivalent trust for the benefit of his wife. His exemption for 1984 made this amount free of the estate tax. He left the balance of his estate outright to his wife. Upon Mrs. Bannon's death, assuming she died in 1987 or later, she could leave the children up to $600,000 estate tax free by using her exemption available for that year.

As a result, upon Mr. Bannon's death there was no estate tax on the $325,000, or on the balance of his estate that he left his wife because of the unlimited marital deduction. Upon the death of Mrs. Bannon, the $325,000 that Mr. Bannon left in trust would go tax free to the children. The remaining property owned by her would be subject to the estate tax only to the extent that it exceeded the then $600,000 exemption. Thus the Bannons could leave their children $925,000 completely exempt from the federal estate tax.

From the above example, it is clear that both spouses should own property up to the exemption levels. If the husband has a large estate and his wife a relatively small one, he should give her sufficient property to bring her estate up to the current-year exemption level and continue to do so until 1987. No gift tax is incurred because of the unlimited gift tax marital deduction which permits any amount, no matter how large, to be given to a spouse.

A word of warning. When a spouse gives appreciated property to the other spouse within one year of death, and the appreciated property returns to the donor, the property will not be entitled to a stepped-up cost basis.

"Using the marital deduction" is an expression often employed in estate planning. In most cases this means that the deceased spouse is leaving this much of his or her estate to the surviving spouse. And no matter how much property this may be, it is exempt from estate tax.

Thus we can make the statement that using the marital

deduction (after using the unified credit), to the extent that this will eliminate the estate tax at the death of the first spouse, will produce the maximum benefit for the survivor. Even in larger estates this is true, although dividing the estate into two equal parts might seem to be the better way to reduce estate taxes. It is not, when the interim benefits to the survivor are considered.

Mr. and Mrs. John Flynn had combined property worth $1,500,000. They were retired and in good health, and spending all of their income. In their estate planning they concluded that both of them would probably be alive in 1987, that their respective estates would be the same size, and that each would have a $600,000 exemption. They also assumed, because Mrs. Flynn was considerably younger, that she would survive him by at least ten years. Mr. Flynn had a $900,000 estate and Mrs. Flynn had a $600,000 estate.

If Mr. Flynn left one-half of his $300,000 (above his exemption) to his wife, each would pay $55,500 in estate taxes for a total of $111,000, for each spouse would die possessed of $750,000. However, the extra estate tax cost, if Mr. Flynn should leave his wife the entire $300,000, would be only $3,000. By looking at the unified tax table, they found that Mr. Flynn would pay 37 percent on the $150,000 if he retained it in his estate, and if he left this sum to his wife she would pay 39 percent. (Two percent of $150,000 is $3,000.)

But the interim benefits would be greater than this amount for Mrs. Flynn. If Mr. Flynn did not retain $150,000 in his estate but left this sum to Mrs. Flynn, his estate would not have to pay $55,500 in estate taxes to the IRS. This is the same thing as obtaining an interest-free loan from the government, for certainly if she inherited the $150,000 from her husband, she would not owe any interest to the IRS during the time she had the use of the $55,500 in saved estate taxes.

If it is assumed that she could earn 9 percent on this money for ten years, this would provide $49,950 for Mrs. Flynn (before income taxes). By paying an additional $3,000 in estate taxes, Mrs. Flynn would enjoy a higher income during the years that she survived her husband. Of course, if she died shortly after Mr. Flynn, there wouldn't be any interim economic benefits, but the extra cost to her estate would still be only $3,000.

If both husband and wife have large estates, and especially where both are up in years, balancing the two estates may be desirable. Two estates of $1,250,000 incur less of an estate tax than one estate of $2,500,000. The tax saving is $107,000 in 1987. When both spouses are advanced in years, it should be recognized that the opportunity for interim tax savings may not be present.

Trusts and wills entered into prior to September 12, 1981, should be reviewed and probably redrawn. Prior to that date the marital deduction was one-half of the estate, or $250,000, whichever was the larger. The Internal Revenue Service has ruled that trusts and wills that were entered into before September 12, 1981, must abide by the rules that were in effect at that time. Thus the exemption that is available in the year of death after 1981 cannot be used if these legal documents are not revised or revoked. For example, if only $250,000 is available by the terms of a pre-1981 will, and death occurs in 1986, $250,000 of the exemption will be lost.

If a new trust agreement is drawn before 1987, it should be clearly stated that it is the testator's desire to use the unlimited marital deduction, and that whatever the amount of the exemption may be at the time of death, this is the sum that is willed to the survivor either in trust or outright. This will automatically make use of the exemption no matter in what year the testator may die.

There is another way to make use of the marital deduction. If you are not sure of the best way to divide your estate between the marital and nonmarital deduction, you can give your wife a "blank check." You can leave the decision open until after your death when all the facts are known. This way your wife and her advisers can decide whether or not she should use the unlimited marital deduction.

The tax code provides a disclaimer provision that helps in

after-death tax planning. Your wife may disclaim any portion of your bequest, and if she does, that part pours over into an income trust for her for life, with distribution to the children or other beneficiaries upon her death. No gift tax will be incurred if the disclaimer is used. When such a trust is used, it is sometimes referred to as a Q-Tip trust.

The disclaimer must be exercised within nine months after death, but it gives the widow this length of time to decide how best to divide the estate for tax purposes.

There are special conditions laid down if the disclaimer provision is exercised.

1. The disclaimer must be a written and irrevocable refusal to accept an interest in the property.
2. The written disclaimer must be delivered to the legal representative of the estate, or to the legal owner of the property, no later than nine months after the transfer was made, or when the disclaimant is age twenty-one, if later.
3. The disclaimant must not have accepted an interest in the property or any of its benefits prior to making the disclaimer. The benefits include:
   (a) exercise of a power of appointment; and
   (b) acceptance of any consideration in return for making the disclaimer.
4. As a result of the exercise of the disclaimer provision, the interest in the property must pass to someone other than the disclaimant without any direction by the disclaimant.

This can be a very desirable way to make use of the marital deduction. The testator should have confidence, however, in the judgment of the surviving spouse and his or her advisers. If used, however, the disclaimer provision gives the surviving spouse responsibility for deciding how to divide an estate most advantageously between a marital and nonmarital bequest.

At any time before 1987, married persons with property worth $600,000 (or less) should revoke any existing trusts originally drawn to save estate taxes. After these trusts are revoked, property should be held in joint tenancy with right of survivorship.

For example, assume that it is October of 1985, in which event the exemption per individual is $400,000. It will be only fifteen months until the exemption for each spouse is $600,000, and only three months until it is $500,000. It is worth the gamble that only *one* spouse will die before 1987, when the entire estate in the hands of the survivor will be estate tax exempt because of the $600,000 exemption. Ease of estate settlement for the surviving spouse should be the important consideration, not saving estate taxes for the heirs.

What would happen if the surviving spouse should die unexpectedly in 1986 owning property worth $600,000 because the deceased spouse revoked a previously existing trust to make use of the unlimited marital deduction? The estate tax in that event would be $37,000 out of a $600,000 estate. Is this so bad, really? Especially when the alternative is considered, for with the trust in effect (because it wasn't revoked), the survivor would have to go through probate, and be saddled with a trust and annual fiduciary reports, possibly for many years. We repeat, it's worth the small risk involved to revoke the trust at any time before 1987. Assuming good health, it is highly unlikely that both spouses will die within a period of fifteen months.

We have been discussing relatively small estates. Trusts in large estates set up years ago to avoid successive estate taxes in following generations should, of course, be kept intact.

Today, because of the generation skipping tax, sheltering estates from successive estate taxes is difficult. To have a generation skipping transfer, three generations have to be involved. The decedent must be in the oldest generation, and he or she must leave an interest in the property to a younger generation, which eventually passes to an even younger generation member or members. A typical example is where a father leaves his estate in trust for the benefit of his daughter, paying her the income for life, with ultimate distribution to her children when she dies.

Such a trust triggers the imposition of the generation skipping tax upon the daughter's death. The daughter is the skipped generation. No estate tax is levied on the trust property, but the generation skipping tax applies. This tax is computed as if the trust property were included in the daughter's estate on top of all the estate that she owns. There is one advantage. The generation skipping tax is paid out of the trust assets, not from the daughter's estate. The tax is in lieu of, not an addition to, the estate tax.

Fortunately, with a trust involving three generations, there is a $250,000 grandchild exclusion for trust property that passes to grandchildren. This in most instances can completely eliminate the estate tax and any generation skipping tax that might otherwise be assessed. The $250,000 exclusion applies to each child of the original donor, not to each grandchild.

Mr. Landsdale had three children. Child A had three children, Child B had two children, and Child C had one. Mr. Landsdale was able to shelter $750,000 from the generation skipping tax when his three children died, because $250,000 was available for each child. The three children of Child A each inherited one-third of $250,000, the two children of Child B each inherited $125,000, and the one child of Child C inherited $250,000. There was nothing he could do about the uneven distribution to the grandchildren under the terms of the grandchild exclusion. The amount excluded was per child, not per grandchild.

Fortunately, there are other transfers to which the generation skipping tax does not apply.

An outright transfer will not trigger the tax, no matter how many generations are skipped. A property owner may leave assets outright either during life or at death to grandchildren and great grandchildren without the tax being imposed.

The tax is not assessed where only one younger generation

benefits from the trust. A man may leave property in trust for his wife, with distribution to their children upon his death, and there is no generation skipping tax. In this case only two generations are involved. For the purpose of the law, a wife is considered to be of the same generation as her husband, no matter how much younger she may be.

There is no tax where a husband leaves property in trust for his wife, with distribution to the grandchildren upon her death. Once again only two generations are involved.

Where a beneficiary has a future interest or a future power granted by the testator in the trust agreement, the tax does not apply when the future interest or power terminates.

Assume that Mr. Francis has a son and one grandson, and creates a trust for the benefit of his grandson. The income from the trust is to be paid to the grandson until age thirty-five, at which time the trust terminates. The trust provides that if his grandson should die before age thirty-five, with no descendants, the trust property is to be distributed to the son.

If the grandson should die before age thirty-five, no generation skipping tax is imposed because the son had a future interest in the property, and a taxable event does not occur because the future interest terminates. Obviously the son would have a present interest in the property upon the death of the grandson, but this makes no difference.

When trusts are created for the benefit of beneficiaries or to reduce estate taxes, or both, powers of appointment are frequently used to lend flexibility to the trust.

Mr. Linsey left his entire estate in trust for his wife, giving her the right to withdraw up to 5 percent of the principal annually on a noncumulative basis. He further stipulated that she could not withdraw more than 50 percent of the trust assets during her lifetime. The right to withdraw principal was a power of appointment to his wife. It gave her the right to appoint the trust principal to herself, but only under certain conditions and up to a definite limit.

Often it is advisable for a testator to give the beneficiary the right to change the order of distribution "down the line," particularly if his wife is considerably younger. If the couple has children, it is possible for one of them to become permanently disabled, or one of them to become wealthy. Should either event occur, it would be advantageous if the surviving spouse could have the right to alter the plan of distribution. A larger share of the trust assets could be given the child with the disability, or the wealthy child could be skipped entirely, often at his or her suggestion. Such a power of appointment in a trust can be valuable by giving the surviving spouse a chance to reassess the family circumstances if conditions should warrant it.

There is another reason why trusts drawn prior to September 12, 1981, should be reviewed and redrawn if necessary. Formerly, only a general power of appointment could be granted a spouse. The surviving spouse had to be given the right to withdraw all of the trust principal, or the power to appoint all of the trust principal to herself or to her estate.

Today the surviving spouse does not have to be given this general power in order for the trust to qualify legally. The grantor of the trust can retain the right to control the ultimate disposition of the trust property. This is an important change, for the first spouse to die can state in the trust agreement that the trust property upon the death of the surviving spouse must be distributed to their children, and to no one else. If the surviving spouse should remarry and have children by her second husband, she cannot leave any part of the trust property to them. The trust assets must be distributed only to the children by the first marriage.

A daughter-in-law is frequently the forgotten heir when trusts are created, but she need not be. A married son with small children can be given a power to appoint the income from the trust to someone else besides himself and his children. If in his will he gives the income from the trust to his wife, and he dies, she has the means to raise the children. This is an important power to give the son, particularly if he has a small estate.

Because of the generation skipping tax, trusts are increasingly created for the benefit of grandchildren. In such cases the trusts can last for a considerable period of time.

Powers of appointment should be given grandchildren the same as those given to children, and even more so when the time element is taken into account. Here a second look down the line on the ultimate distribution of the property can lend important flexibility to the trust.

Most trusts name a bank as trustee. This is because lawyers draw trusts, and they work closely with bank trust departments. A bank is named, too, because as an institution it has perpetuity, where an individual does not. Many things besides death can happen to an individual which will make it impossible for that person to serve as trustee. A bank will always be available.

Where a trust is created for the benefit of an income beneficiary, a bank trustee is normally given the power, at the bank's discretion, to pay out not only the income but principal to the income recipient for basic needs such as support, education, and medical expenses.

To give a bank trustee the power to pay out principal *solely at its discretion* is a mistake. Yet lawyers when drawing trusts grant a bank this power as a matter of course. The bank trustee usually refuses to distribute principal because the bank maintains that it must basically work for the heirs, who will eventually inherit the trust, not for the income beneficiary. This is a lot of nonsense. The truth of the matter is that the bank will not relinquish any part of the principal unless forced to by the terms of the trust.

This is a basic attitude on the bank's part, for if control of the principal is retained, the bank will still collect the full trustee fee, and when you are talking about billions of dollars, this is a lot of money.

As a matter of fact, the grantor of the trust would not have created the trust to begin with if the testator was aware of this attitude on the part of the bank. The purpose of a trust for an income beneficiary is to protect that individual, not the eventual heirs, whoever they may be. (An additional powerful reason, of course, is to reduce estate taxes.)

Mr. and Mrs. Wilson left their combined estate in a bank trust (with her consent), with the income to be paid to her for life and the principal to be paid at her death to the heirs named in the trust agreement. Principal was to be paid to Mrs. Wilson for her support, maintenance, and medical bills at the discretion of the bank. The sole purpose of the trust was to protect Mrs. Wilson financially because she knew nothing about money. The Wilsons didn't have an estate tax problem; the estate was valued at only $80,000.

Mrs. Wilson survived her husband by many years. Finally she asked the bank to distribute part of the principal to her because, with rising costs due to inflation, she could no longer maintain a decent standard of living. The bank refused, so she turned for help to an investment representative who was recommended to her by a close friend.

The representative told Mrs. Wilson that the first thing he had to do was to read her copy of the trust. After they were both seated comfortably at his office desk, he read the agreement carefully.

Looking up, he said: "Mrs. Wilson, I'm sorry. I can't help you. There is nothing I can do. The bank has sole power at their discretion to distribute principal from the trust."

"But somebody has to help me, Mr. Jones. I simply don't have enough income. I have to be very careful just to meet my basic expenses."

"And what does the bank say?"

"I have been to the trust department several times. They just won't give me any money."

"Why did you and your husband create the trust in the first place?"

"To protect me, so I would have an adequate income for the rest of my life. I don't know anything about money. He was afraid that I might spend what little we had."

"What do you want me to do?" the representative asked.

"Go to the trust department with me," Mrs. Wilson replied. "Maybe, because you are in the investment business, they will listen to you."

"OK," the representative replied reluctantly. "I'll go, but don't expect too much."

At the bank the next day they sat down at a long table in a

conference room with two officers of the trust department. They went over Mrs. Wilson's monthly expenses in detail. At the end of their examination, they again told her that she didn't need any more money, that apparently she had $16 a month left over for nonessential expenditures, and this was enough.

At this point the investment representative spoke up for the first time.

"Gentlemen, I disagree, of course. Why won't you give her some of the principal? After all, it is her money, not the bank's."

"Because as trustee the bank must protect the interest of the eventual heirs who will inherit upon termination of the trust."

"But, gentlemen," the representative protested, "I have read the trust agreement. The heirs [upon Mrs. Wilson's death] are first of all Mr. Wilson's three brothers, but they are all dead. There is one heir left, which is a school for boys. It certainly wasn't Mr. Wilson's intention at the time he created the trust to have Mrs. Wilson barely able to meet her expenses, so their eighty thousand dollars could be kept intact for an educational institution!"

But the trust officers stayed with their decision. The result was that Mrs. Wilson was not only furious with the bank, but also with the attorney who drew the trust. But when she eventually died, the $80,000 was left intact to a school for boys.

How should the lawyer have drawn the trust agreement? Mr. Wilson should have given his wife a power of appointment, with the right to ask for 5 percent of the principal of the trust, evaluated annually, *at her discretion.* This way she would have been adequately protected from dissipating the trust assets, and she would not have had to beg the bank to give her some of her own money, only to be turned down.

Only lawyers can draw trust agreements, but that doesn't mean they don't work closely, and many times too closely, with the banks.

If you are contemplating having a trust drawn with an orphan exclusion clause, the Tax Reform Act of 1984 eliminated this provision. The orphan exclusion clause provided that if a surviving parent should die orphaning a child (or children), then $5,000 times the number of years the child was under twenty-one could be excluded from the estate tax. Thus a child orphaned at age seventeen would entitle the estate to a $20,000 exemption (four times $5,000).

If you are counting upon your retirement plan being excluded from your estate valuation, it is no longer a possibility. The amount used to be excluded; then it was reduced to $100,000; and in 1984 this deduction was eliminated entirely.

A legal representative has always been able to choose between two dates when evaluating an estate, the date of death or six months later. This still holds true, but in 1984 the rules were changed slightly. The later date can be chosen only if it will decrease the value of the gross estate and the amount of the tax. This removes a previous advantage for an estate with little or no tax liability. *If practically no estate tax is owed* (and this is an important provision), a higher evaluation six months after death would result in a higher cost basis. Now if the heirs should sell the assets at a profit, they would have less of a capital gain tax to pay. Since the estate did not owe an estate tax anyway, the election of an alternate valuation date which provided a higher cost basis was a tax advantage.

Under former law, the election to use the alternate valuation date could be made only on a timely filed estate tax return. The Tax Reform Act of 1984 allows the election to be made on a late return, provided the return is filed within one year. The election when made is irrevocable, and must be made on the first estate tax return that is filed. The new rules apply to the estate of a person who dies after July 18, 1984.

The Tax Reform Act of 1984 eliminated a former tax break for a trust or estate that distributed appreciated property. Prior law allowed a trust or an estate to avoid a capital gain tax on appreciated property by distribution of such property in kind to a beneficiary. The beneficiary reported the full value of the asset as income, the asset assumed a new cost basis, and the appreciation was not treated as a capital gain by either party.

The Act ends this break for taxable years ending after June 1, 1984.

The trustee or legal representative can elect to realize gain or loss on the distribution as though the property were sold at its fair market value. If the election is not made, the distribution is net income only to the extent of the lessor of (a) the fair market value of the property at the date of distribution, or (b) the cost basis of the property to the estate or trust.

The last-minute purchase of flower bonds can reduce federal estate taxes. These are Treasury obligations that sell considerably below their face value because of their low interest rate. The Treasury allows these bonds to be accepted at their face value for payment of estate taxes upon the death of the testator. The low yield of these bonds makes them unsuitable for long-term investments, but as a last-minute purchase just before death their purchase can be "found" money for an estate and its beneficiaries.

The problem lies in the testator's ability to make a last-minute purchase because of illness. This can be solved by arranging for their purchase in advance. A margin account, with sufficient collateral, should be established with a broker and a power of attorney given to a responsible relative. Now a substantial purchase can be made by a phone call because flower bonds can be bought with a low down payment.

William Whelass saved estate taxes by this method, purchasing $200,000 worth of flower bonds entirely on borrowed money. The Internal Revenue Service in the case of Whelass 72 TC 470 did not question the tax saving. In very wealthy estates millions can be purchased this way.

State Inheritance Taxes

The various states impose their own death taxes.

Many states tie their tax to the federal estate tax. In those states where a federal estate tax is not imposed, there isn't a state estate tax. If a federal estate tax is owed, those states assess a tax equal to the state death tax credit.

Tom Cook died in California in 1983, leaving a taxable estate of $318,927. After deducting the unified credit of $79,300 (and other allowable deductions such as funeral expenses), the executor found that he owed the IRS $15,065 in federal estate taxes. Since California did not impose a state inheritance tax, he assumed that no state tax was due. The probate attorney advised him, to his surprise, that he would still have to file an estate tax return for California (even though California had revoked its inheritance tax law). This was because California was entitled to the state death tax credit allowed on the federal return. The executor had to pay the state $4,336. However, this did not cost the estate any more money in total estate taxes. After deducting the state death tax credit, the federal tax was $10,729 ($15,065 minus $4,336).

In those states where they have their own estate tax, it is actually an inheritance tax. The tax is not imposed on the total value of the testator's estate, but on the amount that each individual inherits under the terms of the will.

The law in those states varies widely so it is hard to generalize, but, broadly speaking, the inheritance tax rate varies between 2 and 6 percent. The amount that is exempt for each individual heir and the tax rate depend upon the heir's relationship to the deceased. A widow normally obtains a generous exemption and a low rate, with minor children obtaining the next most beneficial tax treatment. Strangers receive the worst treatment, as high as a 10 percent rate and virtually no exemption.

Because of the wide difference in state laws, when making a will the property owner should not trust anyone as to the situation in the state where he resides except the personnel in the inheritance tax department at the state capital. There is too much misinformation and wrong information to do otherwise.

When trusts are drawn to save estate taxes, the grantor (who is the property owner creating the trust) should realize that state inheritance taxes are imposed against the eventual heirs of the trust at the time of the grantor's death, even though the heirs will not inherit the corpus of the trust until the trust terminates, which may not be for many years. Therefore the grantor should instruct his executor to pay these taxes out of the estate.

Gift Taxes

As we have previously stated, a spouse has an unlimited gift tax marital deduction. This enables a gift to a spouse of any amount, even millions. As we have seen, this is a valuable privilege where spouses have estates of unequal amount, with one spouse not having enough property to take advantage of the exemption equivalent. The spouse with the larger estate may give the required amount of property to the other spouse without incurring a gift tax liability.

Lifetime gifts to children under the annual gift tax exclusion can provide sizable estate tax savings. Any individual can give every year up to $10,000 of property gift tax free to as many recipients as he or she chooses. If a spouse gives her consent (simply by signing the consent clause on the gift tax return), a couple may give $20,000 each year to any number of recipients.

Mr. and Mrs. Dublin owned a sizable amount of property and had three children. They decided to start giving part of their estate to their children to reduce estate taxes. They instituted a program to give $20,000 a year to each of their children, which meant they could give them $60,000 a year. In ten years this would amount to $600,000, completely free of both estate and gift taxes. Since they were worth $3,000,000, with a current estate tax rate of 55 percent, this would save $330,000 in estate taxes.

Let's further assume that the Dublins in 1987 had property that was rapidly appreciating in value. In addition to their annual exclusions, they decided to give this property which was worth $300,000 to the children. Assuming this property tripled in value by the time the Dublins died, the $600,000 of increased value would completely escape the estate tax. In addition, upon the advice of their financial planner, they didn't pay a gift tax on the $300,000, but invaded their 1987 unified credit by this amount instead. Since each of them had a unified credit of $192,800, which is an exemption equivalent of $600,000, they reduced each individual exemption equivalent to $450,000 by filing a gift tax return, with a zero gift tax obligation.

When the Dublins died, however, their estates would be entitled only to the reduced exemption equivalent, and its correspondingly reduced unified credit. If they hadn't given property that was rapidly appreciating in value, but cash or its equivalent instead, there wouldn't have been a tax saving. They simply would have traded one tax for another, both with the same tax rate. The saving by giving what the IRS calls a taxable gift (because it exceeds the annual exclusion) results in a saving only if the donated property is *appreciating* in value.

The Dublins had to pay either a gift tax on the $300,000 at the time of the gift, or an estate tax on the $300,000 later when they died, because all previous taxable gifts have to be included in the estate appraisal. And since it is a Unified Gift and Estate Tax Schedule, the rates are the same. The tax saving was the result of having the $600,000 *increased value* escape the gift and estate tax entirely. The other advantage, of course, was not having to pay a gift tax out of their living estate. The tax would be paid from estate assets after they died.

The unified credit can also be used for gifts made to a trust.

Remember, the $10,000 annual exclusion is available only if the gift is one of a present interest, which means the donee must enjoy the economic benefit now. A gift of a future interest means that the donee will enjoy the economic benefit at some time in the future. A gift of a future interest is subject to the three-year rule. This rule states that the gift is a taxable gift unless three years have elapsed since the date of the donation. All taxable gifts must be included in the estate when it is appraised upon the testator's death.

Gifts to a trust that exceed the annual exclusion may be divided between gifts of a present interest and gifts of a future interest. Each gift of an income interest will qualify for the annual exclusion as a gift of a present interest. The remainder of each annual gift will be a remainder interest. The remainder interest is a taxable gift, but no tax will be payable until the accumulated value exceeds the unified credit of the grantor of the trust.

If a married couple has more income than they can spend, such income will be subject first to the income tax, and ultimately to the estate tax.

If we assume that the couple is in a 50 percent income tax bracket, and a 41 percent estate tax bracket, very little of the excess income is left. In this situation, less than 30 percent will eventually pass through to the children, or other heirs. One dollar of taxable income taxed at a 50 percent rate leaves 50 cents. And when this 50 cents is taxed at an estate tax rate of 41 percent rate, this leaves 29½ cents.

In larger estates gifts to grandchildren should not be ignored, for this increases the number of annual exclusions available.

Mrs. Haskell was a widow worth $2,000,000, give or take a few thousand dollars. She had two sons, both married, and each had two children. When in her late sixties, she decided it was time to make use of gifts to save estate taxes. As a single person it was the only avenue left open to her. Besides giving $10,000 a year under her annual exclusion to each of her two sons, she also included her two daughters-in-law and her four grandchildren. This enabled her to give $80,000 a year and still keep money within the family. If she lived ten years, she could thus give $800,000 of her $2,000,000 away. Assuming that Mrs. Haskell began her gifts in 1987, her program would save $353,000 in estate taxes ($588,000 minus $235,000).

One of the traditional tax-planning guidelines is not to sell appreciated property during life, but to hold the property until death. This way there wouldn't be a capital gain tax because the property wasn't sold during the owner's lifetime.

And there wouldn't be a capital gain tax after death (assuming no increase when the heirs sold) because the property would take on a stepped-up cost basis upon the death of the owner.

Mr. and Mrs. Fremont had a $1,500,000 estate. They decided to use the unlimited marital deduction because she was twenty years younger than her husband. The probable interim savings would far offset any small estate tax saving by placing Mr. Fremont's exemption equivalent in a bypass trust.

Mr. Fremont was terminally ill. A good portion of their estate was in vacant land acquired many years ago for $48,000, now worth $500,000. They had a firm offer on the property from a real estate agent, and Mrs. Fremont didn't know whether to accept it or not, so she consulted a financial planner who was their adviser.

He told her that she could not sell the property because of the capital gain tax involved. She could, however, accept the offer by inserting a condition in the sales agreement that the property could not be sold until after her husband died. Her adviser also told her that she had to immediately change the ownership from joint tenancy to community property. (Fortunately, they lived in a community property state.) This way probate would be avoided, and the entire property would receive a stepped-up cost basis when the estate was appraised.

When Mr. Fremont died shortly after that, the capital gain tax saving was 20 percent of $452,000, or $90,400. (The probable imposition of the alternative minimum tax is ignored.) Such sound advice is not easily obtained. Mrs. Fremont was fortunate to have a knowledgeable financial planner.

Let's mention one more point that could be overlooked. Payments on the behalf of a student to an educational institution for tuition and for medical care are excluded for federal gift tax purposes.

Conclusion

Estate tax savings are achieved by understanding the Unified Rate Schedule for Federal Estate and Gift Taxes, and its ramifications, and by comprehending the gift tax rules. It's amazing how many wills are drawn without any consideration being given to the impact of death taxes upon the estate. As a consequence liquidity is frequently overlooked, and estate taxes are paid to the Internal Revenue Service that could have been considerably reduced by proper planning in advance. Even the state inheritance tax department in many states will take too large a share because state inheritance taxes have escalated along with all other forms of taxes in recent years. Much of what the property owner strove so mightily to build by acquiring a living estate is now destroyed by taxes imposed against the death estate.

Lawyers don't provide much help. Many of them are completely ignorant about estate and gift taxes, and if they do have some knowledge, they ignore the problem. When they draw a will, they know that most of the time the executor will name them as probate attorney. Thus it's in their best interest to arrange for an estate to be as large as possible so their fees will be larger.

As we stated in the probate chapter, there is more misinformation and lack of information on the subject of estate planning than in any other area of money management. There is even confusion among those who are supposed to know, including lawyers, trust officers, and accountants.

In the last analysis you can't trust anyone in this vital area. It's up to you to obtain the facts.

Bear in mind that the only good estate plan is an up-to-date estate plan. If your will or trust agreement is dated prior to September 12, 1981, you must review it, for probably it should be redrawn.

In addition to this date, you should review your will or trust agreement when any of the following events occur.

1. A change in the family, such as a birth, a death, or a divorce.
2. A sizable increase or decrease in your assets.
3. A change in your priorities.
4. A change in the law.

**Affidavit
Death of Joint Tenant**

Dated..19........

Affidavit - Death of Joint Tenant

STATE OF CALIFORNIA

County of .... } ss.

...., of legal age, being first duly sworn, deposes and says:
That ...., the decedent mentioned in the attached certified copy of
Certificate of Death, is the same person as ....
named as one of the parties in that certain...................................dated.....................................
executed by ....
to ....,
as joint tenants, recorded as Instrument No..................., on ...., in
book ...., page ...., of Official Records of ....
County, California, covering the following described property situated in the ....
...., County of... State of California:

That the value of all real and personal property owned by said decedent at date of death,
including the full value of the property above described, did not then exceed the sum of $...................
....

Dated ....

SUBSCRIBED AND SWORN TO before me

this .... day of...   ....

Signature ....

....
Name (Typed or Printed)

(This area for official notarial seal)

Title Order No. .... Escrow or Loan No. ....

11

Financial Planning Principles

EVERY PROPERTY OWNER should be aware of the eleven estate planning principles that can provide simplicity, add cash flow, improve investments, further protect the heirs, and assure long-term growth to counteract the inroads of inflation. They will enable the testator to better enjoy his living estate and give his heirs maximum value and earnings from the property they will inherit.

These eleven estate planning principles are not necessarily listed in the order of their importance.

1. *When retired, take an income from all of your assets.*
The habit of a lifetime of saving is hard to break. It is surprising how many people, for instance, will retain a substantial sum in government E bonds even though they are retired. E bonds do not pay a current income. The interest is compounded every six months. Retaining them after retirement is saving interest for eventual heirs. If these bonds are never redeemed, their increased value will be left to the next generation. They should be cashed so the money can be put to work earning current income. Or they can be exchanged for government H bonds which pay interest every six months.
If you have retired, you should be enjoying the

income from all of your assets. Life expectancy at age sixty-five is just fifteen years. A retired property owner should not, out of habit, continue to save money.

Mr. and Mrs. Bristol were in their late sixties, retired, and worth $1 million, besides receiving income from Social Security and a company pension. They told their investment representative one day that they had too much in their checking account. When he asked them how much it was, they said it was $60,000! Then they admitted, laughing at his surprise, that it had been in their checking account just a short time because they had sold a piece of property.

At the representative's suggestion they invested the money in securities, and Mr. Bristol told him to automatically reinvest the dividends because they didn't need the money.

Their adviser disagreed.

"I wouldn't do that if I were you," he said.

"Why not," Mr. Bristol asked, "when we don't need the income?"

"Because you are retired," the representative replied, "and you should take all of your income. You might find that you will enjoy the dividends. If not, at the end of the year you will know it is excess money, and you can give it to your heirs. If you compound the dividends by buying more shares, you will simply increase the value of your estate and pay more in estate taxes someday. By taking the dividends you can use your annual gift tax exclusion, instead of throwing the exclusion away as you do now. If you don't use it, the exclusion for that year is gone forever."

So Mr. and Mrs. Bristol took his suggestion. They didn't spend the dividends, but they did give the money to their heirs gift tax free to enjoy now, rather than to inherit it at some indefinite future date.

Dr. Morgan, a dentist and a bachelor, retired early

at age sixty-two. He lived in a $200,000 home, which he couldn't afford, but he loved the old place and couldn't bring himself to sell it. He had $20,000 in the bank, and $150,000 in a balanced mutual fund from which he was taking only $450 per month. In addition, he received $620 a month from Social Security.

He told his investment adviser that he didn't need more money, that he was getting by on his monthly income. His representative persuaded him to take $750 per month from his mutual fund instead of $450, pointing out that based on the doctor's average price per share, and the previous ten-year record of dividends and capital gains, the fund's shares would not be diminished by paying the 6 percent.

To Dr. Morgan's surprise he did enjoy the extra income, living much better as a consequence. Sometimes it takes the objective thinking of an outsider to evaluate what you are doing with your estate and persuade you, if this is necessary, to increase the income from your assets when retired.

2. *If you are taking all of the income from your property, and still need more retirement income, spend part of your capital in order to live better.*

Most of the millions of people who are now retired were raised on the concept that they should spend only their income in order to be certain the capital would always be there. In these days of high living expenses and high taxes, this principle, for the most part, should no longer be followed. If you want to live better retired, and who doesn't, you should consider spending a small percentage of your capital each year to increase your cash flow. Admittedly this is a jolt to the way you always thought you would manage your finances. It raises the specter of running out of money some day, a frightening prospect.

But let's take a second look. Supposing you spent 3 percent of your capital each year. This would only be

30 percent in ten years, which would mean leaving 70 percent of your estate to your heirs instead of 100 percent. In addition, you could quit spending capital anytime, although you might be having too much fun to stop.

You could always revert to spending only your income in order to conserve your capital for an extreme old age that may never come, or for that catastrophic illness that may never happen. If you face facts squarely, it's the first ten years after you retire that you want to be on the go the most. After that it might be more fun to stay home and enjoy your friends and your grandchildren.

There are several ways to invest money so you can spend part of the capital while you are spending all of the income.

You can invest in a mutual fund and take a systematic payout. This method is widely used by millions of mutual fund owners. The shareholder decides how much he wants to receive each month, and the fund's disbursing agent sells a sufficient number of shares and fractional shares to equal that month's payment. At the same time, the fund reinvests the dividends and the capital gains during the year to replace shares that have been liquidated. If these shares equal the number of shares sold every month, there is no change in the total number of shares in the account. If more shares are sold than are replaced, the shareholder has spent some capital.

With a systematic payout from a mutual fund, the shareholder doesn't have a contract where he must receive the amount he has chosen. He may change the payments, stop receiving checks altogether, or cash his account at any time for its then current value. If the owner should die, the remaining shares will be inherited by his heirs.

Many retired people find this an ideal way to

spend part of their capital and all of their income on a controlled basis. In addition, since a mutual fund is a cross section of securities managed by professionals, it is a way, too, of providing management and diversification for eventual heirs.

Another method used by some people is to place a part of their estate in a mutual fund and deliberately dissipate it to zero in ten years. When using this method the shareholder receives a payout in excess of 10 percent with the guarantee that, regardless of the amount of the check each month, the shares in the account will not be dissipated until ten years have elapsed.

The income is in excess of 10 percent for a very simple reason. If the investor put $12,000 in a safe deposit box where it earns no interest, and spent $1,200 a year, he would know that the money would last ten years before it ran out. If the $12,000 is invested in a mutual fund, the shareholder would receive the same 10 percent, plus the dividends and realized capital gains, and the growth if any, with this amount being actuarially computed by the fund each month.

Mr. and Mrs. Lantz owned a valuable commercial property on which they had unfortunately signed a low-income lease many years before. After they had first signed the lease, the county in which they lived had become one of the fastest-growing communities in the United States, causing the property to increase tremendously in value. They desperately needed more income because the property taxes had badly escalated as well.

Mr. and Mrs. Lantz wanted to retain the property, not only for themselves but for their children, but they were going to lose it unless something was done. Fortunately they had some money which they could invest. Their financial planner suggested they put this sum in a mutual fund and deliberately dissipate the account to zero to coincide with the termination of the low-income lease. This saved the property for them and their children.

Another method of spending capital as well as income is to invest in a fixed-dollar no-refund annuity issued by an insurance company. This method should be used with care, with complete understanding on the part of the purchaser that an annuity principle is being used based on life expectancy, with the capital and income both being spent to zero. The policy is attractive to many people because the monthly income is guaranteed for life.

Mrs. Merrill was a widow, age sixty-eight, who elected a lifetime income on a $25,000 no-refund annuity, arranging for the first monthly payment to start when she became seventy years of age. When her only daughter found out what her mother had bought, she called her investment representative and asked his help in cashing the policy. She felt that the entire $25,000 could be refunded since the first monthly payment had yet to be paid.

When she was told that, no matter when her mother died, the entire $25,000 was gone because she had purchased a no-refund annuity, the daughter almost went through the roof of her modest home.

Mrs. Merrill, however, was not disturbed for the policy had been carefully explained to her, and she had what she wanted, which was a guarantee of a monthly income for life so she would be financially independent of her daughter. Fortunately for the daughter's peace of mind her mother had another $25,000, which she was perfectly willing to invest. The investment representative explained to both Mrs. Merrill and her daughter that if the $25,000 were invested in blue-chip stocks, and the dividends were used to buy more shares, there was a possibility with time that the stocks could be worth $50,000. The daughter quieted down when she saw an opportunity to inherit the $50,000, after all. Both women realized, of course, that there was no guarantee this would happen, but they were willing to take the risk.

The life underwriter who sold Mrs. Merrill the policy was not completely fair with her. He should have explained that she could buy a *refund* annuity, with only a slight reduction in the monthly payment. This way, if she died before her life expectancy, her daughter would receive the remaining cash value of the policy.

Mrs. Roper, a widow, and her spinster sister were retired and lived together out of financial necessity because the sister was completely without funds. Mrs. Roper was barely able to pay their bills, even though they lived frugally.

When an investment representative was consulted to determine if their situation could be improved financially, he found that they were living so poorly because they weren't receiving all of the income from Mrs. Roper's assets. Nor were they spending any of the capital, even though Mrs. Roper's only heir was her sister.

Her assets consisted of $200,000 in securities at an average return of 5 percent, $10,000 in cash in a safe deposit box, and $25,000 in matured E bonds. When Mrs. Roper was asked why she was trying to get along on approximately $800 per month in dividends, she replied that she didn't know what else to do, for these were the assets her husband had left her. She knew that if she spent only the income, the capital would always be there.

By using principles one and two, the representative was able, with Mrs. Roper's delighted consent, to drastically alter the two sisters' way of life. He had her cash the $225,000 in securities and E bonds, and invest $200,000 in utility bonds paying an average of 12 percent, which gave her an income of $24,000 a year. He suggested that she spend the remaining $25,000. Over the years, since her husband had died, her apartment had become so shabby she was ashamed of it, so she spent $5,000 refurbishing it, and with the other $20,000 Mrs. Roper booked herself and her sister on a world cruise! This is a drastic example, but it clearly demonstrates how principles one and two can be used to an advantage by retired people.

3. *Don't leave your heirs too much cash.*

"Easy come, easy go," is an old expression, but still a true one. Cash will too often be spent. Your heirs are normally much younger and less experienced than you, and therefore you should exercise your mature judgment and invest the money. If heirs are left a sound investment with a good income, they are more inclined to leave it alone.

If your heirs don't spend the cash, and through lack of experience make bad investments, the money will again be gone, but more tragically dissipated, because no one will have enjoyed the inheritance. It is true that decisions are difficult, and when you are retired and getting along on what you have, it is easier to do nothing. But in the best interests of your estate, you should make the decision and invest your excess cash.

Mr. and Mrs. French had accomplished the difficult task of accumulating $200,000, made particularly noteworthy because neither one of them had gone beyond the sixth grade in school, and Mr. French had never made much money. They had one son, who unfortunately had not inherited his parents' acquisitive instincts and, in addition, was a ne'er-do-well who couldn't seem to hold a job much longer than six months. Mr. and Mrs. French's estate, outside of their home, was entirely in cash.

Repeated efforts by both their bank's trust department and a financial planner to have them either invest the money or create a trust for their son's protection were to no avail. When the son eventually inherited the estate, it was all gone within two years.

This seems almost impossible today with the federal and state laws that protect the investor. But since the son knew nothing about money, he was easy prey for an unscrupulous real estate promoter. The scheme was underfinanced, and eventually was declared bankrupt. In a very short time the boy lost an estate that had taken a lifetime to build.

4. *If you need more income, stop paying premiums on permanent life insurance when you are retired.*

Whole life insurance has a cash value which, when needed, should be used at retirement in one of three ways that are called nonforfeiture options by the insurance company.

(a) You can take the cash, which is always less than the face amount of the policy, but by doing so both you and your wife can enjoy the money, rather than have her enjoy alone the higher death benefit.

(b) You can take the reduced paid-up option with the cash. This is a policy for less than the face amount that stays in force for life without any further premium payments. There is an important difference; it is now paid up. On a $10,000 whole life policy taken out age thirty-five, a reduced paid-up policy would have a death benefit of approximately $7,500.

(c) You can take an extended term option with the cash. By this method the entire face amount of the policy is in force for a certain number of years and days. Once again, no further premium payments are due. In a typical $10,000 policy taken out at age thirty-five, the full amount of the policy would be in force at age sixty-five for almost thirteen years. At age seventy-eight, however, the insurance would terminate because the insured had outlived the term of the policy.

If your decision is not to use the first option and take the cash, you would elect the reduced paid-up option if your health is excellent, but take the term option if it is not. In most states, when using the last two options, the remaining cash value in the policy continues to be available if you should change your mind. In any event, no matter which of the three options you choose, your income is increased because you stop paying premiums.

Your death estate would be reduced, however, by using the first two options, and by the full amount of the policy by using the third option if you outlive the extended term insurance.

Mr. and Mrs. Berger were retired, trying to get along on $1,200 per month and having a difficult time of it because they were living in one of the highest cost-of-living areas in the United States. Mr. Berger was still paying premiums on three small whole life policies totaling $26,000.

When he arranged a meeting with his life underwriter to find out what could be done, the agent suggested writing the three insurance companies involved for the necessary information. They were told the combined cash value of the policies was $20,000, the reduced paid-up amount was $22,800, and the extended term insurance would last for twelve years.

Since Mr. Berger's health was apparently excellent, the extended term insurance for the full $26,000 was ruled out. The reduced paid-up insurance was high, which would mean only a small loss to Mrs. Berger, the beneficiary, if her husband should die and, in addition, no further premium payments would have to be paid.

After much discussion, Mrs. Berger elected to take the cash. She said she would rather enjoy the money with her husband now, instead of taking the larger sum later after he died, only to enjoy it alone. So they cashed the policies, only to have Mr. Berger die of a heart attack ninety days later. But Mrs. Berger did not make one complaint to her life underwriter, for she had fully understood her decision.

5. *If income real estate is presenting such a management problem that you cannot retire and enjoy your golden years, you should sell it and invest your money elsewhere.*

Real estate has been an excellent estate building vehicle for a great many people; however, in too many cases it is not a good retirement investment. Retired people no longer want the management headaches. Many of them are physically incapable of taking care of real estate themselves. They have to call a painter every time that an apartment has to be painted or a plumber when a leaky faucet needs to be repaired. The high cost of such repairs materially reduces their net income. It might be advisable, under the circumstances, to sell the real estate and invest the money where it does not require personal daily attention. No one is truly retired while still managing property.

Mr. and Mrs. Athens owned a twelve-unit apartment house in a northern metropolitan city. They had purchased it many years before with a small down payment and, after many years of effort, had succeeded in paying off the mortgage. By the time Mr. Athens was sixty-seven years old he had a bad back, which his doctor kept reminding him might improve if he would move to a warmer climate. The couple lived in one of the twelve apartments in the building and managed the property themselves, pleased that they had done very well financially.

A friend finally persuaded Mr. Athens to meet with a financial planner who suggested, as one of his recommendations, that Mr. and Mrs. Athens, now that they had reached retirement age, should use the dividends from $40,000 in stocks they owned, rather than reinvest them. This would give them an additional income of $2,400 a year.

"But if we took the money," Mr. Athens objected, "we couldn't spend it."

The representative was surprised. "Why not?" he asked.

"Because we are tied down to this apartment house seven days a week, that's why," Mr. Athens replied. "We don't have the time to spend any money. As a matter of fact, I shouldn't be talking to you right now. If I don't repair the lock to the hall door on apartment fourteen before dark, the tenant will move out!"

Mr. and Mrs. Athens estimated their building was worth $500,000. In addition, they had the $40,000 in stocks, and another $40,000 in cash. Yet despite this sizable net worth, Mr. Athens was still working seven days a week.

It took the financial planner many interviews to convince them, but after two years of discussion, they finally sold their apartment house for $100,000 down, taking back a $400,000 first mortgage at 10 percent. After they invested the down payment in a money market fund, they had an income of over $50,000 a year, plus their Social Security. They then took his doctor's advice and moved to a warmer climate, where Mr. Athens's back improved, and they found themselves enjoying their retirement years.

6. *If you own securities and you have inexperienced heirs, either create a bank trust or start training them in how to manage your investments.*

It is surprising how different your stocks and bonds look to you when you think of them in the hands of your heirs. If you are deeply concerned about the future management of your property, you should create a testamentary bank trust; or, better yet, transfer some of your securities to your heirs and observe how well they handle them. They may surprise you, and if they do, or if they learn under your direction, then a trust will not be necessary. They can inherit the property outright, which is the best possible solution.

7. *Don't own too many assets.*

Too many assets present a management problem for you in your living estate, and extra work for your executor in your death estate. Not many property owners can keep track of as many as thirty different securities effectively. If you will review them with your broker, you should be able to reduce your portfolio to a manageable number of ten or twelve stocks and bonds that meet your overall objective, and this move might even improve your investment results as well.

Mr. Foster owned over forty stocks and bonds, three mutual funds, several parcels of real estate, and his own business. He was successful and had acquired a sizable estate. Since his results had been excellent, he felt that he was doing a good job of managing his living estate, until his investment representative complained to him that over the past two or three years he had not made one investment decision. Mr. Foster was so busy keeping track of what he owned, he no longer had time to improve his portfolio or analyze any of the several excellent suggestions made to him by his broker.

When this was pointed out to him, and particularly when he realized the unnecessary work he was presenting to his executor with the concomitant long delay in settling his estate, he trimmed his investment portfolio drastically.

8. *Don't keep assets that have a small monetary value.*

Assets that have little value clutter up your living estate and your death estate. Five shares of a $5 stock are worth $25.00, and a small matured E bond is worth $100. Such assets are not worth keeping in your estate, yet people do retain them. They should be sold for they present a nuisance factor to both you and your executor. Small assets that are acquired over a lifetime are often retained through sheer inertia on the part of the property owner; frequently he has forgotten how he happened to acquire them in the first place.

9. *Be careful about making gifts, for you may lose your financial independence.*

You should enjoy your living estate, remembering

that saving estate taxes by making gifts may not always be the right thing to do. Gifts should be made where there is an estate tax problem, but the donor should be careful to retain enough property and income to remain financially independent.

Mrs. Brand, a widow, was well-to-do, with an only son who was an auditor. She owned sizable real estate holdings. Over the course of several years her auditor son persuaded her to dispose of all of her property and invest the money in securities, which he put in his name only, in order, he said, to avoid probate and save estate taxes.

Eventually he placed his mother in a retirement home at the relatively young age of sixty, after which he condescended to see her once or twice a year.

Mrs. Brand, while not in want, became a very unhappy and lonely woman. She should have made substantial gifts to her son, for her net worth warranted it, but she should not have reduced herself to a point of complete financial dependence upon him.

10. *Don't make yourself financially responsible for your grandchildren.*

If your son or son-in-law is insurable and he does not believe in life insurance, and therefore refuses as the breadwinner to protect his young family by an adequate life insurance program, you should take out insurance on his life and pay the premiums.

Life insurance is the only way that a sizable estate can be created for a widow and dependent children when the head of the family hasn't had the time or the inclination to save. By the stroke of a pen and the payment of a premium an estate can be immediately created where none existed before. Life insurance is the only way this can be done.

You may not object to acting as a baby-sitter if your son or son-in-law should die prematurely, but you shouldn't put yourself in the position of having to help your daughter or daughter-in-law financially, or to send the grandchildren through college. A $100,000 reducing term policy for twenty years at a premium of around $40 per month (depending upon the age of the insured) is a lot easier to pay than $100,000 in cash.

11. *Even a small estate can benefit from estate planning.*
Due to lack of information, many people are unnecessarily concerned about problems with probate, taxes, delays, and costs, which are easily solved and, in some cases, almost nonexistent.

Mrs. Kaspar, a widow, was seventy-four years of age with two married daughters. Her total estate consisted of $98,000 in a savings and loan account. Her two daughters and their husbands, and Mrs. Kaspar, became concerned about what was going to happen to her money when she was gone. They had read about probate, and a recent account in their local newspaper, relating the taxes and costs involved in a large estate, triggered them into asking for a conference with a financial planner who was experienced in estate planning.

He met with all five of them one afternoon, with everyone crowded around the kitchen table of Mrs. Kaspar's modest rented apartment. They wanted advice about many things—probate, lawyers' fees, death taxes, delay—but mainly they were concerned that there would be little left of Mrs. Kasper's $98,000. The financial planner was able to allay their fears by giving them the information they so badly needed. He told them that a will could be drawn for a small fee, but this wouldn't be necessary if they followed his suggestion and put the money in joint tenancy with her two daughters.

With everyone's enthusiastic consent, the representative placed $80,000 in two separate $40,000 mutual fund accounts, with each daughter as a joint tenant. He suggested a balanced mutual fund with a systematic payout in the form of a monthly check. The remaining $18,000 in the savings and loan account he put in joint tenancy with Mrs. Kaspar's older daughter, after satisfying himself that this was a closely knit family, with everyone having complete trust in the others. Upon Mrs. Kaspar's death each fund account could be transferred to the appropriate daughter, and the older child could divide with her sister what was left of the savings and loan account after paying final expenses. The investment representative pointed out that all three names could be on the savings and loan account, but the younger sister voted against it.

The investment representative showed them from his tax tables that there wouldn't be a federal estate tax because of the $400,000 exemption equivalent enjoyed by every estate ($600,000 by 1987), and that the state inheritance tax in their state, because of a $5,000 exemption for each daughter and a 3 percent rate, would be only $2,100.

When the conference broke up, everybody in the family was tremendously relieved and thanked the financial planner for his information and suggestions.

In addition to these eleven estate planning principles, there are fundamental rules to follow that have been brought out in preceding chapters and which should be emphasized here.

It should be understood by everyone who saves money that two estates are built during a lifetime—a living estate and a death estate. Too often the living estate receives all of the attention, and the death estate none, which, we have seen, is a serious mistake. People should learn about the complex problems that are created when their property is transferred to their heirs. Those who take over from them should not feel that, in their case anyway, probate was the most expensive undertaking establishment in the world.

Assets cannot be left intact to someone else. Death creates

debts that did not exist before, and the payment of final expenses, administration costs, and death taxes have to be met before the heirs can inherit anything. The long delay of probate can be very frustrating, and when your assets are listed down to the last penny as a matter of public record, the resulting lack of privacy can be nerve-racking, at least for some people.

You can avoid probate if you like, and how to avoid it is simply a matter of correct ownership. You have three choices: joint tenancy with right of survivorship; naming a beneficiary; or creating a living trust, the last one being used only where large estates are involved.

Everyone should have a will drawn by an attorney, even though, when joint tenancy is used between spouses, the will is ignored upon the first death. Where large estates are in involved, a trust has to be created in order to reduce estate taxes.

Be careful about gifts for your own protection and financial independence, but remember, too, that there is a lot of truth in the old cliché that nobody lives longer than rich relatives. If you have more property than you need, let the younger generation enjoy now some of the fruits of your lifetime of labor. This will also reduce your estate taxes.

Once you have completed your estate plan, don't mistakenly feel that the job has been accomplished for all time. Resolve to review your plan periodically, especially when there has been a marriage, death, divorce, or birth in your family, or a change in the law.

A lawyer must be consulted when drawing a will or trust agreement, for he is the only one who can ensure it will be legal. But you can't always trust him to do it right. Lawyers work too closely with bank trust departments, and they want you in probate court. You should insist that your attorney draw your will or trust agreement the way you want it. After all, it's your property and your heirs.

And remember, estate planning is a must if you are to transfer your assets to your heirs with the least trouble and expense.

12

Real Estate

BUYING PROPERTY as an investment is difficult because of high interest rates and high prices, especially when comparing today's prices with the values of commercial property in 1974.

Even if the property can be bought for $100,000, it would require a down payment of 20 percent. Most potential real estate investors don't have $20,000 to put down, nor can they meet the monthly mortgage payments. In too many cases the asking price is so high that the property has a negative cash flow, meaning that the rents are not sufficient to pay the operating costs; therefore the deficiency must come out of the prospective buyer's pocket.

Commercial real estate is also harder to evaluate, which requires the prospective investor to trust the real estate agent even more than, say, when buying a home. If the buyer isn't knowledgeable, this compounds the problem.

Nevertheless, investing in real estate can be highly profitable. Many of the great family fortunes in the world have been established by investing in real estate. People starting with only a few thousand dollars have become millionaires in a few short years, and many more will become wealthy for the first time this year because they invested their money in property.

All of them, of course, took a businessman's risk. There

weren't any guarantees they would make money. Many have tried investing in real estate and lost. Yet more money is invested in real estate than in any other way, including the stock market. Men of prominence and enormous wealth have extolled the virtues of investing in property.

John D. Rockefeller said: "The fortunes of the future will be made in real estate." Andrew Carnegie said: "Ninety percent of all millionaires acquired their wealth by owning real estate. The wise young man or wage earner invests his money in property." And Marshall Field, the great retailer, said: "Buying real estate is not only the best way, the quickest way, and the safest way, but the only way to become wealthy."

Real estate has great attraction as an investment, aside from its profit potential, because it is tangible. You can see it and walk on it. It's not like a stock investment, which is intangible, for which you receive just a piece of paper, a stock certificate. Land will always be here, and there is only just so much of it. With an expanding population, land has a built-in growth factor, as more and more people compete with one another to buy it.

Time works against us most of the time. We ourselves grow old, and the things we own and use become obsolete. But not land. Even the Internal Revenue Service recognizes this basic fact and will not permit land to be depreciated for tax purposes. They allow depreciation on buildings (except your home), and on machinery, furniture, and equipment, but never on land. And this is true no matter to what use, or no use, it may be put.

Even if you agree that real estate is a wonderful investment, how can you buy it in today's economic environment?

The best way to invest is in a real estate limited partnership, or in a real estate investment trust. Let's consider the limited partnership first.

Real estate limited partnerships invest in multifamily and commercial properties to provide investors with the following benefits.

CAPITAL APPRECIATION OVER THE LONG TERM

Growth in the form of increased property value is definitely the major objective. This takes time. The investor should not expect real estate to sell at a good profit under five to seven years.

CASH FLOW FROM THE NET RENTS

The general partners of a limited partnership will not buy a property that does not provide an economic benefit, meaning a net income after operating expenses. Negative cash flow might evolve because of unexpected developments, such as a softening of the rental market in the area where the property was purchased, but it will not be present at acquisition. Cash distributions are relatively low, generally 3 to 5 percent annually, because the balance of any net income in excess of this is spent improving the property to accelerate growth. These distributions typically are not subject to federal income tax because of depreciation deductions.

TAX SAVINGS

A flow-through of tax deductions, in excess of the cash distributions. These deductions (besides depreciation) are primarily start-up expenses of the partnership, interest on the mortgage, and property taxes. They shelter other income and can amount to as high as 60 to 70 percent of the original investment in the first five years.

EQUITY BUILDUP

One source of capital growth is mortgage reduction (i.e., paying down the loan principals), resulting in an increase in equity, which is eventually realized in cash as properties are sold or refinanced.

Besides the above benefits, there are other advantages.

A PROFESSIONALLY CHOSEN PORTFOLIO

Because the general partners are experienced in real estate, they are able to appraise expertly and negotiate favorable terms when purchasing properties.

DIVERSIFICATION

This is a proven and sound investment strategy. Normally (except in private placements, explained later), several properties are purchased, thus lowering investment risk.

CAPITAL POOLING

With millions of dollars of purchasing power available, particularly in the larger public partnerships, acquisition is made easier and at more favorable prices. In addition, the property management team can buy on a national scale at wholesale prices for their necessary supplies, thus holding down costs.

A VALUE ADDED STRATEGY

Each property is targeted for improvements that will enhance value. This continues during the entire time the property is held.

AN INTEGRATED THREE-STAGE CYCLE

Each property goes through the three stages of acquisition, property management, and sale. These stages are clearly kept in mind from the outset. As an example, no property is purchased without the prior approval of the property management team. As the head of one partnership's management department told the vice president of acquisition: "Look, your department has to make a decision once; we have to manage the property at a profit for years. We have to know the problems in advance."

Since the investor is a limited partner, the law in regard to partnerships should be understood.

Unless otherwise specified, each partner in a business enterprise is a general partner who is a principal and fully active in the management of the business. A general partner has the authority to act for the partnership within the scope of its activity and is fully responsible for its debts, even to the extent of his or her personal wealth (including cash and a home).

A limited partner is neither active in the business nor liable for any of its debts. As such, a limited partner cannot lose any more money than the amount that he or she has invested in the partnership. Nor can this person be assessed for an additional investment.

In short, the general partners manage the business. The limited partners, being passive investors, do not have any say in the day-to-day operations.

Real estate limited partnerships are broadly divided between public and private partnerships, the latter frequently being referred to as private placements.

A public partnership is registered with the Securities and Exchange Commission. As the name implies, the units are offered to a wide spectrum of the general public, who usually reside in several states, and in the larger partnerships, nationwide. This can result in millions of dollars being raised, as much as $50 million to $100 million in a single partnership. When all of the units in the partnership have been sold, the partnership is closed. From then on, no additional limited partners are admitted to that particular partnership. When all the money has been committed, the partnership is fully invested. The acquisition stage is then complete, and the portfolio enters the long property management stage of the three-stage cycle.

Besides the equity real estate limited partnerships that purchase properties already built, there are other real estate partnerships available to the investor.

TRIPLE NET LEASE PARTNERSHIPS

The primary objective of these partnerships is to provide a good current income for the limited partners. The partnership buys a large commercial building that is already owned and occupied by a big corporation, and then leases it back to the same corporation. The term *triple net lease* derives from the fact that the leasing corporation pays for all three of the basic expenses of taxes, insurance, and operating costs. The only expense incurred by the partnership is the monthly payment on the mortgage.

The corporation sells the building, and then leases it back, in order to obtain working capital as a result of the sale. Some of the largest banks in the country sell their headquarters building for this purpose. One bank built its headquarters office building for $30 million and sold it several years later for $450 million, as an example. In addition to occupying two-thirds of the property, the bank had a long list of prime tenants which made the building very attractive to a buyer.

There are other real estate limited partnerships that buy vacant agricultural land and develop it. This gives investors the opportunity to participate in the potential gain from creating new income streams by purchasing and controlling land, and then developing it for specific purposes, such as building shopping centers, apartment houses, and office buildings.

In a land development limited partnership, the responsibilities of the fund's general partners include working with the various governmental agencies in securing the zoning and variances necessary for the project; obtaining environmental-impact studies, final tract maps, and building permits; and arranging for the necessary financing. Throughout the life of the partnership there is a continuing endeavor to maximize gain in the shortest possible period of time.

This type of real estate development requires management skills and experience beyond that of mere ownership. In these limited partnerships in particular, you have to trust the judgment of the general partners.

No income is paid in the early stages of a development fund, for there isn't any income from vacant land. Tax advantages are meager initially because deductions are derived solely from interest on the mortgages and from start-up expenses (which are high, as much as 25 percent). The appreciation is greater, however, than in other real estate limited partnerships, because the creation of income property from raw vacant land takes an expertise that is recognized by potential buyers.

Real estate partnerships are further divided into public partnerships and private partnerships.

Normally, private partnerships are not registered with the Securities and Exchange Commission; therefore they do not come under federal jurisdiction. They are governed by state law where they are domiciled. Usually they are offered in only one state and then only to a total of thirty-five investors. The individual investor is not limited, however, in the amount that he or she invests; therefore the amount of money raised varies widely. In any event, it is small compared to the big public partnerships. Therefore private partnerships quite often invest in just one property.

Private partnerships are usually structured as a tax shelter. They generally require a commitment by the limited partner to a series of payments over a period of four to five years. This obligation requires the limited partner to sign a promissory note for the unpaid portion, which is a legally enforceable document, with interest penalties if the note is not paid when the installments are due.

The risk is greater in a private placement; only one, or at the most two or three, properties are purchased because of the limited amount of money raised. But the rewards can be greater as well, for one property acquired at the right location and at the right price can exceed in value the average of many properties that provide the safeguard of diversification. While a high tax shelter is the principal objective, appreciation is a major goal.

A sample offering taken from the sales brochure of a successful general partner is given on the next page.

OFFERING HIGHLIGHTS

Size of program $2,960,000
Minimum investment $74,000 payable over six years.
Cumulative write-off 160% of cash invested
Estimated holding period 5 to 7 years

PROPERTY PROFILE

A garden-style complex consisting of 202 apartment units approximately eight miles from downtown Portland, Oregon.

The property includes nineteen two- and three-story buildings containing a total of 141,079 leasable square feet.

Amenities include a swimming pool with a wood deck for sunbathing, a sports court, and a children's play yard, surrounded by attractively landscaped grounds.

Total purchase price represents an average cost per apartment unit of $25,742, or $36.85 per leasable square foot.

Investment in a real estate limited partnership involves risk. No public market for the units is likely, which means the money invested is not liquid. Accordingly, the units are suitable only for those who have adequate financial means and desire a long-term investment.

Units of a *public partnership* can be sold only to an investor who has, and who also represents in the subscription agreement that he has, either: (1) a net worth (exclusive of home, home furnishings, and automobiles) of $30,000, plus a minimum annual gross income of $30,000: or, in the alternative, (2) a minimum net worth of $75,000 (exclusive of home, home furnishings, and automobiles), irrespective of annual gross income. These qualifications are not high as to income, but they would exclude many people because of the net worth requirements.

Units of a *private partnership* have even higher suitability standards because they are sold primarily as a tax shelter; therefore they should be sold only to those in a high tax bracket. (Please refer to the chapter on income taxes for the suitability standards of private parnerships.) These qualifications definitely exclude all but the well-to-do.

There are disadvantages to investing in real estate limited partnerships. Your money is not liquid for a period of many years. It is managed by someone else. Many people prefer to make their own decisions, right or wrong. The costs are high; therefore you have to decide they are worth it considering the net results you expect to obtain. These charges include securities sales commissions from 7 to 10 percent of the original investment, acquisition and sales fees, a yearly property management fee of 5 percent of the gross rents, and 14 percent to 20 percent owed the general partners from the net sales. This last charge, however, is subordinated to the limited partners retrieving first 100 percent of their invested capital, plus a minimum cumulative annual return. This return varies from 6 percent (the usual minimum by state law) to as high as 18 percent.

An investment in a real estate limited partnership requires complete confidence in the general partners. An investment should not be made unless the investor is satisfied that the management personnel has the necessary expertise generated over a period of several years, and a track record with satisfactory results. If the investor establishes this to his satisfaction, trust of the general partners is justified.

Real Estate Investment Trusts

Although many people cannot qualify to invest in real estate limited partnerships because of the high income and net worth required, they can invest in real estate investment trusts which have no such suitability standards. These trusts invest in commercial real estate, and offer advantages and benefits similar to the limited partnerships. They fill a need, too, for a real estate investment vehicle for the small investor because the initial investment required is low.

These trusts are of two types. The equity real estate investment trust and the mortgage real estate investment trust.

The equity real estate investment trust, as the name implies, invests in existing commercial properties for the triple advantage of income, long-term profit, and tax advantages.

The concept of the equity real estate investment trust originated in the middle of the nineteenth century. At that time Massachusetts law prohibited a corporation from investing in real estate except in the land on which its offices and factories were located. As a result of this law, an organization that was ruled *not* to be a corporation came into existence. It was called the Boston real estate trust. Similar trusts were soon formed, and they became so popular that when they ran out of attractive large investment properties in Boston, they started investing in other big cities across the country. These trusts received a setback, however, when a federal court decision in 1936 reversed previous decisions and ruled that the Boston trust was in fact a corporation and therefore had to pay corporation taxes.

This ruling made the individual investor in equity trusts subject to double taxation; not only did the trusts have to pay a corporation tax, but the investors had to pay income taxes on any distribution of income. As a consequence, equity real estate investment trusts became economically unattractive as an investment.

For a quarter of a century thereafter, the concept of the equity real estate investment trust lay dormant. Then in 1960 the United States Congress took recognition of the tax inequity faced by real estate trusts and passed a law that applied the conduit theory to the distributed income. Thenceforth, as long as the trust paid out 95 percent of its investment income to its shareholders it was not subject to the corporate tax. Actually, the conduit theory of passing through income to the investor tax free had already been in effect with respect to mutual funds since the passage of the Federal Investment Company Act of 1940.

When passing the law in 1960, Congress not only took recognition of the tax inequity in existing law, but also incorporated in the bill comprehensive provisions to protect the small investor.

These provisions are:

(a) To ensure true public ownership, an equity trust must have at least one hundred shareholders, and no more than 50 percent of its outstanding shares can be owned by five persons or fewer.

(b) At least 75 percent of the gross income of the equity trust must come from real estate.

(c) An equity trust cannot directly manage any property that it owns. This provision is designed to prevent the small individual shareholder from being victimized by a professional management group. Any group that managed the property could, by clever manipulation, milk it and pay the shareholder little or nothing.

(d) An equity trust cannot deal exclusively in land development or land sales, for this could result in zero income.

(e) An equity trust must have shares that can be freely transferred. This provision is designed to keep the investment liquid. Since the trust is a publicly held corporation, the shares may be sold at any time.

Despite the protection provided by law, the investor should realize that the success of an equity real estate investment trust rests with its management. No more than 10 percent of the money invested by the shareholder should accrue to the promoters of the trust. Ninety percent of all money received should go into actual investment in real estate properties.

The management should have a long and successful experience in real estate investments, and they should be people of proven business ability and integrity. Accounting practices should conform to approved procedures, and leverage (borrowing money) should be used with restraint, even though this is a significant way to maximize profits. If the trust is allowed to borrow, according to its official prospectus, it should be for only a reasonable percentage of the total amount invested.

Like all investments, real estate investment trusts (REITs) have their disadvantages. Since by law they must distribute 95 percent of their investment income, very little money is left for improvement of the properties, which we have seen is a very effective way of increasing value. Some trusts have experienced management difficulties for they have bought properties that were too high priced. Others bought in areas that were overbuilt, thus experiencing high vacancy percentages which made it difficult, or impossible, to provide a return to the investor.

Mortgage real estate investment trusts invest exclusively in mortgages. This instrument is strictly an income vehicle serving as a substitute for investments in money market funds, bonds, utility stocks, and limited partnerships whose primary objective is income. Like equity investment trusts, there are no suitability standards, with the minimum investment low, usually $500. Also like equity real estate trusts, the shares are liquid because they are publicly traded on a stock exchange.

The trust's adviser should have long experience in real estate and a proven record. Sales literature of one nationally known sponsor supplied the following information.

"The sponsor has been in business since 1969, and in that time has formed 12 real estate limited partnerships and 3 mortgage trusts. Total capital raised to date is $1.2 billion invested by 138,000 investors nationwide. The 3 trusts have made 672 million dollars in loans."

With that kind of a record an investor should invest with confidence, provided the objectives of the trust coincide with his own.

Many mortgage lenders, seeking the highest income consistent with safety, make short-term loans so they can continue to provide their shareholders with a high current yield, rather than tie up the money for long periods of time. They are also looking for capital appreciation by insisting upon equity participation agreements in the event the property on which the loan is being made increases in value.

They maintain conservative loan-to-value ratios. For example, if the loan-to-value ratio is 70 percent, the value of the collateral is 43 percent higher than the amount of the loan (43 percent of 70 percent is 30 percent, and 70 percent plus 30 percent equals 100 percent). They also maintain cash reserves in excess of 10 percent of the loan balances.

The benefit to the investor in a real estate mortgage trust is a relatively high income compared to other forms of investment, a low initial payment, liquidity, professional management and diversification, plus an opportunity for gain from equity participation in the loans.

Oil and Gas Exploration And Development

This is also an investment in real estate, albeit a risky one. It is common knowledge that fortunes have been made in oil and gas, especially in exploratory drilling. It is also common knowledge that all too often investors in this type of real estate have not realized their objective, and if wildcat drilling for new oil is involved, they could lose 100 percent of the money they have invested.

Much of the money that has been lost has gone into the unproductive drilling of one or two wildcat wells by an oil promotor who has sold the idea to investors that a well will "come in" if only the necessary capital can be raised. Of course, if an oil discovery is made, the rewards are immense. In far too many cases, however, the well turns out to be a dry hole that has to be abandoned.

There is a way for investors to invest in oil and gas on a more sensible basis and with better hope for success. This is by an investment in oil and gas limited partnerships. There are two types: those that invest in exploratory wells, and those that buy already existing wells for income.

*   *   *

The chief attraction of an oil and gas exploration program is the possibility of a major discovery, which could mean handsome profits. But because of the great risk involved, the prospective limited partner should insist that the following minimum requirements be met before placing his trust in the general partners.

1. The general partners must have proven integrity and long experience in oil and gas exploration.
2. The partnership's objective should be a major discovery of oil or gas, or both. Drilling wells adjacent to proven fields simply to find limited amounts of oil and gas in order to prove that the general partners are in fact drilling productive wells will not produce a satisfactory return to the limited partners. This tactic is used where the general partners own all of the subsidiary companies associated with the complicated drilling process, such as the companies that lease the rigs, those that supply the mud, etc. In this case the general partners don't care whether they find oil and gas because they will make money from the subsidiary companies as long as they are drilling.
3. The general partners must be obligated, and financially able, to develop any field that is discovered. The limited partners' money is used for drilling exploratory wildcat wells, but after a well comes in, it should be the responsibility of the general partners to drill the development wells that will determine the size of the field.
4. The recovery of the costs involved should be clearly stated. That is, the limited partners should recover their costs of drilling a successful exploratory well *before* they have to share any of the income from that well with the general partners. By the same token, the general partners should recover their costs of drilling a successful development well *before* they have to share any of the income from that well with the limited partners.

5. After recovery of the costs, the division of income from all of the producing wells (the limited partners' exploratory wells and the general partners' development wells) should be in favor of the limited partners. A favorable split would be 60 percent for the limited partners and 40 percent for the general partners, and for a good reason. If no oil or gas is found, the limited partners will have put up all of the money for the program, and the general partners will have put up none because they are required to drill wells only *after* an oil or gas field is discovered.

6. The general partners' charges should be limited to 20 percent of the amount of money invested by the limited partners. This assures that 80 percent of the money invested will be spent in drilling for oil and gas.

7. The general partners should not be able to make any money unless oil and/or gas is discovered.

The limited partner in an oil and gas exploration limited partnership should realize that he is essentially playing a numbers game, because only one wildcat well out of ten comes in as a commercially productive well. Therefore the objective of the partnership should be to raise enough money to drill approximately fifty wells.

The limited partner receives two tax deductions which may be used to reduce other ordinary income.

Most of the expenses incurred in oil and gas exploration are intangible, and they may be taken as a tax deduction. These expenses are for wages, fuel, hauling, and the supplies that are necessary for the drilling and preparation of a well for production. The investor may deduct intangible drilling costs up to a maximum of 100 percent of his investment. (The investment for each limited partner is a minimum of $5,000.)

The second tax deduction is for the oil depletion allowance. The theory behind the depletion allowance for oil is similar to the depreciation deduction for real estate. Oil and natural gas when taken from the ground will eventually be dissipated, or depleted. Some day the source will dry up. When it does, there should be enough money set aside to drill another well. The depletion allowance for independent oil producers is 15 percent of the first 1,000 barrels of oil a day. In a limited partnership each partner is considered to be an independent producer.

The second way to invest in oil and gas limited partnerships is through an income fund. In this type of program the general partners do not drill wells at all. The capital of the partnership is invested primarily in fully developed *producing* oil and gas properties for the purpose of providing an income that is comparable to, or better than, other income investments. The income is not tax deductible, but it is reduced by the amount of the depletion allowance.

The best way for an individual to invest in real estate is to buy units in a real estate limited partnership, or shares in a real estate investment trust. The cost of real estate and the interest on the mortgage are too high for the average person.

The individual investor, too, does not have the necessary expertise or the time to find desirable properties. Nor does he or she have sufficient money to diversify, or the ability to properly manage real estate, which is one of the keys to selling later at a profit.

With the professional management that is available from the general partners of a limited partnership, and the results that they have been able to achieve, it is hard to make a case for the individual investor to invest in real estate on his own.

Oil and gas limited partnerships that have as their avowed purpose exploration for oil and gas should not be considered by an investor unless he wants to deliberately speculate in the hope of receiving unusual profits. The investor should also be economically able to stand a loss of 100 percent of his original investment.

13

Stockbrokers

OVER 42 MILLION PEOPLE own stocks and bonds in the United States. They buy them from approximately 300,000 registered representatives of the big commission houses, such as E. F. Hutton and Dean Witter-Reynolds, and from hundreds of independent broker/dealers. Obviously a great many people trust stockbrokers when making their investments. But it is an open question how much of this trust is justified.

Most registered representatives have faith in the daily and weekly recommendations of the research department of their home office. They feel that the due diligence department of their particular firm (which is the trade name for research) is the best available, which is why they are working for that particular commission house or independent broker/dealer. But here, too, that faith is too often not warranted.

Those who trusted their broker and bought J. David & Co. (briefly mentioned in Chapter 1) lost $100 million in fraudulent currency trading. A loss of this magnitude made headlines in the *San Francisco Examiner*.

The article went on to say that the promise of enormous profits in the little-known world of international currency trading prompted fifteen hundred investors to place their faith and more than $100 million in the hands of J. David Dominelli.

The Securities and Exchange Commission and the U.S.

Attorney's office investigated the cause of the collapse of J. David & Co., the company name under which Dominelli operated. A federal grand jury looked into possible tax-law violations and fraud.

It turned out that Dominelli, forty-three years old, a Marine veteran and a former securities salesman, was possibly the only one who knew where all the cash went. Part of it did go into high living, purchasing expensive homes, luxury cars, and gifts for his partner and live-in girl friend—who had enough money to make a personal loan of $130,000 to a former Del Mar mayor, Nancy Hoover.

Subsequent articles in the *Examiner* disclosed that Dominelli fled to Plymouth, Montserrat, in the Caribbean to escape prosecution, but was subsequently extradited and brought back to the United States and jailed, first in Miami, and later in San Diego, where he faced charges of fraud and conspiracy.

Nor was this all of the story, for several prominent brokerage firms were sued by disgruntled investors for misrepresenting to them the performance of J. David & Co. in the currency trading market. At this writing it is anybody's guess as to how much, if any, of the $100 million will be recovered.

If articles like this don't throw a scare into you, I don't know what will. It even made me nervous, and I'm in the investment business.

Here is another headline taken from the *San Francisco Chronicle* just a month or so later:

TAX FRAUD TRIAL OPENS FOR FIVE SENTINEL TRADERS

Five Wall Street secutities traders contrived false tax losses for their celebrity customers who claimed $130 million in deductions on their income tax returns.

All five were executives of Sentinel Financial Instruments and Sentinel Government Securities who went on trial in one of the biggest tax fraud cases ever tried in the United States.

Their wealthy customers included television producer

Norman Lear, actor Sidney Poitier, composer Henry Mancini, New York TV weatherman Storm Field, and many prominent business executives.

Be assured that none of these prominent individuals was prosecuted. They were not accused of wrongdoing, but their tax returns were introduced as evidence in the trial, and certainly their tax deductions were disallowed. Lear, for example, earned $4.3 million in the year in question, and put in for a $1.8 million deduction through his investments with Sentinel. In this case very prominent people trusted the wrong stockbrokers.

At the conclusion of the trial, Judge Richard Owen of the District Court in Manhattan, New York, sentenced Michael Senft, forty-four, founder of the two Sentinel companies, to fifteen years in prison and fined him $80,000. Walter Orchard, thirty-five, of Somers, New York, former head tax trader for both companies, was sentenced to a four-year prison term and ordered to pay a fine of $15,000. Two other convicted executives were sentenced at a later date.

The commission houses in these transactions were among the biggest and most trusted in the United States. And these examples are only two out of many similar stories that could have been mentioned. In view of this, the individual investor should view the recommendations of a stockbroker, if not with apprehension, certainly with skepticism and considerable caution. It is difficult to believe in the competence of a research department that is unable to uncover fraud, much less make a recommendation of a fraudulent company to its customers.

The brokerage community also conducts its business in a manner that encourages you to make a snap judgment. Obviously this is not the best way to make a decision on an investment that quite often involves thousands of dollars. A registered representative of a commission house seldom leaves his or her office. Business is conducted almost entirely over the telephone. For example, let's say you are busy at work and your registered representative calls you.

"Tom?" he queries.

"Yes, it is," you reply.

"This is Joe Blow, your stockbroker. You got a minute?" You really don't, but you'll listen. "What do you have in mind, Joe?"

"You know your two oil stocks? Well, they're not going anywhere, as you probably know. Our research boys in New York feel you should get out of oils, considering the current world oil glut. We think you should be in retail trade right now and are recommending Sears. What do you say?"

Since you are busy, you make a fast decision. After all, you have to trust somebody, and you don't know too much about stocks. It's not your business.

"OK, Joe," you reply, "if you think Sears is a good buy, go ahead."

This is not a sound way to buy securities, in a two-minute telephone conversation with your registered representative. Yet this is the way stocks are traded, thousands of times all over the country, during the normal course of a stock market day.

And who sold you the two badly performing oil stocks in the first place? Your stockbroker friend, Joe, of course.

Now I realize that the stock market has a tremendous attraction. Its fascination rests with the possibility of making a lot of money in a hurry. If you can only choose the right stock at the right time, it's possible for it to go up in price in a few short months by as much as 50 percent, or even 100 percent. This is certainly preferable to bank interest. And if you are using other people's money with a margin account, the result can be even more spectacular. You can even trade in puts and calls, or options, and possibly make a killing.

So if you want to speculate in the stock market to make a fast dollar, go ahead. It's not as bad as gambling in Las Vegas, and your chances of success are better; but you should realize, as in Nevada, not too many people attain their objective.

Stocks are also bought, not for speculation, but as sound investments. When fifteen hundred wealthy people were polled about their favorite investment, they said they preferred growth common stocks or growth mutual funds. But you can be sure that when they bought them, they didn't buy them on rumors or hunches, or because of a short telephone conversation with their broker.

They bought them after careful analysis, with the objective of holding them for a reasonable period of time.

Whether you intend to speculate or invest conservatively, you should, as with real estate, protect yourself from placing too much trust in others by knowing as much as you can about securities.

At the risk of being too elementary, let's understand that you can invest in American industry in three different ways. You can buy common stocks, preferred stocks, or bonds. When you buy common stock, you become a part owner of the business, thereby taking a risk. If the business prospers, the stock will go up in value and the quarterly dividends will be good. Then you have made a wise investment. If the stock doesn't go up and the dividends are just fair, then you have made a mediocre investment. If the stock goes down, stays down, and the dividends are zero, then you will have made a poor investment. Or, if you are really unfortunate, you could lose your entire investment if the business is declared bankrupt. If that should happen, the bondholders get paid first; the preferred stockholders get paid second; and the common stockholders divide what is left.

Investors buy common stock for the quarterly dividend, if any, and for the possible appreciation in price. Of the two, the opportunity for a profit is the stronger motive. Over the long term, both stock prices and dividends have kept abreast of inflation.

There are two basic types of common stock. They are either blue-chip stocks or growth stocks.

For a corporation to have its stock classified as a blue chip, it must be a leader in a major industry, such as food, automobiles, or electronics, with an unbroken record of paying dividends during good times and bad, and with the prospect of being able to continue to do so.

A growth stock is usually a younger company, with a better-than-average increase in the price of its stock over a relatively short period of time. Earnings should be compounding at an unusually high rate, 30 percent per year, and more. It should be a leader in the right growth industry at the right time. And herein lies the problem. You must have the luck, the intuition, or the ability to make the right choice.

When buying stocks, you should not trade them frequently, although at first it might seem to be the best way to make a profit. The seasoned individual investor, and the professional, buy to hold for at least a year, and most of the time for several years.

A recent survey covering a period of ninety-one years disclosed that if an investor sold within one to five years, a profit was made approximately 60 percent of the time. But if the sale was made after ten years, the chance for a profit increased to 84 percent; and if the sale was made after twenty years, the profit percentage increased to 94 percent.

The prices of common stocks are quoted every day in the newspapers; therefore a word of caution. If daily price fluctations are going to get you upset, stay out of the market. Knowing what your investments are worth every day of the week can be very upsetting to some people.

Also, suffering through bear markets and bull markets can be hard on the nerves.

A bull market exists when the broad trend of the market is up and has been on this upward trend for some time. Most of the economic indicators, such as the gross national product, the number of people employed, corporation profits, personal income, total savings, and the availability of credit, are favorable. A general optimism prevails. The volume of shares traded on the stock exchanges is high and has a broad base, meaning that most of the issues listed are participating in the rise. The number of issues reaching new highs for the year is impressive, and the number reaching new lows is small. A bull market will last for several years. Normally the rise is not spectacular but steady. There are, of course, fluctuations as it goes along, when the market averages will temporarily decline, which is the unnerving part.

It would be good to know when a bull market is coming to a close because that would be the time for you to sell and, by having your money in a cash position, wait out the subsequent down market. Then when the market bottoms out (gradual leveling of market prices after a long and steep decline), you could again invest at much lower prices. Unfortunately even the professionals have a hard time doing this.

A bear market exists when the market is going down rather abruptly over a period of many months. Usually future business conditions and the international scene appear unfavorable. Unfortunately the general market quite often anticipates this future condition by as much as six months and starts going down before the individual investor is aware of what is happening. Profits and earnings are still reported as good and everyone is optimistic. Nevertheless, the future is not bright. It is this inability to foresee the future bad times that gives so few people the insight to know that a bear market is forming and that it is time to sell and wait for improved market conditions. While the topping out of a bull market is very difficult to determine even for the professionals, the bottoming out of a bear market is more obvious. This is because the downturn is already a matter of record. The market averages have already gone down 20–35 percent, and many individual issues will have gone down more. It is simply a matter of deciding when they have stopped declining. Investors who stay with a bear market suffer appreciable losses, at least on paper. The point at which the general market hits bottom will not be apparent immediately. If it doesn't go any lower over a period of several months, in spite of continued bad news about general business conditions, it might be reasonable to conclude that the bear market is over.

What yardsticks should an investor use in evaluating common stocks? There are enough books on the subject to fill a library. The most common yardstick is the price-earnings ratio, which is used so widely that it is quoted in daily newspapers along with the stock prices. This ratio is determined by dividing the current market price of a share of stock by its earnings. For example, if the current market price is $80 per share and its earnings for the previous year $4, the price-earnings ratio would be 20 to 1 (80 divided by 4).

For stocks in general, a price-earnings ratio of 10 to 1 is considered to be low. On the other hand, a growth stock with a price-earnings ratio of 30 to 1, while considered to be high, is not necessarily excessive.

Stock market averages are also used as a yardstick. While they primarily show the price level of the entire market, the averages are also used in evaluating individual issues. If the general market is relatively high, it might be a good idea not to buy at all.

The oldest and best known of the averages is the Dow Jones Industrial Average (DJIA). The DJIA is an index consisting of 30 industrial stocks that are considered by Dow Jones to be sufficiently representative of what the market is doing as a whole. This index dates from 1884 when Charles Henry Dow added together the trading prices of 11 industrial stocks and divided the sum total by eleven. Over the intervening years the composite stocks have changed so that now they are thirty in number, with only two left of the original eleven. Today, to compensate for the numerous stock splits that have taken place over the years, instead of dividing by 30, a divisor of 1.132 is currently used.

In addition to the DJIA, Dow Jones publishes an average for 20 transportation stocks, 15 utilities, 65 common stocks, and 40 bonds. Other stock market averages that are also widely watched are Standard and Poor's Index of 500 common stocks, the New York Stock Exchange Index of the average price of all stocks listed on its exchange, and the American Stock Exchange Index.

During the stock market crash in 1929, the Dow Jones Industrial Average plummeted from 381.17 to a low of 41.22 in 1932. By 1946 it was back up to 163.12, and then went on over the next twenty years to a high of 1,000 in 1966, only to fall back to near disaster to below 650 in May of 1970. Again it recovered, only to fall badly in October of 1974, when it went below 600. But once more, as the stock market has a habit of doing, the DIJA came back in 1976 to go over the magical mark of 1,000, only to decline again to 776.92, on August 12, 1982. On that date the stock market started its most spectacular short-term rise in its history. From a DJIA of 776.92 on August 12, it went to a high of 1151.12 in March of 1983.

Individual stocks, of course, do not necessarily follow the averages. Over a long term some of them can spectacularly out-perform any cross section of the market. Listed on the following pages is the performance of 35 well-known stocks over a 56-year period, from 1928 to 1983. This figure assumes an initial investment of $10,000 in each of the 35 companies, with all dividends taken in cash. You might want to look at the first page to test your ability to choose the top performer, then move on to page 2. Note that the performance of the top 11 companies was truly remarkable, for the investor's original investment in each of them was worth more than $100,000 at the end of 1983. The leader, Coca-Cola, was worth over $500,000! Note also that if an investor had invested in the bottom two stocks, the original investment of $10,000 would have been worth less than $10,000 at the end of 1983.

The individual investor should decide on his objectives before investing in the stock market. He should not do as the man did in the famous quotation by Stephen Leacock, "He flung himself upon his horse and rode madly off in all directions."

Certainly a young couple in their thirties should have a different objective from a widow or a retired couple or, for that matter, a person who is only a few years away from retirement. Those investors who are trying for maximum appreciation should be young and have time on their side. If they should lose, they could always save again. Widows and retired people should have as their objective maximum income consistent with safety.

After deciding on objectives, the next step is to choose a

Test Your Skill as an INVESTOR

Hindsight is better than foresight.
Let's go back to March 1, 1928 and pick the five stocks from this list
of well known U.S. corporations that you think would have proven
to have been the best investments through the years.
Put $10,000 in each of the five stocks you picked......
Then...turn the page to see your results...

Dow Jones Industrial Stocks	March 1, 1928 Invest
Allied Chemical	$10,000
Aluminum Company of America	10,000
American Brands	10,000
American Can	10,000
American Telephone & Telegraph	10,000
Bethlehem Steel	10,000
Coca Cola	10,000
Chrysler	10,000
DuPont	10,000
Eastman Kodak	10,000
Esmark	10,000
Exxon	10,000
Firestone	10,000
General Electric	10,000
General Foods	10,000
General Motors	10,000
Goodyear Tire & Rubber	10,000
Hershey Foods	10,000
International Harvester	10,000
International Nickel	10,000
International Paper	10,000
International Telephone & Telegraph	10,000
Kraft Cheese	10,000
Nabisco	10,000
Procter & Gamble	10,000
RCA	10,000
Sears, Roebuck	10,000
Singer Manufacturing	10,000
Standard Oil of California	10,000
Texaco	10,000
Union Carbide	10,000
United Technologies	10,000
U.S. Steel	10,000
Westinghouse Electric	10,000
Woolworth	10,000

Common Stock Investing Does Require Skill

Stock	Original Investment Mar. 1, 1928	Value* Dec. 31, 1983
Coca-Cola	$10,000	$507,423
Eastman Kodak	10,000	312,654
Hershey Foods	10,000	304,324
Goodyear Tire & Rubber	10,000	288,363
Procter & Gamble	10,000	278,603
Exxon	10,000	245,922
Sears Roebuck	10,000	245,729
General Electric	10,000	228,331
International Paper	10,000	174,910
Standard Oil of California	10,000	165,243
Firestone	10,000	163,728
Aluminum Company of America	10,000	158,581
Texaco	10,000	150,808
United Technologies	10,000	131,781
Kraft Cheese	10,000	124,524
Westinghouse Electric	10,000	109,389
DuPont	10,000	103,986
General Motors	10,000	82,305
Union Carbide	10,000	81,850
General Foods	10,000	67,909
RCA	10,000	67,661
Esmark	10,000	65,076
American Brands	10,000	64,802
Bethlehem Steel	10,000	64,524
American Telephone & Telegraph	10,000	41,127
Chrysler	10,000	39,482
Allied Chemical	10,000	35,900
Nabisco	10,000	24,563
International Telephone & Telegraph	10,000	21,337
U.S. Steel	10,000	20,215
Woolworth	10,000	14,701
International Harvester	10,000	12,224
American Can	10,000	12,212
International Nickel	10,000	9,030
Singer Manufacturing	10,000	6,321

*It was assumed that the full $10,000 was invested in each stock and that fractional shares were purchased where required to use up the full amount. No brokerage charges were included in the cost. Adjustments were made for all stock splits and stock dividends. No adjustments for cash distributions have been taken into consideration.

broker. You can only buy securities from someone who is registered with the Securities and Exchange Commission. You should choose three old-line firms that are members of the New York and American stock exchanges, the largest in the country. Tell the manager of each of these stockbrokerage firms that you want to be assigned to a registered representative who has been at least five years in the business. Remember that you have sought them out, they have not found you; therefore you have the right to ask for someone who is experienced.

After your conversation with each of these three representatives, decide which one gave you the most information, treated you right, and in whom you felt you could have the greatest confidence. Then go back to him or her and sign a cash agreement, which is a standard form for opening an account with a broker. You are now in a position to invest.

Information about the history of the New York Stock Exchange is also helpful. When the United States was a young nation, huge amounts of capital were needed to finance industrial expansion. Iron ore and copper had to be discovered and mined, steel mills had to be founded, and factories built. After the discovery of gold in California, there was a need for telegraphic communication between the east and west coasts. Railroads had to be built to take the place of covered wagons and the sailing ships that took months to round the tip of South America and make the long voyage north to San Francisco.

The young burgeoning corporations turned to the general public to obtain the necessary money by offering ownership in their companies in the form of common stock. The only way this vast demand for funds could be met was through a central marketplace, where investors could buy and sell stocks and bonds, which represented the money they had invested.

On May 17, 1782, over fifty years before gold was discovered in California, twenty-four farseeing businessmen and auctioneers agreed to meet at the same time every day under an old buttonwood tree on Wall Street to handle the public's orders in stocks and bonds. The following year the Tontine Coffee House was built, and the men moved inside. Thus was born the New York Stock Exchange. During the first half of the nineteenth century its location was changed a dozen times, until finally it was housed on Broad Street, where it has been ever since. The present building was built in 1903. Today the NYSE has close to fifteen hundred members, most of them partners or officers of over four hundred stock-brokerage firms who execute orders for their companies on the floor of the exchange amounting to millions of shares every trading day.

The investor in securities has to have faith in the future of America. In a few years it will be the twenty-first century. The changes that will take place in the American economy, mainly because of technology, the myriad of new products that will be available, and the growth of the gross national product (which is the sum of all the goods and services in the United States in one year), will be astonishing. There is nothing nebulous about the long-term growth of America, and most Americans don't doubt her future. The United States is the most powerful nation on earth. We arrived at world leadership at the end of World War II, only a short forty years ago. In the light of history, America should retain its leadership for another two hundred years. The increase in the national wealth has been phenomenal. In some years its *increase* has been equal to the entire production of Canada.

To protect the investor who invests in American corporations, common stockholders have certain preemptive rights.

1. The right to hold and transfer stock certificates.
2. The right to receive corporate reports, such as semiannual and annual financial statements.
3. The right to vote at stockholders' meetings. If you don't want to exercise this right personally (and most people don't), companies will mail you a proxy statement, and you can authorize someone else to cast your vote for you.

4. The right to receive dividends as declared by the board of directors.
5. The right to participate in any new stock offering.
6. The right to share in the assets of the corporation if it is dissolved.

Stockbrokerage firms are called commission houses for the obvious reason that they charge a commission for executing orders to buy and sell securities, a part of which is paid to their registered representatives. An order for 100 shares is called a round-lot order, and an order for less than 100 shares, an odd-lot order. You have to pay a penalty for an odd-lot order of ⅛ of a point, or 12.5 cents per share for a stock that sells at $55 per share or less, and ¼ of a point, or 25 cents a share, for a stock selling at more than $55.

Commissions are negotiable, and because of competition they are about the same from one brokerage firm to another. The investor should plan on paying about 1 percent of the amount of money invested to buy a stock, and about 1 percent to sell. For those investors shopping for a bargain, there are discount houses. They charge as little as 25 percent of what it costs to do business with the regular brokerage firms, but you don't receive any information, advice, or service. For the experienced investor who makes his own decisions, the discount houses are a cheap and convenient way to buy and sell securities. A telephone call will place your order, and it's executed in a matter of minutes.

Either way, the broker will send you a confirmation of your purchase, which tells you how many shares you bought or sold, the price, the commission charged, and the taxes, if any. Also included will be the trading date and the settlement date. The trading date is the date the stock was bought or sold. The settlement date is the date you must pay for the stock or, if you sold it, the date your broker owes you. Currently the settlement date is five business days after the trading date.

Before you place an order to buy a stock, you should learn

as much as you can about the corporation and its management. Besides information supplied by your broker and the investment services, no one should buy a stock without first analyzing the latest annual statement of the company. Corporations publish these reports to provide financial information to their shareholders, and federal law requires them to do so.

There are two major parts to an annual report: the balance sheet and the income statement. The balance sheet is a listing of what is owned and what is owed by a company on a specific date. The income statement is a summary of the income and the expenses of the company for a definite period of time, usually a year. It is obvious that both reports are important to an investor. Is the company making money, and is it worth anything? Certainly a prudent investor would like to know the answer to both questions.

In addition, most firms include in their annual report a ten-year financial summary in very easy to understand form. You should have such information before you invest.

Sixteen Rules for Investing in Common Stocks

BEFORE YOU INVEST

1. *Commit just a percentage of your excess cash to stocks.* Many stockbrokers recommend only 50 percent. This may be too little or not enough; it depends upon your finances and what you think of existing market conditions. At any rate, it is sound advice not to invest it all.
2. *Buy on facts, not on rumors or hunches.* Never invest unless you have seen the latest annual financial statement of the company. No matter how much you trust your broker, a recommendation over the telephone that you invest in a stock that you don't know much about is not good enough.

3. *Set your sights high.* Try for 50 percent in one year. You probably won't get it, but you certainly won't if the stock doesn't have a ghost of a chance of doing that well. If you only realize 25 percent, you will double your money in four years.

4. *Come to grips with the fact that no speculative investment is a sound investment.* If you are deliberately speculating, you should stand ready to lose everything. Speculation should be reserved for the young, for they have time on their side. If they lose, they can start all over again.

5. *Avoid short-term trading.* If you trade frequently your broker will love you, but your pocketbook won't. People who make money in the market hold their stocks for several years. It takes time for money to make money.

6. *Long-term trading is a must.* The time has gone by when you could buy blue-chip stocks, put them in your safe deposit box, and years later find yourself wealthy. The economic times are too volatile, especially in this age of high technology.

7. *Invest in stocks for growth, not dividends, when you are still years away from retirement.* Those companies that pay out most of their earnings in dividends have little left for expansion. Research and capital investment is the name of the game if you want your stocks to go up. Research provides new products for the company to sell. Investment in new plant and equipment modernizes these facilities, which increases production. Top management helps, too, witness the remarkable recovery from near bankruptcy of the Chrysler Corporation after Lee Iacocca became president.

8. *Invest in stocks that pay high dividends, like utilities, if you are retired or close to retirement.* This is the other side of the coin from the advice given in rule seven.

9. *Look at a stock's potential, not its high price.* Many investors will not buy a stock whose price is over $100 a share. Remember, there is no such thing as a too high-priced stock (in terms of dollars) if its potential for growth is good.

10. *Buy a stock only when it is going up in price, never at any other time.* Risk in the stock market is all on the down side. It is true if you wait until a stock starts up, you will miss part of the rise. But if the stock is a good buy, there will be plenty of profit left.

AFTER YOU INVEST

1. *Supervise your investments all of the time.* Don't be so busy that you forget to monitor the market, and be aware of how your stocks are faring. Many people make a lot of money and do a miserable job of investing their excess cash because they say they don't have the time. Don't you be one of them.

2. *Diversify your investments.* It's one of the soundest investment principles around. Don't put all your eggs in one basket. All of us have heard of that rule. It's a good one.

3. *Dollar cost average in a stock only when it is going up, never when it is going down.* A stockbroker will advise you to double up on your investment when a stock has gone down. This way, he says, you will reduce your average cost per share. It's true, you will. But why throw good money after bad? Why stay with a loser? Admit you were wrong and get out; don't buy more.

4. *Reinvest all of your dividends while you are still employed.* You are probably saving the income on your bank accounts, and in your money market funds; why not on stocks? Over 1,300 corporations will arrange for you to automatically buy more of their stock with your

dividends, and at no commission. It's a great way to build a stock portfolio.

5. *Sell high and buy low.* We would all like to do that. But don't be too greedy. Don't try to sell at the very top of a bull market. You never will, unless you're lucky. Be satisfied to sell when you have a fine profit. What you don't want to do is the opposite, which is to ride a bear market down, get disgusted, and sell at a loss.

6. *Get rid of bad stocks.* Everyone makes a bad investment once in a while. Too err is human, and this is never more true than in the marketplace. Never for any reason ride a bad stock down. It will kill you. Admit you were wrong and get out.

Preferred Stock

The second way to invest in American industry is to buy preferred stock. Note that it is still a stock, but it has preferential treatment in that its dividends must be paid first before the common stockholder receives anything; and in the event the corporation is dissolved, the preferred stockholder has a claim on the assets ahead of the common stockholder.

The preferred stockholder also receives a stated amount of dividends. The par value is usually $100 a share, and has considerably more significance than the par value of a common stock (which is usually no more than a bookkeeping entry). If a company issues a 6 percent preferred stock, the dollar amount of that dividend relates to its par value. If the par value is $100, then $6 will be paid. If the par value is $25, however, then a 6 percent preferred stock will pay 6 percent of $25, or $1.50. If a preferred stock doesn't have a par value, then the amount of the dividend will not be expressed in terms of a percentage, but in terms of a dollar, such as $5.

The dividends must come from profits. If there are no profits, the board of directors has the right to pass the dividend. The company has no obligation to pay dividends on the stock, common or preferred, such as it has with debts of the company. Preferred stockholders cannot force a corporation into receivership, for they do not have any of the rights of creditors, or of bondholders (who are also creditors). Preferred stockholders do not have any of the preemptive rights enjoyed by common stockholders. Preferred stocks do have, however, features that are peculiar to them; they may be participating, callable, convertible, or cumulative.

Participating preferred stockholders participate in the profits with the common stockholders under certain conditions. Usually the stated preferred dividend is paid first, then the common stockholder is paid (in a stated amount), and then both stockholders share equally in any dividends that are declared by the board of directors after that.

Owners of *callable preferred stock* are subject to having their stock redeemed, at a certain time and at a certain price, at the option of the company, usually at a premium above their par value. For example, a $100 preferred stock may be callable at $105. Corporations issue this type of preferred stock because they want to have the option to retire the issue at some time in the future. The corporation's charter states the terms under which it may call its preferred stock and the earliest date at which it may exercise this option.

Stockholders who hold *convertible preferred stock* have the right to exchange it for the common stock of the company under certain conditions. The option of exercising this privilege is left up to them. This feature is offered when, in the opinion of the company's underwriter, it must be included in order to make the stock more attractive.

For example, let us say that some time ago you purchased a convertible preferred stock at a price of $105, with the right to convert this into five shares of common stock after a certain date. If at any time after that date, the price of the common stock is quoted at $21 per share there would be no reason for you to exercise the conversion privilege. If you did you would have, after the conversion, five shares of common stock worth

$105 instead of one share of preferred stock also worth $105. You would have gained nothing, and at the same time you would have lost the fixed yield on your preferred stock. Anytime the common stock is selling at $21, or below, you would not exercise your conversion privilege.

However, if the common stock should go up to, say, $30 per share, you could convert and buy five shares for $105, which would immediately be worth five times $30, or $150. You could then sell them in the open market and make approximately 50 percent on your investment.

A *cumulative preferred stock* provides that all dividends that are in arrears accumulate, and this amount must be paid before the common stockholders can receive anything. Great care should be exercised, however, when buying cumulative preferred stock to obtain the dividends that are in arrears. The board of directors passed these dividends because the company was in financial difficulty. One has to be convinced that the company is recovering so it will be able to pay all of the arrears on its cumulative preferred stock when the company is again profitable.

A very large firm, such as a utility corporation, sometimes has several series of preferred stock. These are differentiated from one another by being called by such names as first preferred, second preferred, prior preferred, or preferred A and preferred B, because they were originally offered to the public at varying dates and under different conditions of the money market. They could differ materially in their rate of return, and in their prior claim on assets if the corporation should be dissolved.

The prices of preferred stocks fluctuate, but for a different reason than common stocks. Because of their set rate of return, they fluctuate inversely as to interest rates. If interest rates go up, preferred stock prices go down, and if interest rates go down, preferred stock prices go up. The time to buy them is when the dividend they pay is historically high. But always remember that you buy preferred stock because you want income.

Bonds

The third way to invest in American industry is to buy bonds. A corporate bond pays interest and is evidence of a debt of the corporation. It is almost always issued at a face value of $1,000. The following three facts should be remembered about bonds.

1. A bond is an evidence of a debt.
2. The corporation issuing the bond is a borrower.
3. The investor purchasing a bond is a creditor.

A bond states the issuer's promise to pay the lender the face amount of the bond at a specified time known as the maturity date. It also promises to pay interest on the principal of the loan at a specified rate. Failure of the issuer to pay either the principal or the interest when due constitutes a legal default; therefore legal action may be taken by the bondholder to force payment.

Bonds are known as senior securities, and stocks as junior securities. The term "senior" is used to describe bonds because bondholders have a prior legal claim over the common and preferred stockholders on both the income and the assets of a corporation. The bondholders must be paid their interest in full before the stockholders are entitled to receive any dividends. In the event the firm is dissolved, the bondholders must be paid their principal before the stockholders are entitled to receive any of the assets of the corporation.

Sometimes bonds are better understood when stocks and bonds are compared to real estate. One could think of common stocks as property owned, and bonds as a mortgage on the property. Dividends on the common stocks could be considered as net rent, and the interest on the bonds as interest on the mortgage.

The bond market at first glance seems simple. On the contrary, understanding bonds is more difficult than comprehending common stocks. There are hundreds of thousands of bonds, and their value depends upon the credit rating of the corporation involved, which is not easy to ascertain. It therefore behooves the investor to know as much as he can about bonds.

There are three different types of corporate bonds, differentiated by the kind of collateral they offer as security, the way they pay the interest, and the manner in which they pay the principal.

The collateral behind bonds is often a mortgage on the real estate or the equipment that the corporation owns. If it's a mortgage on the real estate, the collateral can be one of two kinds: a first mortgage on a particular piece of property, or a general mortgage on all of the fixed capital assets of the corporation.

If the mortgage is on the equipment, it is called an equipment trust certificate. Airlines and railroads are the companies that usually issue them. Jet aircraft cost millions of dollars each, and it is difficult for airlines to finance them by conventional methods. When equipment trust certificates are issued, the airlines pledge title to the aircraft to a trustee. The bondholders' interest is protected by having the bonds mature long before the equipment is fully depreciated in value. Railroads use the same borrowing method, offering their rolling stock as collateral.

Debenture bonds are issued by corporations with excellent credit because no collateral is required. A debenture is simply a promise to pay, similar to a personal promissory note. Investors are willing to buy these bonds without collateral because of the outstanding reputation of the company. For example, the American Telephone and Telegraph Company (especially before the split-up of that concern) has no difficulty borrowing money by issuing debentures.

Bonds that are classified according to the method by which they pay interest to the bondholder fall into three types. They are either income bonds, registered bonds, or coupon bonds (often referred to as bearer bonds).

Income bonds are a misnomer. One would assume that these bonds would guarantee the income, but they do not. Income bonds guarantee only the principal at maturity, with the interest being paid only when and if it is earned.

Registered bonds may be either fully registered or partly registered. When a bond is fully registered, the name and address of the owner of the bond is recorded on the books of the issuing corporation, with the owner's name also appearing on the face of the bond. Interest when it is due is mailed to the bondholder. The bond may be cashed at maturity, or transferred to someone else, only when it is properly endorsed.

When a bond is partly registered, the name and address of the owner are again listed on the company's books, and the owner's name appears on the face of the bond. But unlike the fully registered bond, a partly registered bond is registered for payment of the principal only, not the interest. The bond has coupons attached to it, and when interest is due the coupons are detached by the owner and presented to a bank teller for cashing. When the bond is cashed or transferred, however, it must be endorsed by the owner.

A coupon or bearer bond is not registered. Most corporate bonds are bearer bonds because investors prefer that type of ownership. Whoever is in possession of these bonds owns them and may transfer them to someone else without an endorsement; no owner's name appears on the face of them. Like partly registered bonds, coupons are attached to them for payment of the interest.

A word of warning. Great care has to be used in handling bearer bonds. If they should be lost, whoever has possession of them owns them, with no endorsement necessary. If you own bearer bonds, they should be kept in a safe deposit box.

There are several methods used for the eventual repayment of the principal to bondholders. Bonds can be sinking-fund bonds, serial bonds, callable bonds, or convertible bonds.

When sinking-fund bonds are issued, the corporation issuing them is required to set aside, at stated intervals, a specific sum of money for the purpose of retiring them. Sinking-fund bonds are issued originally to obtain the necessary funds to buy excessively expensive machinery, such as printing presses for newspapers. In order to have the necessary cash to redeem the bonds at maturity, the corporation has to accumulate the necessary amount over the course of many years.

Serial bonds mature at different times and on successive dates as specified by the serial numbers on the bonds. Those with the shortest maturity have the highest interest rate, and conversely those with the longest maturity have the lowest interest rate.

Callable bonds may be redeemed on or after a specific date at the option of the corporation. This is not a desirable feature as far as the investor is concerned because the company will call the bond only when it is in the best interests of the corporation to do so. For example, when existing conditions of the money market allow the company to borrow money for less interest than called for by the bonds, then the corporation would probably redeem them. When a company calls the bonds, it is known as a refunding operation.

Convertible bonds may be converted into another type of security, usually common stock, at the option of the holder during a specified period of time. Because of their convertible privilege, these bonds have some of the profit potential of common stocks.

Bonds, like common and preferred stocks, are quoted in the daily newspapers and in the *Wall Street Journal*. This is because they are seldom worth their original purchase price of $1,000 per bond. And for a very good reason. Their prices vary inversely as to interest rates. When interest rates go up, bond prices go down; and when interest rates go down, bond prices go up.

To illustrate: let us say you own a $1,000 bond that pays 8 percent, and long-term interest rates rise to 12 percent. Under these conditions your 8 percent bond will no longer command a market price of $1,000. It will go down in value because no one will pay the face value for a bond that yields 8 percent when they can obtain 12 percent elsewhere. If you want to sell the bond, you will have to sell it at a discount. On the other hand, if you own a bond yielding 8 percent, and long-term interest rates go down to 6 percent, you will be able to sell your bond for more than $1,000, or at a premium.

An investor may buy municipal bonds as well as corporate bonds. Municipal bonds—or municipals, as they are frequently called—are obligations of states, local governments and authorities. Bonds issued by a state are municipal bonds, and so are bonds issued by the Pennsylvania Turnpike (an authority) or school bonds issued by Podunk, which could be any small town in the United States.

Municipal bonds are bought mainly because the income from them is exempt from federal income taxes. This feature is important only to those who are in a high income tax bracket. If you are in a 40 percent tax bracket, for instance, a tax-exempt municipal bond that pays 9 percent is equivalent to a taxable interest of 15 percent. You determine this by dividing the tax-exempt portion of your income by the yield of the municipal bond (9 divided by 60 equals .15). Municipal bonds are subject to state income taxes, unless they are issued by the state in which the investor is domiciled.

The market price of a corporate or municipal bond is quoted in the daily newspapers and is expressed in two parts. The first part is a percentage in round figures of its face value, and the second part is a fraction of $10. For example, a bond that is quoted at 92 ⅜ is selling for $923.75. This is 92 percent of its face value which is $920, plus ⅜ of $10.00 which is $3.75. The total price of this bond is therefore $923.75.

Because a bond seldom sells for exactly $1,000, there are several ways of expressing its yield. The nominal yield is the interest that is stated on the face of the bond. This is the interest that is paid regardless of the bond's market value.

The current yield of a bond takes into consideration its market value. Current yield is the annual income of the bond divided by its current price. The current yield of an 8 percent bond that is selling for $920 is 8.695 percent (8 divided by 920).

The yield to maturity takes into consideration three things: the current yield, the market price, and the time period to maturity. For example, if you purchase a bond for $970 with a current yield of 10 percent, which matures in three years, your yield to maturity is 11 percent. This is because the bond matures for its face value in a known time period of three years. You will make an additional $30 in three years, or $10 a year, or 1 percent, which is added to the current yield.

The above example of yield to maturity is a rule-of-thumb method. It's not accurate because it fails to take into consideration the average cost of the bond to maturity, but we are not going into that. Brokerage firms have bond tables that compute this for you, if you really want to be that precise.

Bonds are rated by investment advisory services. The two best known are Moody's Investors Service and Standard & Poor's Corporation. These bonds are rated like a school paper: A, B, C, and D. Each letter is further divided into three parts, such as AAA, AA, and A. Triple A is the highest rating. Many experienced bond buyers will not buy a bond that is rated lower than A.

Mutual Funds

What is a mutual fund? It's a pool of money contributed by many people and invested by professional money managers in a cross section of American industry.

Arthur Wiesenberger and Company, the recognized authority on mutual funds, prefers a broader and longer definition: "It is a corporation or trust whose only business is the proper investment of its shareholders' money, generally in common stock, or a combination of stocks and bonds, in the hope of achieving a specific investment goal. It brings together the investable funds of many people with similar needs and purposes, and it undertakes to do a better job of investing those funds and managing the investments than the people, individually, could do for themselves."

So, if you don't have the interest or the time to invest in securities, you can buy mutual fund shares. Approximately 50 million people have invested billions of dollars in several hundred mutual funds. Because of their large number, it has become increasingly difficult to select the right investment company. Which one of the many fund managers are you going to trust with your money?

The only solution is for an investor to find out as much as he or she can about mutual funds before making a decision.

Mutual funds are either open-end or closed-end funds. An open-end fund continuously offers new shares to the investing public and redeems those shares anytime at their true or asset value. A closed-end fund does not actively sell its shares, nor does it stand ready to redeem them. The investor who buys a closed-end fund must purchase the shares from someone who already owns them. The funds of both types are bought through stockbrokerage firms or independent broker/dealers, just like stocks and bonds.

All mutual funds state their investment objectives in their official prospectus and accompanying approved sales literature. An investor should choose a fund whose stated goals most nearly coincide with his or her own. When considering objectives, mutual funds fall into two broad categories. They are either balanced funds or common stock funds.

A balanced fund invests in a combination of common stocks, preferred stocks, and bonds. The average mix is about 65 percent common stocks and 35 percent preferred stocks and bonds, with the percentage changing in response to how aggressive or defensive management wants to be at that particular time. The objectives of a balanced fund are to provide a reasonable return, conserve the value of the investments, and to achieve long-term appreciation on an investment rather than a speculative basis.

A common stock fund, as its name implies, invests all of its money in common stocks. But since common stocks have a

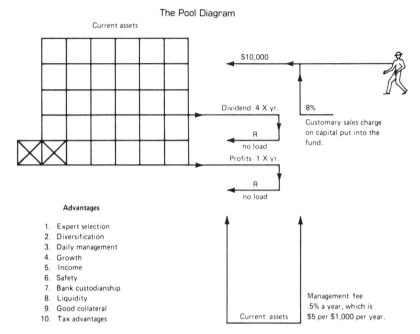

The Pool Diagram

Current assets

$10,000

Dividend 4 X yr.

R
no load

Profits 1 X yr.

R
no load

8%

Customary sales charge on capital put into the fund.

Advantages

1. Expert selection
2. Diversification
3. Daily management
4. Growth
5. Income
6. Safety
7. Bank custodianship
8. Liquidity
9. Good collateral
10. Tax advantages

Current assets

Management fee .5% a year, which is $5 per $1,000 per year.

range from blue-chip stocks to aggressive growth stocks, these funds are further divided into three groups: growth-income funds, growth funds, or maximum-appreciation funds. The name of each fund discloses its major objective.

A good way to explain how a mutual fund operates is by a pool diagram, which is illustrated above. The diagram also lists ten advantages of mutual funds.

The drawing in the upper right-hand corner represents an individual investor. Any sum of money (as low as $100) may be invested initially on the line where $10,000 is chosen as the opening amount. After the account is opened, some funds allow an additional investment as low as $10. The grid on the upper left portion of the pool diagram represents the investments in the portfolio. The two X's in the lower left corner of the grid show that a fund manager might delete an investment and add another.

The two arrows extending out to the right from the grid demonstrate that the funds pay a dividend four times a year, and a year-end capital gain distribution once a year. These may be received in cash, or reinvested at the option of the shareholder at no sales charge (explained later). The ten advantages of mutual funds are:

EXPERT SELECTION

Mutual funds have expert investment analysts and port-folio managers who work full time choosing investments that will meet the portfolio's objectives. They follow and chart the performance of several hundred stocks, utilizing the most modern computer techniques. No one is infallible, of course; therefore mutual fund managers do make errors, but for the most part they are minor.

DIVERSIFICATION

We have already extolled the virtues of this advantage.

DAILY MANAGEMENT

This is beyond the capabilities of the individual investor, busy as the average person is with the all-consuming task of just living, and making a living. Investments of a mutual fund portfolio are continuously being substituted for others to meet changing conditions, often adding as many as ten or twelve stocks, and eliminating as many more, all in the space of six months. Such activity on an intelligent basis can only be accomplished by professionals working full time.

GROWTH

Appreciation over the long term is the objective of the majority of mutual funds. The difference among them in the pursuit of this objective is the aggressiveness with which growth is pursued.

INCOME

How much income a mutual fund produces is influenced by the primary objective of that particular fund. If income is number one, then the investor should expect a good income. If maximum appreciation is the fund's main objective, then the investor should expect a low income.

SAFETY

Safety of a mutual fund is derived mainly from the first three advantages of expert selection, diversification, and daily professional management. While these three will not guarantee that the investor will not suffer a loss, especially in a bear market, they do considerably reduce the down-side risk inherent in securities. A mutual fund, like any other investment, does not guarantee the return *of* your money or a return *on* your money.

BANK CUSTODIANSHIP

This is one of the requirements of the Federal Investment Company Act of 1940. Mutual fund shares are *not* insured by an agency of the federal government, nor by anyone else. But bank custodianship of the assets of a mutual fund should give a feeling of security to the shareholder.

LIQUIDITY

An open-end mutual fund shareholder may redeem any or all of the shares anytime at their true asset value, which may or may not be what that individual paid for them.

GOOD COLLATERAL

Mutual fund shares are considered to be excellent collateral for a loan. Lenders view them more favorably than individual stocks because of a mutual fund's diversification and professional management.

TAX ADVANTAGES

They are small, but they do provide some tax relief. The dividends of a mutual fund qualify for the dividend exclusion, and the realized gains, if any, are entitled to the capital gain exclusion of 60 percent of the distribution.

The charges imposed for investing in a mutual fund are high when compared to investing in individual securities. When an investor opens a mutual fund account, and when he adds to it, there is a sales charge, which by federal law cannot be more than 9 percent of the amount invested. Because of the sales load a mutual fund investor must view his purchase as a long-term investment. Recovery of the sales charge can only be derived from an increase in the price per share.

The shareholder qualifies for a quantity discount of the sales load when he reaches a breakpoint. The amount of investment required to reach this point varies from fund to fund. It is granted most frequently at the $10,000 level. It is also granted by signing a letter of intention. For instance, a shareholder may invest initially only $5,000, but if he invests a total of $10,000 (the breakpoint amount) within the ensuing thirteen months (and the investor signed a letter of intent to that effect when he opened the account), then when this point is reached, the entire $10,000 (including the first $5,000) receives the reduced breakpoint sales load.

All funds charge a yearly management fee. This is ½ of 1 percent up to $250 million, with reductions in this percentage when the total assets of the fund surpass this figure.

There are also many no-load funds. They are purchased directly from the funds themselves. Since the investor never sees a salesman, the choice of which fund to buy is entirely up to him or her. For an experienced investor this might be a wise thing to do, since a case can be made that the performances of the load and no-load funds are strikingly similar.

But once again, because of the sheer numbers of no-load funds, the decision of whom to trust is again a problem.

The performance of mutual fund shares has to be viewed for positive results over at least a ten-year period. We admit this is a long time, which restricts investment in mutual funds to those who are fifty-five years of age and younger (assuming a retirement age of sixty-five. In examining the results of mutual funds over a shorter period, the record is not good enough to recommend that an investor consider a briefer term.

Long-term results are better, too, if one does not invest a large lump sum initially, but instead invests a modest $500 to open the account and then adds regularly at the rate of $100 a month. This is for two reasons. First, a modest initial amount eliminates the guesswork as to whether it is the right time or the wrong time to open a mutual fund account. Secondly, investing regularly (referred to as dollar cost averaging) reduces the average cost of all the shares purchased by automatically buying more shares in a down market, because the shareholder invests the same number of dollars each month regardless of price.

When reviewing the twenty-five-year results of a conservative common stock fund that has been in existence for over fifty years, whose management consistently buys stocks for their intrinsic value, we find that dollar cost averaging as described above has had excellent results. The amount invested over a twenty-five-year period is $30,400. There have been fifteen twenty-five-year periods starting with 1945 and ending in 1983. In this time the minimum result for the $30,400 invested was $104,317, and the best result was $192,906. This assumes, of course, that all of the quarterly dividends were reinvested in shares. This kind a result should be very gratifying to any investor.

Eight Guidelines for Investing in Mutual Funds

BEFORE YOU INVEST

1. Choose a mutual fund as carefully as you would an individual security. The fund's objectives, the length of time it has been in business, and its past performance are all important. But remember that past performance is only a guideline; it is not a guarantee of how well the fund will do in the future.
2. When making a single, large investment, timing is of the utmost importance. If at all possible, avoid making a sizable investment at the cresting of a bull market. It's better to wait in a cash position, even for a fairly long period of time, to avoid making a serious mistake. You may never recover from a single large mutual fund commitment made at too high a price.
3. If you are young and have only a small amount of money to invest initially, and you plan on saving regularly every month for many years, there is no better investment vehicle than a well-chosen growth-income or maximum-capital-appreciation fund.
4. If your heirs are inexperienced or too young, invest in mutual funds so they can inherit professional management and diversification which they might badly need. Don't leave your heirs too much cash. "Easy come, easy go" is an old saying, and never truer than when it is applied to an inexperienced younger generation. Cash is too easily and quickly spent, but your heirs might retain a sound investment.
5. If you have enough money, diversify management by buying several funds. Note that this guideline applies only to the wealthy.

AFTER YOU INVEST

1. Monitor your fund's performance as far as your individual account is concerned in relation to the record of other funds in its same category. You can easily do this by obtaining from the reference desk in your public library a copy of Wiesenberger Services' *Investment Companies*, which is the number one authority on mutual funds. This publication contains a wealth of information about mutual funds and their past performance. In addition, the publisher supplies a quarterly supplement of dividends, realized capital gains, and changes in asset value.
2. View your account as a liquid investment. You can't trade your mutual funds as you would stocks, particularly if you have a small account subject to the maximum sales charge. But you shouldn't stay with a badly performing mutual fund for years because you would have to pay another sales load if you shifted to another fund.
3. If you need part of your capital in a down market, don't liquidate your shares at a loss. In this situation, if an emergency arises where you need some or most of the money in your mutual fund, you should borrow at a bank, using your shares as collateral for the loan. Later, when the market goes back up, you can pay off the loan by selling the necessary number of shares in your account.

Money Market Mutual Funds

Money market mutual funds are a phenomenon of just the last ten years. In that period of time their growth has been spectacular; their assets have increased from $1.7 billion to over $250 billion, and the number of their shareholders from less than 2 million to approximately 50 million.

A money market fund invests in short-term credit obligations (three months to one year) that yield high interest and provide relative safety. They are not as safe as the money market accounts that are available at a bank because they are not insured by an agency of the federal government. Since an account may be opened for as little as $1,000, and thereafter added to in increments of $100, the small investor is able to obtain the high yields that were formerly available only to the affluent.

Money market mutual funds are of three types: general-purpose funds, broker/dealer funds, and institutional funds.

Mutual funds organizations offer the general-purpose funds, providing the usual service, plus catering basically to the small investor. Over one-half of the general-purpose fund shareholders view their accounts as a part of their long-term savings program, despite the fact that they are liquid and have the privilege of writing three checks a month free of charge. These funds mail a statement to the investor anytime there is an addition or a withdrawal from the account.

Broker/dealer mutual funds are available to a broker's customers. An investor who opens a broker/dealer mutual fund account is usually already a customer of that particular commission house and is using the mutual fund as a place to "park" money while he awaits a more favorable time to invest. Saving money is not the objective of shareholders of broker/dealer mutual funds. Short-term high yield and liquidity are the objectives. Because of the size of the average individual account, the broker/dealer mutual funds have a much larger share of the money market business.

Institutional mutual funds are also offered by broker/dealers. These are available only to large institutions such as pension funds, trust departments of banks, and insurance companies.

Money market mutual funds are also classified as to how they invest.

Diversified money market funds invest in all types of short-term obligations such as commercial and bank CD's, repurchase agreements, commercial paper, bankers' acceptances, Eurodollars, and U.S. Treasury bills and notes.

Single-purpose money market funds invest solely in U.S. Treasury obligations. The objective is not only high yield and liquidity, but the ultimate in security. Certainly nothing is safer than a promise to pay by the United States Treasury. In exchange for this greater security, however, investors in these funds sacrifice 1 or 2 percentage points in interest on their account. Under conditions of economic uncertainty, investors turn to the single-purpose mutual funds to obtain the greater safety they provide.

Tax-free money market mutual funds. These funds invest exclusively in tax-exempt bonds, thus providing the professional selection and diversification that the individual investor cannot obtain by investing in municipal bonds on his own.

Money market mutual funds are quoted in a separate list in the daily newspapers, usually just once a week. Price per share is not important because the investor buys at $1.00 per share and sells at $1.00 per share. What the list does show is the average maturity of the portfolio in number of days, the annualized yield for the previous seven-day period, and the annualized yield for the previous thirty-day period. The investor is thus able to compare the yield on his or her account with all other tax-free money market mutual funds to determine how well his or her particular fund is performing.

When investing in a mutual fund you place your trust in the management; therefore you should choose your mutual fund with care.

14

Financial
Planners

A FINANCIAL PLANNER is an investment representative
who analyzes your present financial situation, and then provides you with a written comprehensive plan on how to improve it.

He asks you to fill out a questionnaire that describes your
net worth, listing in detail your assets and liabilities. He
wants you to provide him, too, with your family relationships,
your present and probable future income, your age, and your
financial goals. He wants and needs a copy of your federal and
state income tax returns for the last three years; a copy of any
will, trust agreement, or divorce settlement; and copies of
your life and disability insurance policies.

After a careful analysis of all this information, he will submit a written plan for your financial future. It will include a
balance sheet of assets and liabilities, a cash-flow statement,
the client's financial objectives, the impact of taxes on earnings, and the client's tax bracket. No matter what the goal or
goals may be, an educational fund for the children, retirement
income, tax and estate planning, a method of achieving these
objectives will be submitted. It should be emphasized, however, that only the client can put the plan into action. If he or
she does not implement the plan (no matter how good it may
be), it is worthless, and the client has spent time and money
which is completely wasted.

Financial planning is an infant service industry with a lot

of growing pains. There is no government regulation, federal or state, of a financial planner, nor is any license required. Anyone connected with the financial services industry—an investment representative, an insurance agent, a banker, an accountant—can be a financial planner. As a consequence there is a wide spectrum of competence, from no ability to a very knowledgeable professional.

You hear a lot today, especially on television, about total financial planning. Sears, Roebuck will offer you a financial plan for $100. Stop by their financial booth, give them the information, and when you are through with your shopping they will provide you with a computerized plan. Such a computer analysis is practically worthless. Stockbrokerage firms and banks are also getting into the act. Many of them offer a financial plan of some kind. Too often, however, it is not any better than the computerized plan offered by Sears.

Why all the furor? Because more and more people are moving into an income bracket of $25,000 and more, and they don't know how to achieve their financial goals. Many of them don't even know how to define them. In addition, there is an increasing awareness that it is difficult in today's environment to keep track of what one is doing with available excess dollars. This is especially true of two-income families because of even greater demands on their time. Continuing inflation, ever increasing taxes, and economic uncertainty have created a financial wilderness.

For help in getting through this economic maze, people don't want to continue to deal with a half-dozen different persons, each one expert in only one discipline. The public is hungry for an expert who can take the broad view and advise on all areas of personal money management. Such a person is hard to find. A financial planner *who is well qualified* (and we must emphasize this point) is one who is able to fill this need. The unified approach recognizes the interrelationship and the need for balance among insurance programs, investments, taxes, and estate planning that is appropriate to an individual's particular financial needs and desires.

It is becoming increasingly apparent that the ability to

make money, and the expertise necessary to manage it successfully, are seldom found in the same individual. Gerald Loucks of Denver is a classic example. He struck it rich in oil in 1974 and became known as the "Father of the Overthrust Belt," but the gifted geologist found out to his sorrow that he knew little about managing his new-found wealth. "I knew the oil business. What I didn't understand (and still don't) is how to manage the income from my expertise. In a nutshell, I was in a mess," he says. His solution was to find a competent financial planner.

It's common knowledge that many successful people are hard workers, often putting in as much as three hundred hours a month making money, but these same people will spend only an hour or two managing it. Recent market studies found that over 80 percent of people with disposable income felt they needed some kind of financial planning. But this does not necessarily mean, according to *Forbes* magazine, that a financial planner is the solution.

In a recent issue *Forbes* addressed the problem. The cover showed a monkey all dressed up in a three-piece suit standing in front of a blackboard. On the blackboard written in chalk were columns depicting assets, liabilities, estate-planning techniques, tax shelters, etc. The cover title read: "These Days Everyone's a Financial Planner." This included, presumably, the monkey.

The article went on to say there were hundreds of thousands of financial planners, which may have been an exaggeration to demonstrate a point. It also stated that some them *really do financial planning*. And we agree; many of them are very competent.

Forbes brings out that there have been a dozen major changes in the tax laws over the last fifteen years and asks its readers if they are up-to-date on them. To find out, they asked them to try the following questions on for size.

1. What is the maximum tax on total income?
2. Can you roll over only part of your pension plan into an IRA if you change jobs?

3. What is the "net interest exclusion" on your federal taxes?
4. What is currently the holding period for capital gains and losses, effective as to when?
5. How much money can one put into a Keogh account?
6. Is an ex-spouse receiving alimony eligible for an IRA?
7. What is the capital gains exclusion if you sell your home after you reach fifty-five?
8. What is the maximum percentage of your annual income that you can give away to charity and still get a tax deduction?
9. Why is your child's seventh birthday so important if you are planning on sending him or her to college?
10. How much of your estate are you allowed to leave your spouse before it is taxed?

(See the Appendix for the answers)

"If you can answer all of these questions," says *Forbes*, "then read no further. You are a fiscal saint. If you can answer few or none, you are a financial sinner; you must repent and act according to a Plan. Naturally, nearly all of us fall into the sinner category, and therein lies an industry."

The International Association of Financial Planners based at 5775 Peachtree-Dunwoody Road, Atlanta, Georgia 30342, is trying to self-regulate the industry. It boasts about 30,000 members, with the roster growing rapidly. But the qualifications to join are minor, and the program director, Maureen Ordman, admits that the public has a suspicious view of what financial planning stands for. As a consequence, she readily admits, financial planners have an identity crisis.

To become a member, the IAFP only requires that applicants be actively involved in the financial services industry and adhere to a Code of Professional Ethics. The basic objective of the code is to specify and set forth the means to enforce the minimum ethical conduct expected of all members, and to facilitate voluntary compliance with standards considerably higher than the required minimums.

The International Association of Financial Planners maintains that the reliance of the public and the business community on sound financial planning imposes on professionals in this field an obligation to have and maintain high standards of technical competence, morality, and integrity. To this end the following Code of Professional Ethics serves as the guiding document.

Canon 1
    Members as professionals should endeavor to place the public interests above their own.
Canon 2
    Members should seek continually to maintain and improve their professional knowledge, skills, and competence.
Canon 3
    Members should obey all laws and regulations, and should avoid any conduct or activity which would cause unjust harm to others.
Canon 4
    Members should be diligent in the performance of their duties.
Canon 5
    Members should establish and maintain honorable relationships with other professionals, and with all those who rely upon the members' professional judgments and skills.
Canon 6
    Members should assist in improving the public understanding of financial planning.
Canon 7
    Members should use the fact of membership in a manner consistent with the Association's Rules of Professional Conduct.
Canon 8
    Members should assist in maintaining the integrity of the Code of Professional Ethics of the Association.

In addition to the above code, IAFP's philosophy demands a unified approach to the solution of a client's financial problems. The IAFP defines financial planning as a six-step process:

1. Collecting and assessing all relevant personal and financial data
2. Identifying financial goals and objectives
3. Identifying financial problems
4. Providing written recommendations and alternative solutions
5. Coordinating the implementation of recommendations
6. Providing periodic review and update

Besides being a member in good standing of the International Association of Financial Planners, many of the members aspire to a higher professional identity. They do this by becoming certified financial planners after taking a two-year course offered by the College for Financial Planning in Denver, and passing several examinations. Seven thousand members now hold this coveted designation.

In addition, in response to appeals for tougher standards for full-fledged planners, IAFP has established a registry of financial planning practitioners. Qualifications for this select group requires direct involvement in overall planning, three years' experience as a planner, and either a designation as a certified financial planner or a chartered financial consultant (issued by the insurance industry). There are several hundred members of the registry, and the list is growing rapidly. A telephone call or a letter to the headquarters of IAFP will give you the names of those who are registered in your area.

In the fall of 1984 the International Association of Financial Planners began a $1.8 million "Public Awareness" advertising campaign. Specially prepared packages were mailed to those responding to the advertisement, giving them a detailed description of the financial-planning concept. The campaign opened on September 10, 1984, with a three-ad series in the

Wall Street Journal. Other publications in which the advertisement subsequently appeared were *Business Week, Newsweek, Time, Changing Times,* and *Money.*

In the first six months, 65,000 written responses to the advertisement were received in IAFP's headquarters in Atlanta. The "Public Awareness" advertising program is now a permanent part of the association's plans. Most financial planners agree that the campaign was a long-overdue public education program from which the industry and the public will both benefit. They foresee that tens of thousands of individuals will know more about financial planning, and many of them will seek the services of a qualified, professional planner. Financial support ranging from $10,000 to $100,000 per contribution has come from mutual fund organizations, syndicators of limited partnerships, and trust companies.

"We have discovered," said Herky Harris, executive director of the association, "that there is a great public demand for an objective advisor. The public is also looking for someone who is doing more than selling a single concept (such as insurance or mutual funds). People don't want to deal with five or six different individuals, each person selling one product. They want to deal with one individual who has a broad view."

The IAFP is also talking with the securities administrations of the various states, and with the Securities & Exchange Commission, about setting up minimum legal standards for financial planners, and the possibility of requiring a license for them to operate. But there are dissenters about the advisability of this among professional financial planners. One of them is Doug Thorburn, a certified financial planner writing in a publication of the California Association of Financial Planners.

He claims that because of the *supposedly high standards* set by licensing authorities, the general public has the false impression that because a person is licensed, that individual must know what he or she is doing. On the contrary, he says, licensing permits the less competent to raise their ability (in the eyes of the public) to the level of the true professional. What it actually does is to lower the expertise of everyone in the profession down to the level of that licensee who receives the lowest passing grade on the government examination, for this is how the public judges you. You passed; therefore we can trust you.

Thorburn goes on to say that while licensing requires applicants to pass examinations, these examinations are not relevant to the profession. For example, the test to become a registered representative (stockbroker), while difficult, does not test one's understanding of how to analyze investments, nor teach one how to determine what investments are appropriate for a particular client. Thorburn actually goes on to make a rougher statement than that. He writes, "The real estate and stockbroker exams are exercises in rote memorization of irrelevent nonsense."

So what would be accomplished, Thorburn asks, by passing licensing laws for financial planners? Is it likely that the truly incompetent will not pass the licensing requirements? Yes. But there will be many who will go through the motions to become licensed who are not competent by the standards of the truly professional financial planner, and thus they will deceive the public. Is it possible to make the licensing rules and/ or examinations better than those required for real estate agents and stockbrokers and others? Yes. But what are the odds for this when a licensing authority does not have to compete in the open market as do those conferring private or voluntary designations, such as the one for certified financial planner?

In summation, Thorburn says, licensing financial planners will backfire, no matter what the requirements may be. Instead, professional financial planners should devote their energies to self-regulation in a manner that will benefit the general public as well as themselves. Government involvement in licensing has never worked in other disciplines, he maintains; therefore it will certainly not work in this one.

We feel that Thorburn makes a strong case. It remains to be seen whether the IAFP, the lawmakers, or his fellow financial planners will listen.

Financial planners charge for their work, just as we all do.

Nobody works for nothing. They charge either a flat fee per hour or per plan, or they earn commissions by their clients' investing in products they recommend. Some charge a combination, which is, of course, a fee as well as a commission. Which of the three methods is best for the client is a matter of dispute among financial planners. The fee-only planners maintain their way is more objective. The commission-only planners claim that the fee-only planners throw their clients to the wolves, because they leave it up to the client to implement the financial plan. There is no follow-through to see to it that the client actually benefits from the recommendations that are made.

It appears that all three charge methods are satisfactory. The clients of the fee-only planners are inclined to be wealthy, for the cost can run into thousands of dollars. The clients of the commission-only planners are less affluent, less inclined by nature to follow through on recommendations and therefore need help in decision making, and periodic consultation after that.

There are those, too, who would rather do their financial planning themselves. For these people there are computer do-it-yourself kits. Consumer Financial Institute, 288 Walnut Street, Newton, Massachusetts 02160, will send you one in approximately three weeks after they receive your $175 check. Some brokerage firms and big accounting firms will do the same thing.

The accounting firm of Touche Ross will send you one for $500. Merrill Lynch has a program called Pathfinder. E. F. Hutton has a plan called MAP (for money allocation program) that costs $150. If you're wealthy and willing to sit through several lengthy interviews, E. F. Hutton will provide you with an in-depth personalized plan that can cost as much as $10,000. How wealthy do you have to be? A mere $3 million with an income of $300,000.

If you are an investor with a personal computer, there are software programs on the market that enable you to devise your own plan. One of them is called *Managing Your Money*.

I telephoned them in Massachusetts, and I was told that if I would leave my telephone number someone would return my call in one week. I never heard from them.

As with any business, you can become victimized by an unscrupulous and dishonest financial planner. *Forbes* magazine reported one.

"In New Jersey a financial planner named Thomas Swarts promised clients 14% returns in a special money market account that he was privy to. The cash from five clients, some $125,000, went instead into an office building that he was buying. The deal soured, and Swarts went to jail."

Financial planners and others, including brokerage houses, put on free seminars, advertise them, and urge those who attend to bring their wives. They are often held in the evening to accommodate those who work during the daytime hours. These seminars should be viewed as a means of gaining information. They are well planned, informative, and the speaker or speakers are experts in their field whether it be stocks, real estate, tax shelters, etc. It is true that they are trying to sell you a particular product, but there is no high pressure. Go to one if you want to have an entertaining evening and learn something about investments. If the seminar is conducted by a financial planner, it is one way to judge if you would like to have a personal interview.

What is the best way to find a competent financial planner? Write to the International Association of Financial Planners in Atlanta and ask them to recommend one in your area who has been a member for at least three years. Then arrange an interview and decide for yourself about his level of competence. Ask for references and for a look at a couple of plans that he has proposed to others, with the names and addresses omitted, of course.

Financial planning is here right now, and, looking into the future, it will be the major way that the financial services industry will function. Emerging as the most confident and competent members of this infant industry are the financial planners who offer comprehensive services to their clients.

They can be found usually operating as individuals, associated with independent broker/dealer firms with whom they place orders for the products in which their clients invest to implement their financial plans. They can also be found within a few stockbrokerage firms, some accounting firms, an occasional bank, but almost never in the legal fraternity.

They are technology conscious, using personal computers in their offices. Automation is today a major force in the advancement of the financial services industry, and in the effective practice of financial planning. An automated financial-planning system is the only way the planner of the future will be able to stay abreast of the changes in the law and the economy, and of the proliferation of new products in the marketplace.

By the use of telecommunications, and the ability through a modem to access millions of bits of information stored in mainframe computers around the country, the financial planner can reduce research to hours and minutes that would take months to accomplish by other methods. Stock quotations, research information from the investment-advisory services, daily and weekly recommendations of what stocks to buy or sell are all at his fingertips. The planner's automated system turns out calculations with relative ease and generates a number of different scenarios which will show what product or combination of products is best for a particular client. In addition, many of the broker/dealer offices of the financial planners are also completely computerized, with the information instantly available as long as the financial planner has a personal computer with a modem.

Taxes play an increasing role as more and more people are moving up the income ladder. Software programs that show five years of income tax returns on a single spreadsheet allow the financial planner to change a single entry to see what effect this would have on his client's taxes. And immediately the computer will recalculate all the balance of the numbers on the return to show the effect of the new information that has been inserted.

The computer will allow the financial planner to make frequent and systematic reviews of his clients' investments. As the volume of the financial planner's business increases, automation is the only way the planner can survive and serve his clients efficiently. The information needed by the planner from other sources, such as the syndicators, the products sponsors, and the mutual fund organizations, are all in the process of being automated. This information, too, in the near future will be available to the financial planner. Also available from the planner's automated broker/dealer will be both transaction information and asset performance. Freed from tracking the performance of the various products in his clients' portfolios, the planner can react immediately to any changes in performance that affect his clients.

The ultimate goal is to have a system that connects all four—product sponsor, broker/dealer, information systems, and the financial planner. This connection may even extend in the future to the individual client who will have a new portable notebook-computer by which the investor can communicate with the planner's automated system.

Automation is definitely the only practical way to deal with the phenomenal growth of the financial services industry.

Mere product selling, under the guise of financial planning, is no longer acceptable. In planning a client's financial present and future, coordinating all three phases of plan creation, plan implementation, and plan updating is crucial to a client's welfare.

Plan creation means obtaining all of the facts from the client, diagnosing the problem, defining investment goals, and writing a recommendation of how to achieve them.

Plan implementation is up to the client, with the urging of the financial planner. A written plan is not worth the paper it is written on unless it is brought to life by action. It will never be implemented by procrastination. As someone once said: "On the plains of hesitation bleach the bones of countless millions, who at the dawn of victory, sat down to rest, and resting, died."

Plan updating means periodic review. With some financial planners, updating is glaringly absent. No plan, like a will or a trust, should be carved in stone. Economic and tax changes, change in the financial status of the client, change in family relationships, an unanticipated increase or decrease in product performance can all affect the financial plan. Death of a family member, particularly a spouse, can be a dramatic example.

As a result of all of the above, we heartily recommend the truly professional financial planner, who is fully automated, competent, and dedicated, as someone you can trust.

APPENDIX

Answers to the Questions in Forbes *Magazine*

1. The maximum federal tax on all sources of income is 50 percent, but if you live in a city with a high local income tax, such as New York, you can pay up to 57 percent after the federal deduction for state and local tax payments.
2. You can roll over a portion of your pension plan into an IRA, but the portion you keep is taxable as income.
3. You aren't allowed to exclude any interest income except that from tax-exempt bonds.
4. The holding period for capital gains and losses is six months on property acquired after June 22, 1984, and before January 1, 1988.
5. You can put 25 percent of your total income, up to $30,000, into a Keogh defined-contribution plan. But a defined-benefit plan will allow you to put a lot more into it. Your contributions are limited only in that your accumulated benefits at retirement cannot exceed $90,000 a year or 100 percent of your average compensation over the last three years. If you're fifty-five, earning $150,000 a year and planning to retire at sixty-five, you can contribute $53,865, or 36 percent

of your gross pay, to get the maximum benefit of
$90,000 a year.

6. Yes.

7. $125,000.

8. You can donate up to 50 percent of your total income
   to a recognized charity and claim a deduction. But if
   you donate appreciated property, the deductible
   amount drops to 30 percent, the same as if you give
   cash to a private foundation.

9. If you expect to send your child off to college around
   age eighteen, you should establish a Clifford trust by
   his seventh birthday, since the trust must last ten
   years and one day.

10. All of it.

Form **706** (Rev. June 1982) Department of the Treasury Internal Revenue Service	**United States Estate Tax Return** Estate of a citizen or resident of the United States (see separate instructions) To be filed for Decedents dying after December 31, 1981, and before January 1, 1985, Section references are to the Internal Revenue Code.	OMB No. 1545-0015 Expires 3-31-84

Decedent's first name and middle initial (and maiden name, if any)	Decedent's last name	Date of death

Domicile at time of death	Year domicile established	Decedent's social security number

Name of executor	Executor's Address (Number and street including apartment number or rural route, city, town or post office, State and ZIP code)
Executor's social security number	

Name and location of court where will was probated or estate administered	Case number

If decedent died testate check here ▶ ☐ and attach a certified copy of the will. | ☐ Check here if Form 4768 is attached.

Authorization to receive confidential tax information under regulations section 601.502(c)(3)(ii), to act as the estate's representative before the Internal Revenue Service, and to make written or oral presentations on behalf of the estate if return prepared by an attorney for the executor:

Name of attorney (print or type)	State	Address (Number and street, city, State and ZIP code)

I declare that I am the attorney of record for the executor before the above court and prepared this return for the executor. I am not under suspension or disbarment from practice before the Internal Revenue Service and am qualified to practice in the State shown below—

Signature	Date	Telephone Number

Tax Computation

1 Total gross estate (from Recapitulation, page 3, line 10)	**1**	
2 Total allowable deductions (from Recapitulation, page 3, line 20)	**2**	
3 Taxable estate (subtract line 2 from line 1)	**3**	
4 Adjusted taxable gifts (total taxable gifts (within the meaning of section 2503) made by the decedent after December 31, 1976, other than gifts that are includible in decedent's gross estate (section 2001(b))) . .	**4**	
5 Add line 3 and line 4	**5**	
6 Tentative tax on the amount on line 5 from Table A in the instructions	**6**	
7 Total gift taxes payable with respect to gifts by the decedent after December 31, 1976. Include gift taxes paid by the decedent's spouse for split gifts (section 2513) only if the decedent was the donor of these gifts and they are includible in the decedent's gross estate	**7**	
8 Gross estate tax (subtract line 7 from line 6)	**8**	
9 Unified credit against estate tax from Table B in the instructions	**9**	
10 Adjustment to unified credit. See instructions	**10**	
11 Allowable unified credit (subtract line 10 from line 9)	**11**	
12 Subtract line 11 from line 8 (but do not enter less than zero)	**12**	
13 Credit for State death taxes. Do not enter more than line 12. See Table C in the instructions and **attach credit evidence** (see instructions)	**13**	
14 Subtract line 13 from line 12	**14**	
15 Credit for Federal gift taxes on pre-1977 gifts (section 2012) (attach computation) . .	**15**	
16 Credit for foreign death taxes (from Schedule(s) P). (Attach Form(s) 706CE) .	**16**	
17 Credit for tax on prior transfers (from Schedule Q)	**17**	
18 Total (add lines 15, 16, and 17)	**18**	
19 Net estate tax. (subtract line 18 from line 14)	**19**	
20 Prior payments. Explain in an attached statement	**20**	
21 United States Treasury bonds redeemed in payment of estate tax	**21**	
22 Total (add lines 20 and 21)	**22**	
23 Balance due (subtract line 22 from line 19)	**23**	

Note: *Please attach the necessary supplemental documents. You must attach the Death Certificate.*

Under penalties of perjury, I declare that I have examined this return, including accompanying schedules and statements, and to the best of my knowledge and belief, it is true, correct, and complete. Declaration of preparer other than the executor is based on all information of which preparer has any knowledge.

Signature(s) of executor(s)	Date

Signature of preparer other than executor	Address (and ZIP code)	Date

For Paperwork Reduction Act Notice, see page 1 of the instructions.

Estate of:

General Information

1 Death certificate no. and issuing authority (Attach a copy of the death certificate to this return)

2 Date of birth

3 Decedent's business or occupation. If retired check here ▶ ☐ and state decedent's former business or occupation.

4 Marital status of the decedent at time of death
☐ Married
☐ Widow or widower—Name and date of death of deceased spouse ▶
☐ Single
☐ Legally separated
☐ Divorced—Date divorce decree became final ▶

5a Surviving spouse's name	5b Social security number	5c Amount received (see instructions)

6 Individuals (other than the surviving spouse), trusts, or other estates who receive benefits from the estate (do not include charitable beneficiaries shown in Schedule O). (see instructions) For Privacy Act Notice, see the Instructions for Form 1040.

Name of individual, trust or estate receiving $1,000 or more	Identifying number	Relationship to decedent	Amount (see instructions)

All unascertainable beneficiaries and those who receive less than $1,000 . . . . ▶

Total . . . .

Please check the "Yes" or "No" box for each question.

		Yes	No
7	Does the gross estate contain any section 2044 property?		
8	Do you elect the alternate valuation?		
9	Do you elect the special use valuation?		
	If "Yes," complete and attach Schedule N.		
10a	Have Federal gift tax returns ever been filed?		
	If "Yes," please attach copies of the returns, if available, and furnish the following information:		

10b Period(s) covered	10c Internal Revenue office(s) where filed

11 Are you excluding from the decedent's gross estate the value of a lump-sum distribution described in section 2039(f)(2)? . . . .
If "Yes," you must attach the information required by the instructions.

12 Do you elect to claim a marital deduction for an otherwise nondeductible interest under section 2056(b)(7)? . . . .
If "Yes," please attach the additional information required by the instructions.

13 Was the marital deduction computed under the transitional rule of Public Law 97-34, section 403(e)(3) (Economic Recovery Tax Act of 1981)? If "Yes," attach a separate computation of the marital deduction, enter the amount on line 18 of the Recapitulation, and note line 18 "computation attached".

Estate of:

If you answer "Yes" to any of questions 14–20, you must attach additional information as described in the instructions.

	Yes	No
14a Was there any insurance on the decedent's life that was not included on the return as part of the gross estate? . . .		
14b Did the decedent own any insurance on the life of another that is not included in the gross estate?		
15 Did the decedent at the time of death own any property as a joint tenant with right of survivorship in which (1) one or more of the other joint tenants was someone other than the decedent's spouse and (2) less than the full value of the property was included on the return as part of the gross estate?		
16 Did the decedent, at the time of death, own any interest in a partnership or unincorporated business?		
17 Were any of the contents of any safe deposit box which the decedent either owned or had access to not included on the return as part of the gross estate?		
18 Did the decedent make any transfer described in section 2035, 2036, 2037 or 2038 (see the instructions for Schedule G)?		
19 Were there in existence at the time of the decedent's death:		
a Any trusts created by the decedent during his or her lifetime?		
b Any trusts not created by the decedent under which the decedent possessed any power, beneficial interest or trusteeship?		
20 Did the decedent ever possess, exercise or release any general power of appointment?		

Recapitulation

Item number	Gross estate	Alternate value	Value at date of death
1	Schedule A—Real Estate		
2	Schedule B—Stocks and Bonds		
3	Schedule C—Mortgages, Notes, and Cash		
4	Schedule D—Insurance on the Decedent's Life (attach Form(s) 712)		
5	Schedule E—Jointly Owned Property (attach Form(s) 712 for life insurance) . .		
6	Schedule F—Other Miscellaneous Property (attach Form(s) 712 for life insurance) .		
7	Schedule G—Transfers During Decedent's Life (attach Form(s) 712 for life insurance)		
8	Schedule H—Powers of Appointment		
9	Schedule I—Annuities		
10	Total gross estate (add items 1 through 9). Enter here and on page 1, line 1 . . .		

Item number	Deductions	Amount
11	Schedule J—Funeral Expenses and Expenses Incurred in Administering Property Subject to Claims . .	
12	Schedule K—Debts of the Decedent	
13	Schedule K—Mortgages and Liens	
14	Total of Items 11 through 13	
15	Allowable amount of deductions from item 14 (see the instructions for line 15 of the Recapitulation.) .	
16	Schedule L—Net Losses During Administration	
17	Schedule L—Expenses Incurred in Administering Property Not Subject to Claims	
18	Schedule M—Bequests, etc., to Surviving Spouse	
19	Schedule O—Charitable, Public, and Similar Gifts and Bequests	
20	Total allowable deductions (add lines 15 through 19). Enter here and on page 1, line 2	

Form 706 (Rev. 6–82)

Estate of:

SCHEDULE A—Real Estate
(For jointly owned property that must be disclosed on Schedule E, see the Instructions for Schedule E.)

Item number	Description	Alternate valuation date	Alternate value	Value at date of death
1				

TOTAL. (Also enter on the Recapitulation, page 3, at item 1.) . . . .

(If more space is needed, attach additional sheets of the same size.)

Schedule A—Page 4

Form 706 (Rev. 6–82)

Estate of:

SCHEDULE B—Stocks and Bonds

(For jointly owned property that must be disclosed on Schedule E, see the Instructions for Schedule E.)

Item number	Description including face amount of bonds or number of shares and par value where needed for identification	Unit value	Alternate valuation date	Alternate value	Value at date of death
1					

TOTAL. (Also enter on the Recapitulation, page 3, at item 2.) . . . .

(If more space is needed, attach additional sheets of the same size.)

Schedule B—Page 5

Form 706 (Rev. 6–82)

Estate of:

SCHEDULE C—Mortgages, Notes, and Cash
(For jointly owned property that must be disclosed on Schedule E, see the Instructions for Schedule E.)

Item number	Description	Alternate valuation date	Alternate value	Value at date of death
1				

TOTAL. (Also enter on the Recapitulation, page 3, at item 3.) . . . .

(If more space is needed, attach additional sheets of the same size.)

Schedule C—Page 6

Form 706 (Rev. 6–82)

Estate of:

SCHEDULE D—Insurance on the Decedent's Life

Item number	Description	Alternate valuation date	Alternate value	Value at date of death
1				

TOTAL. (Also enter on the Recapitulation, page 3, at item 4.) . . . .

(If more space is needed, attach additional sheets of the same size.)

Schedule D—Page 7

Estate of:

SCHEDULE E—Jointly Owned Property

Part I Qualified joint interests—interests held by the decedent and his or her spouse as the only joint tenants (section 2040(b)(2))

Item number	Description	Alternate valuation date	Alternate value	Value at date of death

1(a) Totals . . . .

1(b) Amounts included in gross estate (½ of line 1(a)) . . . .

Part II All other joint interests

2(a) State the name and address of each surviving co-tenant. If there are more than 3 surviving co-tenants list the additional co-tenants on an attached sheet.

Name	Address (Number and street, city, State, and ZIP code)
A.	
B.	
C.	

Item number	Enter letter for co-tenant	Description (include alternate valuation date if any)	Percentage includible	Includible alternate value	Includible value at date of death

2(b) Total other joint interests . . . .

Total includible joint interests (add lines 1(b) and 2(b)). Also enter on the Recapitulation, page 3, at item 5 . . . .

(If more space is needed, attach additional sheets of the same size.)

Schedule E—Page 8

Estate of:

SCHEDULE F—Other Miscellaneous Property Not Reportable Under Any Other Schedule
(For jointly owned property that must be disclosed on Schedule E, see the Instructions for Schedule E.)

			Yes	No
1	Did the decedent, at the time of death, own any articles of artistic or collectible value in excess of $3,000 or any collections whose artistic or collectible value combined at date of death exceeded $3,000? If "Yes," full details must be submitted on this schedule.			
2	Has the decedent's estate, spouse, or any other person, received (or will receive) any bonus or award as a result of the decedent's employment or death? . . . . *If "Yes," full details must be submitted on this schedule.*			
3	Did the decedent at the time of death have, or have access to, a safe deposit box?			

3 *If "Yes," state location, and if held in joint names of decedent and another, state name and relationship of joint depositor.*

If any of the contents of the safe deposit box are omitted from the schedules in this return, explain fully why omitted.

4 Did the decedent, at the time of death, own any other miscellaneous property not reportable under any other schedule? .
If "Yes," full details must be submitted on this schedule.

Item number	Description	Alternate valuation date	Alternate value	Value at date of death
1				

TOTAL. (Also enter on the Recapitulation, page 3, at item 6.) . . . .

(If more space is needed, attach additional sheets of the same size.)

Schedule F—Page 9

Estate of:

SCHEDULE G—Transfers During Decedent's Life

Item number	Description	Alternate valuation date	Alternate value	Value at date of death
1	**A.** Gift tax paid by the decedent or the estate for all gifts made by the decedent or his or her spouse within 3 years before the decedent's death (section 2035(c)) . . . . **B.** Transfers includible under sections 2035(a), 2036, 2037 or 2038:	X X X X X		

TOTAL. (Also enter on the Recapitulation, page 3, at item 7.) . . . .

SCHEDULE H—Powers of Appointment

Item number	Description	Alternate valuation date	Alternate value	Value at date of death
1				

TOTAL. (Also enter on the Recapitulation, page 3, at item 8.) . . . .

(If more space is needed, attach additional sheets of the same size.)   **Schedules G and H—Page 10**

Estate of:

SCHEDULE I—Annuities

		Yes	No
1a Was the decedent, immediately before death, receiving an annuity described in the "General" paragraph of the instructions for this schedule?			
1b If "Yes," was the annuity paid pursuant to an approved plan described in the instructions for this schedule?			
1c If the answer to "1b" is "Yes," state the ratio of the decedent's contribution to the total purchase price of the annuity.		/////	/////
2a If the decedent was employed at the time of death, did an annuity as described in paragraph (d) of the "Annuity defined" instructions for this schedule become payable to any beneficiary because the beneficiary survived the decedent? . . .			
2b If "Yes," state the ratio of the decedent's contribution to the total purchase price of the annuity.		/////	/////
3a Did an annuity under an individual retirement account, annuity, or bond described in section 2039(e) become payable to any beneficiary because the beneficiary survived the decedent?			
3b If "Yes," is the annuity payable to the beneficiary for life or for at least 36 months following decedent's death? . . .			
3c If the answer to "3a" is "Yes," state the ratio of the amount paid for the individual retirement account, annuity, or bond that was not allowable as an income tax deduction under section 219 (other than a rollover contribution) to the total amount paid for the account, annuity, or bond.		/////	/////

Item number	Description	Alternate valuation date	Alternate value	Value at date of death
1				

TOTAL. (Also enter on the Recapitulation, page 3, at item 9.) . . . .

(If more space is needed, attach additional sheets of the same size.)

Form 706 (Rev. 6-82)

Estate of:

SCHEDULE J—Funeral Expenses and Expenses Incurred in Administering Property Subject to Claims

Note.—Do not list on this schedule expenses of administering property not subject to claims. For those expenses, see the Instructions for Schedule L.

If executors' commissions, attorney fees, etc., are claimed and allowed as a deduction for estate tax purposes, they are not allowable as a deduction in computing the taxable income of the estate for Federal income tax purposes. They are allowable as an income tax deduction on Form 1041 if a waiver is filed to waive the deduction on Form 706 (see Form 1041 instructions).

Item number	Description	Amount
1	**A. Funeral expenses:**	
	Total	X X X X X
1	**B. Administration expenses:** Executors' commissions—amount estimated/agreed upon/paid. (Strike out the words that do not apply)	X X X X X
2	Attorney fees—amount estimated/agreed upon/paid. (Strike out the words that do not apply)	X X X X X
3	Miscellaneous expenses:	
	Total miscellaneous expenses	X X X X X

TOTAL. (Also enter on the Recapitulation, page 3, at item 11.) . . . .

(If more space is needed, attach additional sheets of the same size.)

Schedule J—Page 12

Estate of:

SCHEDULE K—Debts of the Decedent, and Mortgages and Liens

Item number	Debts of the Decedent—Creditor and nature of claim, and allowable death taxes	Amount
1		
	TOTAL. (Also enter on the Recapitulation, page 3, at item 12.)	

Item number	Mortgages and Liens—Description	Amount
1		
	TOTAL. (Also enter on the Recapitulation, page 3, at item 13.)	

SCHEDULE L—Net Losses During Administration and Expenses Incurred in Administering Property Not Subject to Claims

Item number	Net losses during administration (Note: Do not deduct losses claimed on a Federal income tax return.)	Amount
1		
	TOTAL. (Also enter on the Recapitulation, page 3, at item 16.)	

Item number	Expenses incurred in administering property not subject to claims (Indicate whether estimated, agreed upon, or paid.)	Amount
1		
	TOTAL. (Also enter on the Recapitulation, page 3, at item 17.)	

Form 706 (Rev. 6–82)

Estate of:

SCHEDULE M—Bequests, etc., to Surviving Spouse

	Yes	No
1 Did any property pass to the surviving spouse as the result of a qualified disclaimer? . . . . If "Yes," attach a copy of the written disclaimer required by section 2518(b).		

Item number	Description of property interests passing to surviving spouse	Value
1		

2 Total . . . .

3 (a) Federal estate tax payable out of property interests listed above . . . .

(b) Other death taxes payable out of property interests listed above . . . .

(c) Add items (a) and (b) . . . .

4 Net value of property interests listed above (subtract 3(c) from 2). Also enter on the Recapitulation, page 3 at item 18 . . . .

(If more space is needed, attach additional sheets of the same size.)   Schedule M—Page 14

Estate of:

SCHEDULE N—Section 2032A Valuation

Enter the requested information for each party who received any interest in the specially valued property.

	Name	Address
A		
B		
C		
D		
E		
F		
G		
H		

	Identifying number	Relationship to decedent	Fair market value	Special use value
A				
B				
C				
D				
E				
F				
G				
H				

SCHEDULE O—Charitable, Public, and Similar Gifts and Bequests

		Yes	No
1(a)	If the transfer was made by will, has any action been instituted to have interpreted or to contest the will or any provision thereof affecting the charitable deductions claimed in this schedule? . . . . If "Yes," full details must be submitted with this schedule.		
1(b)	According to the information and belief of the person or persons filing the return, is any such action designed or contemplated? . . . . If "Yes," full details must be submitted with this schedule.		
2	Did any property pass to charity as the result of a qualified disclaimer? . . . . If "Yes," attach a copy of the written disclaimer required by section 2518.		

Item Number	Name and address of beneficiary	Character of institution	Amount
1			

3 Total . . . .

4 (a) Federal estate tax payable out of property interests listed above . . . .

(b) Other death taxes payable out of property interests listed above . . . .

(c) Add items (a) and (b) . . . .

5 Net value of property interests listed above (subtract 4(c) from 3) Also enter on the Recapitulation, page 3, at item 19 . . . .

(If more space is needed, attach additional sheets of the same size.) **Schedules N and O—Page 15**

Form 706 (Rev. 6–82)

Estate of:

SCHEDULE P—Credit for Foreign Death Taxes

List all foreign countries to which death taxes have been paid and for which credit is claimed on this return.

If credit is claimed for death taxes paid to more than one foreign country, compute the credit for taxes paid to one country o this sheet and attach a separate copy of Schedule P for each of the other countries.

The credit computed on this sheet is for _____
(Name of death tax or taxes)

_____ imposed in _____
(Name of country)

Credit is computed under the _____
(Insert title of treaty or statute)

Citizenship (Nationality) of decedent at time of death _____

(All amounts and values must be entered in United States money)

1 Total of estate, inheritance, legacy and succession taxes imposed in the country named above attributable to property situated in that country, subjected to these taxes, and included in the gross estate (as defined by statute) .

2 Value of the gross estate (adjusted, if necessary, according to the instructions for item 2) . . . .

3 Value of property situated in that country, subjected to death taxes imposed in that country, and included in the gross estate (adjusted, if necessary, according to the instructions for item 3) . . . .

4 Tax imposed by section 2001 reduced by the total credits claimed under sections 2010, 2011, and 2012 (see instructions) . . . .

5 Amount of Federal estate tax attributable to property specified at item 3 (Divide item 3 by item 2 and multiply the result by item 4.) . . . .

6 Credit for death taxes imposed in the country named above (the smaller of item 1 or item 5). Also enter on page 1, line 16 . . . .

SCHEDULE Q—Credit for Tax on Prior Transfers

	Name of transferor	Social security number	IRS office where estate tax return was filed	Date of death
A				
B				
C				

Check here ▶ ☐ if section 2013(f) (special valuation of farm, etc., real property) adjustments to the computation of the credit were made (see instructions).

Check here ▶ ☐ if section 2013(g) (generation-skipping transfers) adjustments to the computation of the credit were made (see instructions).

Item	Transferor			Total A, B, & C
	A	B	C	
1 Transferee's tax as apportioned (from worksheet, (line 7 + line 8) × line 34 for each column)				
2 Transferor's tax (from each column of worksheet, line 20)				
3 Maximum amount before percentage requirement (for each column, enter amount from line 1 or 2, whichever is smaller)				
4 Percentage allowed (Each column) (see instructions)	%	%	%	
5 Credit allowable (line 3 × line 4 for each column)				
6 TOTAL Credit allowable (Add columns A, B, and C of line 5) Enter here and on line 17 of the Tax Computation				

☆ U.S. GOVERNMENT PRINTING OFFICE : 1982—O-363-439 23-188-5979 **Schedules P and Q—Page 16**

Index

271